Document Sets for California and the West in U.S. History

Document Sets for California and the West in U.S. History

Iris H. W. Engstrand

University of San Diego

D. C. Heath and Company
Lexington, Massachusetts Toronto

Address editorial correspondence to:

D. C. Heath
125 Spring Street
Lexington, MA 02173

Acquisitions Editor: James Miller
Developmental Editor: Lauren Johnson
Production Editor: Rosemary Jaffe
Designer: Kenneth Hollman
Photo Researcher: Martha Shethar
Production Coordinator: Charles Dutton
Text Permissions Editor: Margaret Roll

Cover: Picking lemons at La Vida Ranch, Spring Valley, California, 1897. San Diego Historical Society, Photograph Collection.

For permission to use copyrighted material, grateful acknowledgement is made to the copyright holders listed on pages 169–172, which are hereby considered an extension of this copyright page.

Published simultaneously in Canada.

Printed in the United States of America.

International Standard Book Number: 0–669–28494–7

Library of Congress Catalog Number: 92–74843

10 9 8 7 6 5 4 3 2 1

Preface

The Columbian quincentennial in 1992 prompted Americans to reflect about their history—to contemplate the far-reaching effects of two worlds brought together five hundred years before by the thread of discovery. That year opened a dialogue about the meaning of conquest, accommodation, assimilation, and resistance. Historic events move in and out of the public spotlight, but especially for scholars and students, the repercussions following turning points such as the encounters of 1492 continue to stimulate investigation, evaluation, and interpretation.

Before the Columbian encounters, two land masses—Eurasia and Africa, and the Americas—had existed for millennia with similar geographic configurations but with different inhabitants and different ways of life. Suddenly, as a result of a significant voyage, the peoples of each region faced one another with curiosity, hope, suspicion, and doubt. By the time Europeans reached California in the mid-sixteenth century, their geographic knowledge had greatly expanded. When Spanish settlers occupied the region in the late eighteenth century, they supplanted their initial search for gold with a program of defensive expansion. Soon other nations also began to covet the Pacific coast, and development of the area rapidly accelerated.

What lessons have we learned from these pivotal events? What role does history play in promoting an understanding of cultural differences? Can the past help us to plan strategies for the future? The documents in this book cannot answer all these questions, but they do provide material for discussion.

This collection of documents—both written and visual—offers a glimpse of the people who inhabited California and the rest of the American West at the time of European settlement, and takes a longer look at those who later came to colonize. Through letters, diaries, firsthand accounts, newspapers, and recordings of oral traditions, it gives readers insights, perspectives, and a sense of the motivations and feelings that these peoples of the past experienced. The limited selections for each time period by necessity can serve only as an introduction—an enticement—to new vistas. Nevertheless, they cover a wide variety of sources and ideas and challenge readers to think critically about the past.

Document Set 1 begins with stories of creation and other events as told by Native Americans and then features descriptions of these Indians by various Europeans—Spanish, English, Germans, and Italians—who visited California and the West from 1542 to 1805. The native peoples of the Rocky Mountains and intermontane regions initially met British, French, and, later, American fur traders arriving from the East. Document Set 2 contains excerpts from the diaries and reports of Spanish missionaries and explorers, as well as documents recounting the founding of Los Angeles. The views of French,

English, and American travelers and the observations of a French visitor to Hawaii are given as the Spanish era in the West comes to an end in 1821.

The third set of documents spotlights the period of Mexican control. It begins with the reflections of a young girl about life in San Diego and offers accounts by British and French sea captains visiting the Pacific coast. The Mexican government secularizes the missions in California and makes land available for private *ranchos*. Protestant missionaries reach Oregon, and the Swiss entrepreneur Johann (John) Sutter arrives on the scene.

Document Set 4 covers the mountain men and the fur trade of the Great Basin, the intermontane West, and the Pacific Northwest. Several ethnic groups are represented, including the French-Canadian Antoine Robidoux, the half-French, half-Indian Jean Baptiste Charbonneau, and the black trapper Jim Beckwourth. Also highlighted is a controversy between Jedediah Smith and the Mexican government in California. Some of the mountain men settled permanently in the West, whereas others returned to the East—perhaps to families or to other business enterprises.

Document Set 5, covering the era of the Mexican War, includes a selection from the Donner party's fateful mountain crossing and a firsthand report of the Bear Flag uprising. American military men John Frémont and Henry Turner report on their activities in California. The Treaty of Guadalupe Hidalgo ending the war defines the status of all the territories gained from Mexico. The sixth set of documents covers the California gold discovery that took place just a few days before the war's end. The mining frontier witnessed remarkable changes among various groups, from the Mormons to the people of San Francisco and the rest of the West. Silver was discovered in Nevada, and miners returning to the East found gold in Colorado.

New stagecoach lines crossed mountains and deserts as communication between East and West became a top priority during the late 1850s. Document Set 7 focuses on transportation by stage and rail. California and the American West, although on the periphery of the Civil War, nevertheless played a role in the conflict. Confederate newspapers talked about secession, and Union barracks were built for the defense of California. The state of Washington looked northward for fishing rights, and the United States purchased Alaska. Americans celebrated the completion of the transcontinental railroad to the Pacific coast with an elaborate ceremony.

Document Set 8 addresses problems resulting from expansion and development. Advertising campaigns attracted new settlers to the West, but the influx of people brought hardship to the Native Americans, who were fast being displaced from their lands. The western states grew, and Americans in Hawaii looked toward the annexation of that territory. The new century, the subject of Document Set 9, was indeed a turning point in western history. Victorian mansions reminiscent of eastern grandeur graced the growing cities. The gold rush to the Yukon Territory began a new era in the Northwest, and railroads expanded to the south. Ambrose Bierce, a columnist in San Francisco, and Katherine Tingley, a theosophist in San Diego, offered interesting insights about life. As newcomers took advantage of the climate and the natural resources, future environmental problems loomed.

Document Set 10 brings into focus the reforms long proposed for California by Governor Hiram Johnson, and the challenges to his ideas. Between 1910 and 1920, women gained the vote, the Progressive Era ended, and World War II commanded the attention of industry throughout the West. The controversial Industrial Workers of the World (IWW) entered California, and the Ku Klux Klan marched into the political arena in Oregon. During the 1920s California's cultural life drew national attention through the activities of William Randolph Hearst, Aimee Semple McPherson, and the nascent film industry in Hollywood.

Document Set 11 covers the Great Depression of the 1930s, an era that saw severe unemployment, the New Deal, and the 1935 San Diego World's Fair. Migratory farmworkers arriving in California or Washington State in this era struggled with poverty and exploitation; many were homeless and hungry. Filipino immigrants faced mistreatment. The government attempted to spark the depressed economy, which finally revived as World War II broke out in Europe. Document Set 12 covers the war years, with a section on Japanese relocation, and the West's dramatic postwar progress. During the 1950s Walt Disney entered television and developed the idea of a theme park. The future of Indian reservations also came into question.

Document Set 13 discusses the promise and problems of the 1960s and early 1970s, including university student protests, the Watts riots, and a well-known author's lighthearted view of California life. Farmworkers found a champion in César Chávez, and the Indians of the Pacific Northwest regained valuable fishing rights. The Métis of western Canada represented the problems of a little-recognized cultural minority. The final set of selections, in Document Set 14, focuses on current issues ranging from economic trends to environmental concerns and from freeways to desalination plants. The role of the American West in the Pacific Rim community brings into focus major trends that will influence the economic future of California and its neighbor states. The Los Angeles riots of 1992 revealed that serious social, cultural, and economic problems still remain. The political awakening of Mexican-Americans has been a step in the right direction, although a complete integration of minorities has not yet been achieved.

In preparing this book, my deepest appreciation goes to my colleagues in western history, many of whom contributed helpful comments and suggestions, and to others whose work served as a source of inspiration and is included herein. Among these are Tom Alexander, James Allen, Ray Brandes, Donald Cutter, Richard Griswold del Castillo, Janet Fireman, Father Francis Guest, Harlan Hague, Albert Hurtado, John Kessell, Patricia Nelson Limerick, Gerald Nash, Clyde Milner, Claus Naske, Doyce Nunis, Kenneth Owens, Leonard Pitt, Andrew Rolle, James Ronda, Carlos Schwantes, Daniel Tyler, and David J. Weber. I want to extend special thanks to my daughter Kristin Engstrand and my good friend Cindy van Stralen, who helped in innumerable ways, from mundane photocopying to careful proofreading, and offered support through each new deadline. I am also grateful to Paul Raymond of D. C. Heath for suggesting me for this project. Finally, I appreciate the confidence and encouragement of James Miller, history editor at D. C. Heath, and the excellent work of developmental editor Lauren Johnson, production editor Rosemary Jaffe, permissions editor Margaret Roll, designer Kenneth Hollman, and photo researcher Martha Shethar, all of whom made this a better book.

I. H. W. E.

Contents

Document Set 1

The Old World and the New: Native Americans Meet Europeans, 1542–1805

When most Americans think about the early history of the United States, they recall events of the seventeenth century—the colonization of Jamestown in 1607, perhaps, or the Pilgrims' landing at Plymouth in 1620, meeting the Indians of the eastern woodlands and desperately attempting to survive their first dangerous winters. From the East, the Europeans pushed slowly across the continent, in search of better lands, fresh economic opportunities, or just the chance to start life anew.

From a western perspective, United States history is a different story. This continent's first inhabitants, the Native Americans, were descendants of travelers who bridged the gap between Asia and America across the Bering Strait sometime between twelve thousand and fifteen thousand years ago. These first visitors continued southward through Canada and on to California, following the Pacific coast. Others traveled along the foothills of the Rocky Mountains and then eastward across the Great Plains into the Atlantic seaboard areas. These Indians probably were organized into bands of a few extended families that numbered under fifty people each. Although the North American population boasted hundreds of distinct linguistic groups, few of them had anything in the way of a migration legend. Many Native Americans assumed that human beings were created first in the regions that they themselves inhabited. Others, however, especially in the Southwest and in southern California, told tales of wanderings from the far north.

Initially, these hunters relied heavily on large game for food, but by 3000 B.C. they had diversified and had added a variety of plant and marine life to their daily fare. These dietary changes led to a population increase and settlement in permanent villages.

In the north lived the Eskimo or Inuit, an ice-hunting people whose culture enabled them to survive the extreme weather. Highly specialized groups of seafaring tribes dotted the northern Pacific coast. They skillfully built watercraft, and the abundance of fish and fur-bearing animals provided enough material sustenance for them to achieve a high degree of artistic culture. Rather than practicing agriculture, they gathered berries, leaves, and roots.

The Central Plains region south of the Great Lakes was inhabited by tribes practicing a mixed economy of hunting and agriculture. The Indians lived in skin tipis that they could move easily during the buffalo-hunting season. They killed the animals with stone-tipped spears and arrows and used strategies to divert herds over cliffs and into other pitfalls. To supplement their diet, they also practiced some agriculture. In Utah, Colorado, and areas farther south and west, Native American culture reached its highest point. Here the Indians dwelled in large villages located along the river valleys. For many centuries, people such as the Hohokam of what is now southern Arizona engaged in agriculture and used sophisticated methods of irrigation. Raids by nomadic tribes from the north forced these people into cliff-dwelling sites or fortified town settlements (pueblos) on the tops of isolated mesas.

In the Rocky Mountain–Pacific coast areas, poor hunting tribes first inhabited the country. After 3000 B.C., as the archaeological remains of mortars, pestles, grinding stones, and mullers reveal, the Indians relied more heavily than before on plants for food. By the time of contact with Europeans, the native population of California reached somewhere between 135,000 and 350,000. Hunters and gatherers, these people spoke some 135 different dialects that have been organized into six major linguistic groups: Algonquian, Athabascan, Penutian, Hokan, Uto-Aztekan, and Yukian. Many of these languages extended into the Rocky Mountains, the Great Basin, and the desert regions.

The prehistoric San Dieguito and La Jolla cultures dating from 7000 B.C. to about 5000 B.C. occupied California's southern coastal area but later were replaced by native peoples from the north. These new migrants, primarily the Kumeyaay, greeted the first Spaniards who appeared in 1542. By this time, explorers and adventurers carrying the Spanish flag had already discovered and charted the Pacific coast, sent expeditions into the great Southwest as far inland as central Kansas, and explored the coastal regions of what are now Florida and the Gulf states. Movements of the English and French on the eastern seaboard often overshadowed these Spanish activities. Nevertheless, sailing expeditions from all of these European countries, as well as from the Netherlands, Portugal, and Russia, reached the Pacific during the next two centuries.

Because we have few firsthand accounts of these times by Indians, we must rely on their oral tradition and the observations of native peoples made by Europeans and Americans who did leave records. Much Native American history has been handed down for generations by word of mouth. Document 1, recorded from the Yokuts of the San Joaquin Valley by traveler Stephen Powers in 1877, explains the origin of the mountains. The second selection, "Mouse Steals Fire," explains why the Indians speak so many different languages. This passage comes from the oral tradition of the Miwoks of Marin County, north of San Francisco.

The third selection, from the log of Juan Rodríguez Cabrillo in September and October 1542, describes the first European-Indian contact in San Diego Bay, on Catalina Island, and along the coast past San Pedro and Ventura. The Indians already knew of other Spaniards traveling in the interior. Document 4 is Sebastián Vizcaíno's account in November 1602 and records Indian reactions at the same places that Cabrillo had visited sixty years before. Members of the Society of Jesus (Jesuits) founded the first mission in Baja California at Loreto in 1697 and expanded their settlements to the north and south until 1767. The fifth selection is a sketch by the Bohemian Jesuit Father Ignacio Tirsch, who served at the tip of Baja California in the 1760s. Document 6 is by a Franciscan father, Pedro Font, and gives his rationale in 1775 for gaining new converts among the Yuma Indians dwelling between Arizona and California.

Document 7 is as close to a firsthand account by native peoples as it is possible to obtain. José Mariano Moziño, a naturalist born in Mexico, lived with the Mowachaht Indians of Nootka Sound on Vancouver Island for more than four months in the spring and summer of 1792, learning the language and becoming familiar with their customs, religion, and history. A trained scientist, Moziño had no agenda to save souls or to achieve economic gains, and so he recorded the Mowachahts' customs objectively. Document 8, from the journal of the exploring expeditions of the *Sutil* and *Mexicana* commanded by Dionísio Alcalá Galiano and Cayetano Valdés of the Spanish navy, describes the Indians in the area of Monterey in 1792. Formerly with the Malaspina expedition of 1791, Alcalá Galiano and Valdés remained to investigate the area of Vancouver Island and the Pacific coast in greater detail. They returned to San Blas with the scientist José Moziño, author of the previous selection.

After 1800 President Thomas Jefferson began thinking seriously about westward expansion and commissioned Meriwether Lewis and William Clark to lead an expedition overland to the Pacific coast. Upon reaching the mouth of the Columbia River, the team returned to the East Coast following the same route. The final document conveys the observations of Captain Lewis in August 1805. One of his guides, the Shoshone woman Sacajawea, also served as an interpreter and no doubt contributed information about Shoshone social organization.

Together these documents provide insights into Indian life and customs. The mission point of view is obvious in those passages written by priests, and their biases must be kept in mind. In studying documents, it is always important to know the writer's background and objectives and the circumstances under which he or she recorded the material. Even then, drawing clear-cut conclusions is difficult.

Questions for Analysis

1. How do Indian stories of the earliest times compare with Christian or other interpretations of how the world began? Do you think that they comforted Native Americans?
2. What aspects of Indian life most interested the Spaniards?
3. Do the accounts in this document set reinforce or differ from views about Spanish-Indian contact that you previously held?
4. What difficulties did the Spaniards face after landing on or crossing over unfamiliar terrain?
5. How did the introduction of horses change Indian life?
6. What were Father Pedro Font's motives in working among the Indians? Do you think that he felt any kinship with the natives?
7. How do the Spaniards reporting on the Indians at Monterey and Nootka Sound differ in their attitudes from those of Father Font?
8. Which characteristics or activities of the Indians do you find particularly interesting?
9. How did the Shoshones treat women?

1. The Yokuts Describe the Origin of the Mountains

Once there was a time when there was nothing in the world but water. About the place where Tulare Lake is now, there was a pole standing far up out of the water, and on this pole perched a hawk and a crow. First one of them would sit on the pole a while, then the other would knock him off and sit on it himself. Thus they sat on top of the pole above the waters for many ages. At length they wearied of the lonesomeness, and they created the birds which prey on fish such as the kingfisher, eagle, pelican, and others. Among them was a very small duck, which dived down to the bottom of the water, picked its beak full of mud, came up, died, and lay floating on the water. The hawk and the crow then fell to work and gathered from the duck's beak the earth which it had brought up, and commenced making the mountains. They began at the place now known as Ta-hí-cha-pa [Tehachapi] Pass, and the hawk made the east range, while the crow made the west one. Little by little, as they dropped in the earth, these great mountains grew athwart the face of the waters, pushing north. It was a work of many years, but finally they met together at Mount Shasta, and their labors were ended. But, behold, when they compared their mountains, it was found that the crow's was a great deal the larger. Then the hawk said to the crow, "How did this happen, you rascal? I warrant you have been stealing some of the earth from my bill, and that is why your mountains are the biggest." It was a fact, and the crow laughed in his claws. Then the hawk went and got some Indian tobacco and chewed it, and it made him exceedingly wise. So he took hold of the mountains and turned them round in a circle, putting his range in place of the crow's; and that is why the Sierra Nevada is larger than the Coast Range.

2. The Miwok Tell the Story "Mouse Steals Fire"

A long time ago, in the very beginning of things, the people in the hills were freezing, for they had no fire with which to keep warm. They gathered in their assembly house to talk over what they could do. There were Black Goose, White Goose, Lizard, Coyote, Mouse, and many others. It was Lizard, sitting on the rock outside of the assembly house, who discovered fire emerging from an assembly house in the valley below.

Later, Mouse, the Flute-player, slipped away unnoticed to go and steal some of the fire from the valley people. He took with him four of his flutes. When he arrived at the assembly house in the valley he found Bear, Rattlesnake, Mountain Lion, and Eagle guarding all the entrances. But Mouse managed, nevertheless, to get into the house. He climbed on top of the house, and while Eagle slept he cut two of his wing feathers which were covering the smoke hole, and slipped in.

Once in, he began to play his flute for the people. The music soon lulled them to sleep, and, when they were all snoring, Mouse safely filled his four flutes with fire and escaped.

When the people awoke they searched all over the hills for the one who had stolen fire from them.

Eagle sent Wind, Rain, and Hail in pursuit, for they were considered the swiftest travelers among the valley people. Finally Hail came up to Mouse, but Mouse had concealed his flutes under a buckeye tree just before Hail overtook him, and so denied having the fire. Hail believed him and departed.

Because Mouse placed his flutes of fire under the buckeye tree, there remains to this day fire in the buckeye tree, and people today obtain their fire with a drill of buckeye wood.

After Hail's departure, Mouse resumed his journey with his four flutes of fire. He met Coyote, who had become impatient fearing some dreadful fate had befallen Flute-player, and had gone out to find him.

Arrived home, Mouse sat on top of the assembly house, playing his flutes and dropping coals through the smokehole.

Coyote interrupted him, however, before he was finished, and so it is that the people who sat in the middle of the house received fire. Those people now cook their food and talk correctly. The people who sat around the edge of the room did not get any fire and today when they talk their teeth chatter with the cold. That is the way the languages began. If Coyote had not interrupted and Mouse had been able to finish playing all his flutes of fire, everyone would have received a share of fire and all would have spoken one language.

Indians today talk many different languages for the reason that all did not receive an equal share of fire.

3. A Summary Account of Juan Rodríguez Cabrillo's Voyage Describes Meetings with Southern California Indians, 1542

. . . On the following Thursday they went about six leagues along a coast running north-northwest, and discovered a port, closed and very good, which they named San Miguel [San Diego]. It is in thirty-four and one-third degrees. Having cast anchor in it, they went ashore where there were people. Three of them waited, but all the rest fled. To these three they gave some presents and they said by signs that in the interior men like the Spaniards had passed. They gave signs of great fear. On the night of this day they went ashore from the ships to fish with a net, and it appears that here there were some Indians, and that they began to shoot at them with arrows and wounded three men.

Next day in the morning they went with the boat farther into the port, which is large, and brought two boys, who understood nothing by signs. They gave them both shirts and sent them away immediately.

Next day in the morning three adult Indians came to the ships and said by signs that in the interior men like us were travelling about, bearded, clothed, and armed like those of the ships.[1] They made signs that they carried cross-bows and swords; and they made gestures with the right arm as if they were throwing lances, and ran around as if they were on horseback. They made signs that they were killing many native Indians, and that for this reason they were afraid. These people are comely and large. They go about covered with skins of animals. While they were in this port a heavy storm occurred, but since the port is good they did not feel it at all. It was a violent storm from the west-southwest and the south-southwest. This is the first storm which they have experienced. They remained in this port until the following Tuesday. The people here called the Christians Guacamal.

On the following Tuesday, the 3d of the month of October, they departed from this port of San Miguel, and on Wednesday, Thursday, and Friday, they held their course a matter of eighteen leagues along the coast, where they saw many valleys and plains, and many smokes, and mountains in the interior. At nightfall they were near some islands which are some seven leagues from the mainland, but because the wind went down they could not reach them that night.

At daybreak on Saturday, the 7th of the month of October, they were at the islands which they named San Salvador [Santa Catalína] and La Vitoria [San Clemente]. They anchored at one of them and went ashore with the boat to see if there were people; and when the boat came near, a great number of Indians emerged from the bushes and grass, shouting, dancing, and making signs that they should land. As they saw that the women were fleeing, from the boats they made signs that they should not be afraid. Immediately they were reassured, and laid their bows and arrows on the ground and launched in the water a good canoe which held eight or ten Indians, and came to the ships. They gave them beads and other articles, with which they were pleased, and then they returned. Afterward the Spaniards went ashore, and they, the Indian women, and all felt very secure. Here an old Indian made signs to them that men like the Spaniards, clothed and bearded, were going about on the mainland. They remained on this island only till midday.

On the following Sunday, the 8th of said month, they drew near to the mainland in a large bay which they called Bay of the Smokes [Santa Monica Bay] because of the many smokes which they saw on it. Here they held a colloquy [dialogue] with some Indians whom they captured in a canoe, and who made signs that toward the north there were Spaniards like them. This bay is in thirty-five degrees and is a good port, and the country is good, with many valleys, plains, and groves.

On the following Monday, the 9th of the said month of October, they left the Bay of the Fires and sailed this day some six leagues, anchoring in a large bay. From here they departed the next day, Tuesday, and sailed some eight leagues along a coast running from northwest to southeast. We saw on the land a pueblo [village] of Indians close to the sea, the houses being large like those of New Spain. They anchored in front of a very large valley on the coast. Here there came to the ships many very good canoes, each of which held twelve or thirteen Indians; they told them of Christians who were going about in the interior. The coast runs from northwest to southeast. Here they gave them some presents, with which they were greatly pleased. They indicated by signs that in seven days they could go to where the Spaniards were, and Juan Rodríguez decided to send two Spaniards into the interior. They also indicated that there was a great river. With these Indians they sent a letter at a venture to the Christians. They named this town the Pueblo of Las Canoas. The Indians dress in skins of animals; they are fishermen and eat raw fish; they were eating *maguey* [Agave americana] also. This pueblo is in thirty-five and one-third degrees. The interior of the country is a very fine valley; and they made signs that in that valley there was much maize and abundant food. Behind the valley appear some very high mountains and very broken country. They call the Christians Taquimine. Here they took possession and here they remained until Friday, the 13th day of said month. . . .

---

[1]These were most likely members of the Coronado expedition traveling into the Southwest from 1540 to 1542.

4. *Sebastián Vizcaíno Also Tells About Indians of Southern California, 1602*

. . . On the 12th of the said month [November], which was the day of the glorious San Diego, the general, admiral, religious, captains, ensigns, and almost all the men went on shore. A hut was built and mass was said in celebration of the feast of Señor San Diego. When it was over the general called a council to consider what was to be done in this port [San Diego], in order to get through quickly. It was decided that the admiral, with the chief pilot, the pilots, the masters, calkers, and seamen should scour the ships, giving them a good cleaning, which they greatly needed, and that Captain Peguero, Ensign Alarcon, and Ensign Martin de Aguilar should each attend to getting water for his ship, while Ensign Juan Francisco, and Sergeant Miguel de Lagar, with the carpenters, should provide wood.

When this had all been agreed upon, a hundred Indians appeared on a hill with bows and arrows and with many feathers on their heads, yelling noisily at us. The general ordered Ensign Juan Francisco to go to them with four arquebusiers,[1] Father Fray Antonio following him in order to win their friendship. The ensign was instructed that if the Indians fled he should let them go, but that if they waited he should regale them. The Indians waited, albeit with some fear. The ensign and soldiers returned, and the general, his son, and the admiral went toward the Indians. The Indians seeing this, two men and two women came down from a hill. They having reached the general, and the Indian women weeping, he cajoled and embraced them, giving them some things. Reassuring the others by signs, they descended peacefully, whereupon they were given presents. The net was cast and fish were given them. Whereupon the Indians became more confident and went to their rancherías and we to our ships to attend to our affairs.

. . .

In this bay the general, with his men, went ashore. After they had gone more than three leagues along it a number of Indians appeared with their bows and arrows, and although signs of peace were made to them, they did not dare to approach, excepting a very old Indian woman who appeared to be more than one hundred and fifty years old and who approached weeping. The general cajoled her and gave her some beads and something to eat. This Indian woman, from extreme age, had wrinkles on her belly which looked like a blacksmith's bellows, and the naval protruded bigger than a gourd. Seeing this kind treatment the Indians came peaceably and took us to their rancherías, where they were gathering their crops and where they had made their *paresos* of seeds like flax. They had pots in which they cooked their food, and the women were dressed in skins of animals. The general would not allow any soldier to enter their rancherías; and, it being already late, he returned to the frigate, many Indians accompanying him to the beach. Saturday night he reached the captain's ship, which was ready; wood, water, and fish were brought on board, and on Wednesday, the 20th of the said month, we set sail. I do not state, lest I should be tiresome, how many times the Indians came to our camps with skins of martens and other things. Until the next day, when we set sail, they remained on the beach shouting. This port was given the name of San Diego.

We left the port of San Diego, as has been said, on a Wednesday, the 20th of the said month [November] and the same day the general ordered Ensign Sebastian Melendes to go ahead with the frigate to examine a bay which was to windward some four leagues, and directed that the pilot should sound it, map it, and find out what was there. He did so, and the next day ordered the return to the captain's ship. He reported to the general that he had entered the said bay, that it was a good port, although it had at its entrance a bar of little more than two fathoms depth, and that there was a very large grove at an estuary which extended into the land, and many Indians:

---

[1]*Arquebusiers* were men who fired a portable but heavy matchlock gun called a harquebus.

and that he had not gone ashore. Thereupon we continued our voyage, skirting along the coast until the 24th of the month, which was the eve of the feast of the glorious Santa Catalina, when we discovered three large islands. We approached them with difficulty because of a head-wind, and arrived at the middle one, which is more than twenty-five leagues around.

On the 27th of the month, and before casting anchor in a very good cove which was found, a multitude of Indians came out in canoes of cedar and pine, made of planks very well joined and calked, each one with eight oars and with fourteen or fifteen Indians, who looked like galley-slaves. They came alongside without the least fear and came on board our ships, mooring their own. They showed great pleasure at seeing us, telling us by signs that we must land, and guiding us like pilots to the anchorage. The general received them kindly and gave them some presents, especially to the boys. We anchored, and the admiral, Ensign Alarcon, Father Fray Antonio, and Captain Peguero, with some soldiers, went ashore. Many Indians were on the beach, and the women treated us to roasted sardines and a small fruit like sweet potatoes. Fresh water was found, although a long distance from the beach.

The next day the general and the Father Commissary went ashore, a hut was built, and mass was said. More than one hundred and fifty Indian men and women were present, and they marvelled not a little at seeing the altar and the image of our Lord Jesus crucified, and listened attentively to the saying of mass, asking by signs what it was about. They were told that it was about heaven, whereat they marvelled more. When the divine service was ended the general went to their houses, where the women took him by the hand and led him inside, giving him some of the food which they had given before. He brought to the ship six Indian girls from eight to ten years old, whom their mothers willingly gave him, and he clothed them with chemises, petticoats, and necklaces, and sent them ashore. The rest of the women, seeing this, came with their daughters in canoes, asking for gifts. The result was that no one returned empty-handed. The people go dressed in seal skins, the women especially covering their loins, and their faces show them to be modest; but the men are thieves, for anything they saw unguarded they took. They are a people given to trade and traffic and are fond of barter, for in return for old clothes they would give the soldiers skins, shells, nets, thread, and very well twisted ropes, these in great quantities and resembling linen. They have dogs like those in Castile. . . .

5. Father Ignacio Tirsch Sketches Indians in Baja California, 1763

Out of the wilderness a heathen and his wife are coming with their daughters and son to the Mission to be converted.

6. Father Pedro Font Describes His Search for New Converts Among the Yuma Indians, 1775

. . . Finally, these people as a rule are gentle, gay, and happy. Like simpletons who have never seen anything, they marveled as if everything they saw was a wonder to them, and with their impertinent curiosity they made themselves troublesome and tiresome, and even nuisances, for they wearied us by coming to the tents and examining everything. They liked to hear the mules bray, and especially some burros which came in the expedition, for before the other expedition they had never seen any of these animals. Since the burros sing and bray longer and harder than the mules, when they heard them they imitated them in their way with great noise and hullabaloo.

As a conclusion to all that I have said, since I have been somewhat prolix in speaking of the Yumas and their customs, I wish to note down a question or reflection which many times came to me in this journey, in view of the ignorance, infelicity, and misery in which live the Indians whom I saw on all the journey as far as the port of San Francisco. For it is true that the Yumas undoubtedly may be reputed as the most fortunate, rich, and prosperous of them all, since at least they have plenty to eat, and live on their lands, and suffer fewer inconveniences. But the rest, whom I saw farther inland, are in constant warfare between the different villages, as a consequence of which they live in continual alarm, and go about like Cain, fugitive and wandering, possessed by fear and in dread at every step. Moreover, it seems as if they have hanging over them the curse which God put upon Nebuchadnezzar, like beasts eating the grass of the fields, and living on herbs and grass seeds, with a little game from deer, hare, ground squirrels, mice, and other vermin.

. . . On this assumption, and since the Apostles asked Christ that question concerning the man who was blind from his birth: *Rabbi quis peccavit, hic aut parentes ejus, ut caecus nasceretur?*[1] I might inquire what sin was committed by these Indians and their ancestors that they should grow up in those remote lands of the north with such infelicity and unhappiness, in such nakedness and misery, and above all with such blind ignorance of everything that they do not even know the transitory conveniences of the earth in order to obtain them; nor much less, as it appeared to me from what I was able to learn from them, do they have any knowledge of the existence of God, but live like beasts, without making use of reason or discourse, and being distinguished from beasts only by possessing the bodily or human form, but not by their deeds.

And this same question, and all the rest which I have said, is applicable to many other tribes who inhabit the unknown lands of the Arctic and Antarctic regions and other parts of the earth. But I know that the answer is, *Neque hic peccavit, neque parentes ejus, sed ut manifestentur opera dei in illo.*[2] And so, since God created them, His Divine Majesty knows the high purposes for which He wished them to be born to such misery, or that they should live so blind, and it does not belong to us to try to inquire into such high secrets, for *Judicia Dei abyssus multa.*[3]

But, considering that the mercy of God is infinite, and that so far as it is His part, He wishes that all men should be saved, and should come to the knowledge of the eternal truths, as says the Apostle St. Paul, *Qui omnes homines vult salvos fieri, et ad agnitionem veritatis venire;*[4] therefore, I cannot do less than piously surmise, in favor of those poor Indians, that God must have some special providence hidden from our curiosity, to the end that they may be saved, and that not all of them shall be damned. For, as the theologians say, if there should be a man in the forest without knowledge of God and entirely remote from possibility of acquiring the necessary instruction, God would make use of His angels to give him the necessary knowledge for eternal salvation. And that man *in sylvis*[5] whom the theologians assume as an hypothesis, is typified without doubt by some of the Indians whom I saw, and by others who must be farther inland and whom I have not seen. For if God has permitted those people to live for so many hundreds and even thousands of years in such ignorance and blindness that they hardly know themselves, or, as I believe, that they are rational beings, what can we infer, especially in view of a God so merciful that *Misericordia ejus superexaltat judicium?*[6]

Shall we think that God created these men merely to condemn them to Inferno, after passing

---

[1]"And his disciples asked Him: 'Rabbi, who hath sinned, this man, or his parents, that he should be born blind!' " (John, IX, 2).

[2]"Jesus answered: 'Neither hath this man sinned, nor his parents; but that the works of God should be made manifest in him' " (John, IX, 3).

[3]"Thy justice is as the mountains of God: thy judgments are a great deep" (Psalm XXXV, 7).

[4]"For this is good and acceptable in the sight of God our Saviour, who will have all men to be saved, and to come to the knowledge of the truth" (First Epistle of St. Paul to Timothy, II, 3–4).

[5]"In the forest."

[6]"And mercy exalteth itself above judgment" (Epistle of St. James the Apostle, II, 13).

in this world a life so miserable as that which they live? By no means! Shall we say that the Devil is more powerful than God, and rules so many souls who live in the shades of a negative infidelity, and that God shall not communicate to them some light, in order that they may be freed from his tyrannical and eternal powers? Even less. Well, then, we must believe that God has some hidden means for saving those souls whom at such cost He redeemed by His most precious blood, an opinion which can be supported by the text of the prophet Joel, chap. 2, verse 32: *Et erit omnis qui invocaverit nomen domini salvus erit quia in monte Sion et in Jerusalem erit salvatio, sicut dixit dominus.*[7] . . .

7. *José Mariano Moziño Describes the Mowachahts of Vancouver Island, 1792*

The government of these people can strictly be called patriarchal, because the chief of the nation carries out the duties of father of the families, of king, and high priest at the same time. These three offices are so closely intertwined that they mutually sustain each other, and all together support the sovereign authority of the *taises* [chiefs]. The vassals receive their sustenance from the hands of the monarch, or from the governor who represents him in the distant villages under his rule. The vassals believe that they owe this sustenance to the intercession of the sovereign with God. Thus the fusion of political rights with religious rights forms the basis of a system which at first glance appears more despotic than that of the caliphs and is so in certain respects, but which shows moderation in others. There is no intermediate hierarchy between princes and commoners. This latter condition includes all those who are not brothers or immediate relatives of the *tais,* and they are known by the name of *meschimes.* The former are called *taiscatlati,* that is to say, brothers of the chief.

The moderation of this system consists in the fact that the monarch, in spite of being convinced of the value of his orations, does not fail to recognize that these would be unfruitful for the sustenance of himself and his subjects if they did not also employ their working efforts in fishing, hunting, lumbering, and so forth. This obliges him to arm them like sons to defend themselves from their enemies at all risk, and to alleviate as much as possible the hardships of life. It would be very boring to express in detail the deeds that substantiate what I have referred to; suffice it to say that in Maquinna I have always observed inexpressible feeling over the loss of one of his subjects by death or flight; that his subjects treat him with familiarity but maintain at the same time an inviolable respect.

The *tais* always travels in the company of two or three princes of his blood and occupies the center of the canoe. At the two ends paddle the *meschimes,* and no one sits at his side except his relatives and his wives. When the chief retires, his men run hurriedly to accompany him, even if they are enjoying themselves, unless he himself occupies them with some other thing, or wishes to walk alone. The *tais* never works, and even to watch over those who assist in the fishing, he ordinarily assigns one of the *catlati.* He is the first minister of sacrifices, and the principal repository of the religious secrets.

I find it extremely difficult to give this religion an adequate name, unless I may call it a kind of Manicheism, because the natives recognize the existence of a God Creator, Preserver of all things. They also believe in another malign deity, author of wars, of infirmities, and of death. They hate and detest this abominable originator of their calamities, while they venerate and exalt the benevolent God who created them. In his observance, the barbaric high priest fasts many days. He constantly abstains from the pleasures of love

[7]"And it shall come to pass, that every one that shall call upon the name of the Lord shall be saved: for in mount Zion and in Jerusalem shall be salvation, as the Lord hath said" (The Prophecy of Joel, II, 32).

all the time that the moon is not full. He sings hymns accompanied by his family, honoring the benefactions of *Qua-utz* (which is what they call the Creator), and in sacrifice the *tais* throws whale oil into the flames and scatters feathers to the wind.

The manner in which they relate the creation of man in the beginning is rather amusing. They say that God created a woman who was left perfectly alone in the obscure forests of Yuquatl, in which lived deer without antlers, dogs without tails, and ducks without wings; that, isolated there, she cried day and night in her loneliness without finding the least means of remedying her sad situation until Qua-utz, sympathizing with her tears, allowed her to see on the ocean a very resplendent canoe of copper in which, with paddles of the same metal, many handsome young men came paddling. Astonished by this spectacle, the island girl remained stunned at the foot of the tree, until one of the paddlers advised her that it was the All-Powerful who had had the goodness to visit that beach and supply her with the company she longed for. At these words the melancholy solitary girl redoubled her weeping; her nose began to run, and she sneezed its loathsome discharge onto the nearby sand. Qua-utz then ordered her to pick up what she had sneezed out, and to her astonishment she found palpitating the tiny body of a man which had just been formed. She gathered it up, by order of the Deity, in a shell appropriate to its size, and was admonished to continue keeping it in other larger shells as it grew in size. After this, the Creator got into the boat again, after having allowed even the animals to share in his liberality, because at the same moment the deer saw antlers grow over his forehead, the dog began to wag a tail—with which he found himself provided—from one side to the other, and the birds were able to lift themselves by the wind and try out for the first time the gift of wings which they had just received. The man grew little by little, passing successively from one cradle to another until he began to walk. Having left his childhood, the first proof he gave of his early manhood was to impregnate his mistress, whose first-born created the family tree of the *taises* while the other siblings formed that of the common people.

I do not know what to say about Matlox, inhabitant of the mountainous district, of whom all have an unbelievable terror. They imagine his body as very monstrous, all covered with stiff black bristles; a head similar to a human one, but with much greater, sharper, and stronger fangs than those of the bear; extremely long arms; and toes and fingers armed with long curved claws. His shouts alone (they say) force those who hear them to the ground, and any unfortunate body he slaps is broken into a thousand pieces. I presume that the story of Matlox has the same foundation as that of the creation of man, to which I have just referred; or that from most ancient times the tribe to which these natives owe their origin received some account of the existence of demons.[1] . . .

8. Dionísio Alcalá Galiano and Cayetano Valdés Comment on the Indians of Monterey, 1792

. . . Among the Runsienes and Eslenes each man was permitted no more than one wife, and their infidelities were neither punished nor hardly even heeded; with the former being careful, nevertheless, to punish severely the accomplice of an adulterer with sticks, wounds, and incisions, from which once in a while she died. Whereas among the second group [Eslenes] it was not only common to repudiate the woman and then even later to readmit her in her same status, but also she

[1]Modern writers list a number of demons or supernatural beings that plagued the lives of the Nootkan Indians. These included the Thunderbird, a huge man living in the remote snow-covered peaks, headless birds, and a mountain lion that walked backward and killed men with a long lancelike tail; even the "souls of Trees" were malignant.

was given at times by the first husband to the new lover, if both transgressors desired it and the latter gave the beads and other goods that the former had given to the family for her purchase.

This method of buying wives was common to both nations, although among the Runsienes the intervention of the families of the sweethearts made the contract much more solemn, those of the man contributing with their share for the purpose, which was divided between those of the bride at the time of handing her over.

They show signs of tenderness toward their children, and like sensitive people, they never leave them, not even in their most tiring occupations, but rather they are frequently seen loaded down with their little ones. They are loving mothers, and they are not indifferent nor unfaithful wives. Very few weaknesses are noted, and they seem to be attentive in fulfilling their duties. The women in general are fertile and strong. In California it is not rare to give birth in the field and for the new mother to undertake her tasks as soon as she has successfully given birth.

Robbery was a crime almost unknown to both nations. Among the Runsienes they also look at the killing of another person with indifference. It is not so with the Eslenes, who punish the delinquent the same way [with death] unless he acted with the permission of the chief, which he had asked for and which is usually given when there is a disturber of public tranquility.

The funeral services that accompany the death of a chief are not equal but similar. Only the family or the entire tribe get together to cry around the corpse, cutting their hair and throwing ashes over their faces. At this ceremony, which at times lasts four days, they keep giving out clothing and beads, dividing finally among the family the few things that comprised the property of the deceased. The Eslenes, on the contrary, did not distribute anything, but rather all of [the chief's] friends and subjects had to contribute some beads, which were burned with him.

We shouldn't stop speaking of the customs of the Indians who are present at Mission San Carlos without reporting on one that the father president [Lasuén] said had been noted among them from the time of arrival of the religious in that place, and which they continue, the religious not having opposed it because it was not considered contrary to morality.

These natives make a circular trench in the ground and then they cover it with a bell-shaped hood, leaving a very narrow door as an entrance to that room, making it an oven. On one side of it they throw some firewood which they burn at the proper time. When the men come in from work, they go off to that heater, which is already prepared with the proper fire. They enter gradually up to the number that it can hold, while those who have to wait amuse themselves with various games.

Those who are inside suffer that unnatural heat that there is inside the heat chamber until they sweat a great deal; when they leave, they scrape their skin with the edge of a shell for that purpose, taking off with the sweat the filth that covers them. Afterwards they bathe in the river and on coming out they wallow in the dirt.[1]

We have not been able to learn whether this action is taken by them as a health preservative or as a means of giving rest to the body. . . .

9. Captain Meriwether Lewis Comments on Shoshone Life and Customs, 1805

. . . [F]rom what has [already] been said of the Shoshones it will be readily perceived that they live in a wretched stait of poverty. yet notwithstanding their extreem poverty they are not only cheerfull but even gay, fond of gaudy dress and amusements; like most other Indians they are great egotists and frequently boast of heroic acts which they never performed. they are also fond of games of wrisk. they are frank, communicative, fair in dealing, generous with the little they

[1]The sweathouse, called a *temescal* by the Spaniards, was commonly used throughout California.

possess, extreemly honest, and by no means beggarly. each individual is his own sovereign master, and acts from the dictates of his own mind; the authority of the Chief being nothing more than mere admonition supported by the influence which the propiety of his own examplery conduct may have acquired him in the minds of the individuals who compose the band. the title of cheif is not hereditary, nor can I learn that there is any cerimony of instalment, or other epoh in the life of a Cheif from which his title as such can be dated. in fact every man is a chief, but all have not an equal influence on the minds of the other members of the community, and he who happens to enjoy the greatest share of confidence is the principal Chief. The Shoshonees may be estimated at about 100 warriors, and about three times that number of woomen and children. they have more children among them than I expected to have seen among a people who procure subsistence with such difficulty. there are but few very old persons, nor did they appear to treat those with much tenderness or rispect. The man is the sole propryetor of his wives and daughters, and can barter or dispose of either as he thinks proper. a plurality of wives is common among them, but these are not generally sisters as with the Minnetares & Mandans but are purchased of different fathers. The father frequently disposes of his infant daughters in marriage to men who are grown or to men who have sons for whom they think proper to provide wives. the compensation given in such cases usually consists of horses or mules which the father receives at the time of contract and coverts to his own uce. the girl remains with her parents until she is conceived to have obtained the age of puberty which with them is considered to be about the age of 13 or 14 years. the female at this age is surrendered to her sovereign lord and husband agreeably to contract, and with her is frequently restored by the father quite as much as he received in the first instance in payment for his daughter; but this is discretionary with the father. Sah-car-gar-we-ah [Sacajawea] had been thus disposed of before she was taken by the Minnetares, or had arrived to the years of puberty. the husband was yet living and with this band. he was more than double her age and had two other wives. he claimed her as his wife but said that as she had had a child by another man, who was Charbono [Charbonneau], that he did not want her. They seldom correct their children particularly the boys who soon become masters of their own acts. they give as a reason that it cows and breaks the Sperit of the boy to whip him, and that he never recovers his independence of mind after he is grown. They treat their women but with little rispect, and compel them to perform every species of drudgery. they collect the wild fruits and roots, attend to the horses or assist in that duty cook dreess the skins and make all their apparal, collect wood and make their fires, arrange and form their lodges, and when they travel pack the horses and take charge of all the baggage; in short the man dose little else except attend his horses hunt and fish. the man considers himself degraded if he is compelled to walk any distance, and if he is so unfortunately poor as only to possess two horses he rides the best himself and leaves the woman or women if he has more than one, to transport their baggage and children on the other, and to walk if the horse is unable to carry the additional weight of their persons—the chastity of their women is not held in high estimation, and the husband will for a trifle barter the companion of his bead for a night or longer if he conceives the reward adiquate; tho' they are not so importunate that we should caress their women as the siouxs were and some of their women appear to be held more sacred than in any nation we have seen I have requested the men to give them no cause of jealousy by having connection with their women without their knowledge, which with them strange as it may seem is considered as disgracefull to the husband as clandestine connections of a similar kind are among civilized nations. to prevent this mutual exchange of good officies altogether I know it impossible to effect, particularly on the part of our young men whom some months abstanence have made very polite to those tawney damsels. . . .

References

1. The Yokuts Describe the Origin of the Mountains
   Stephen Powers, *Tribes of California* (Washington, D.C., 1877), pp. 383–384.
2. The Miwok Tell the Story "Mouse Steals Fire"
   Edward W. Gifford and Gwendoline Harris Block, eds., *Californian Indian Nights Entertainments* (1930; reprint ed., Lincoln: University of Nebraska Press, 1990), pp. 135–136.
3. A Summary Account of Juan Rodríguez Cabrillo's Voyage Describes Meetings with Southern California Indians, 1542
   Herbert Eugene Bolton, ed., *Spanish Exploration in the Southwest, 1542–1706* (1908; reprint ed., New York: Barnes & Noble, 1963), pp. 23–25.
4. Sebastián Vizcaíno Also Tells About Indians of Southern California, 1602
   Herbert Eugene Bolton, ed., *Spanish Exploration in the Southwest, 1542–1706* (1908; reprint ed., New York: Barnes & Noble, 1963), pp. 80–86.
5. Father Ignacio Tirsch Sketches Indians in Baja California, 1763
   Doyce B. Nunis, ed., *The Drawings of Ignacio Tirsch: A Jesuit Missionary in Baja California* (Los Angeles: Dawson's Book Shop, 1972), pp. 89–95.
6. Father Pedro Font Describes His Search for New Converts Among the Yuma Indians, 1775
   Font's Complete Diary: A Chronicle of the Founding of San Francisco, trans. and ed. Herbert Eugene Bolton (Berkeley: University of California Press, 1933), pp. 109–112.
7. José Mariano Moziño Describes the Mowachahts of Vancouver Island, 1792
   Noticias de Nutka: An Account of Nootka Sound in 1792, rev. ed., trans. and ed. Iris H. W. Engstrand (Seattle: University of Washington Press, 1991), pp. 24–28.
8. Dionísio Alcalá Galiano and Cayetano Valdés Comment on the Indians of Monterey, 1792
   Donald C. Cutter, *California in 1792: A Spanish Naval Visit* (Norman: University of Oklahoma Press, 1990), pp. 144–149.
9. Captain Meriwether Lewis Comments on Shoshone Life and Customs, 1805
   The Journals of the Lewis and Clark Expedition, July 28–November 1, 1805, ed. Gary E. Moulton (Lincoln: University of Nebraska Press, 1983), pp. 119–121.

Document Set 2

The Spanish Settle the Pacific Coast, 1769–1821

Spanish settlement of Alta, or upper, California did not come quickly or easily. More than two hundred years passed between the initial contact made by Juan Rodríguez Cabrillo in 1542 and the founding of Mission San Diego de Alcalá in July 1769. The region's wealth in gold and silver was not apparent in the early years, and the Spaniards moved into the area primarily to buttress their defense and to convert the native peoples to Christianity. Gaspar de Portolá led the military, and Franciscan Father Junípero Serra headed the religious branch of the first colonizing expedition—an effort designed to protect Spain's territories from foreign encroachment and to entice new converts into the mission system. In a letter to José de Gálvez (Document 1), the king's representative in Mexico City who had organized the expedition, Lieutenant Pedro Fages, reports on conditions in California.

After a short stay in San Diego, Portolá, accompanied by soldiers and Father Juan Crespí as diarist, set out for the north to find the port of Monterey, which Sebastían Vizcaíno had selected in 1603 as the capital of California. The explorers missed the port but instead discovered San Francisco Bay, a harbor whose narrow entrance from the sea is often obscured by fog and is difficult to see against the mountains in the background. In Document 2, Father Crespí records the event. Portolá's group returned to San Diego to join Serra and the others, and from there California settlement proceeded slowly.

By 1775 the Franciscans had founded five missions. Juan Bautista de Anza from the presidio (fortified settlement) of Tubac, south of Tucson, Arizona, eagerly sought to connect Sonora and California by an overland trail. After a successful journey in 1774–1775, Anza led an expedition of soldiers and families over a difficult desert route (Document 3), and the group, enlarged by eight babies born along the way, safely reached California. In late October 1775, however, several hundred nonmission Indians at San Diego revolted against the Spanish, attacked and burned the mission, and killed the resident priest, Luis Jayme. In Document 4, Father Serra indicates the action that he thought should have been taken. No further large-scale uprisings occurred until 1824, during the Mexican period.

By 1781, the Spanish had founded two towns—San José and Los Angeles. California's isolation discouraged civilians from settling the area, but eleven families finally took advantage of the free land offered at Los Angeles. The first census (Document 5) shows the diversity of those settlers who built houses fronting on the original plaza.

Other European nations eventually took an interest in the Pacific coast region. The British sent Captain James Cook on three globe-circling expeditions during which he discovered the Hawaiian Islands and visited the northwestern coast of America in 1778. The French, not to be left out, launched a major voyage of exploration under the Count of La Pérouse in Cook's wake. The French stopped in Monterey and commented at length on Spain's progress in California and the treatment of Indians at Mission San Carlos (Document 6). Because of the wealth of fur-bearing animals along the northern coast, the Spanish could not keep the area solely to themselves and finally became locked in a confrontation with the British over rights to occupy the region. English navigator George Vancouver met with Juan Francisco de la Bodega y Quadra, the Spanish commissioner, to discuss boundary claims and then spent two years visiting Hawaii and ports along the California coast (Document 7).

The Russians pursued the fur trade actively after a Danish explorer they hired, Vitus Bering, made an initial voyage into the Pacific in 1741. Establishing trading posts at Kodiak Island and Sitka, they attempted to open up trade with the Spaniards in 1806. Their efforts led to a well-publicized romance between the Russian Nikolai Petrovich Rezanov, chamberlain of the czar, and Doña Concepción Argüello, daughter of the San Francisco presidio commander José Darío Argüello (Document 8). Rezanov perished on his return trip to Russia to gain permission for the marriage, and poor Concepción did not learn of her fiancé's death until 1817. The Russians nevertheless established a colony at Fort Ross north of San Francisco Bay in 1812 and hunted sea otter. Concepción Argüello became a nun.

While Spain struggled to settle California and points north, the United States took shape as a nation and sent trading ships from Boston to join in the western coastal trade. John Jacob Astor's *Tonquin* sailed from New York in 1810 to the Oregon coast, delivering goods in 1811 to Fort Astoria at the mouth of the Columbia River. The ship put in at Hawaii, a frequent stopping place for vessels traveling to California. Document 9 provides a glimpse into the Hawaiian royal family in the early nineteenth century. Contact with Hawaii, an important commercial crossroads, continued as the West expanded.

The final days of Spanish California proved relatively peaceful. Indeed, the War for Independence that began in Mexico in 1810 had few repercussions along the Pacific coast, although Hipólito Bouchard, an Argentine patriot, attacked California in 1818 after stopping in Hawaii.

By 1820 Missouri, the first trans-Mississippi state, was admitted to the Union, and Americans began to look farther west. British trappers and traders occupied the Oregon Country, while men of all nationalities roamed the Southwest in search of beaver furs. Only a few travelers had come by sea to settle along the continent's most westerly shore.

Questions for Analysis

1. How would you evaluate the relationship between Indians and Spaniards at first contact?
2. How did the soldiers and Father Crespí survive during their long overland march from San Diego to San Francisco?
3. What is your impression of the status of women during the colonization period?
4. How did Father Serra feel about punishing the Indians for burning Mission San Diego?
5. How does the ethnic mix of the people who settled Los Angeles compare with its present-day composition?
6. What influenced the French view of Indians during the late eighteenth century?
7. How did British military strength compare with that of the Spaniards in 1792?
8. What motivated Russians to expand into California?
9. What was the governmental status of Hawaii during the early nineteenth century?

1. *Pedro Fages Writes a Letter to José de Gálvez Reporting on Alta California, 1769*

Your Illustrious Lordship—My dear Sir: I am remitting to Your Excellency a box of various little things that I have obtained in trade with the pagan Indians of this vicinity. Here their *rancherías* are many; in fact, in seven leagues around this Port I think there are perhaps eight *rancherías* and some of them are well populated.

We went with Don Miguel Costansó to examine the river which empties into this port. It was somewhat swollen when we arrived. In less than three leagues we found three *rancherías* along the bank. The river has dried up although at a depth of two spans [16 inches], by digging in the sand, very good water comes up. All along the banks there are very good water holes and woods; the land appears to me to be very good.

With regard to the Indians, they appear to be docile and alert. We have made very good friends with them and we are never lacking some little rabbits, hares, and fish that they bring to us. We give them some glass beads, but they value very highly any kind of cloth, no matter how poor it might be, since in exchange for some that I had, I received some furs and nets.

I am enclosing a report of what Box Number 1 contains and I will attempt, in exchange for beads and other items that the *San Carlos* carries for that purpose, to acquire more. Despite the fact that these pagan Indians appear of good character, I am observing precisely that which Your Excellency advised me in Instruction No. 9.[1] I also have very well in mind that which is contained in No. 13,[2] in conformance with which we have covered ourselves in a parapet which is armed with the two small cannon taken off the *Príncipe* [*San Antonio*] in preparation for whatever attempt they might make by day. By night I maintain two sentinels and they are changed every two hours. Don Fernando Rivera follows his own system for there are never enough precautions in suspicious country.

We have planted some seeds and later will probably plant corn.

I am desirous of additional orders from Your Excellency and can assure my prompt obedience. I ask that Our Lord guard your life many years.

Port of San Diego, June 26, 1769. Your most devoted servant and subject kisses the hand of Your Excellency.

Pedro Fages

His Illustrious Lordship Don José de Gálvez

Report of What Is Contained in Box No. 1

Large body shields	1
Medium-sized body shields	4
Medium-sized dried gourds	3
Simple straw hats	3
Large otter pelts	6
Small otter pelts	3
Wildcat pelts	3
Double nets for fishing	8
Simple nets for fishing and hunting	7
Feather headdresses of the *Ranchería* chiefs	8
Arrows with which they make war upon each other	18
Mallet painted various colors	1
Piece of red ochre	1

Note

I exchanged the two medium-sized dried gourds with the sailors of the *Príncipe* who had brought them from the pagan Indians of the Islands of the Santa Barbara Channel; all the rest I have traded with the pagan Indians of this area. Regarding the red ochre, they have given indications that there is much in the earth; I will not fail to ascertain this and other matters which might be of interest. In this encampment at San Diego, June 26, 1769.

Pedro Fages

[1] "9th. The natives are to be impressed with the advantages of peace and salvation and protection from foreign insult offered by the Spaniards."

[2] "13th. The natives are never to be fully trusted, but always watched, for the 'common enemy' will surely incite them to mischief."

2. *Father Juan Crespí Reports the Discovery of San Francisco Bay, 1769*

. . . Thursday, November 2.—To-day, All Souls' Day, we two celebrated Mass for the souls in Purgatory, and after Mass some of the soldiers asked permission to go out to hunt, for many deer have been seen. Some of them went quite a distance from the camp and climbed the hills, so that it was already night when they returned. They said that toward the north they had seen an immense arm of the sea, or an estuary, which penetrated into the land as far as the eye could reach, extending to the southeast; that they had seen some beautiful plains well adorned with trees, and that the smokes which they saw in all directions left no doubt that the country was thickly populated with heathen villages. This report confirmed us still more in the opinion that we were on the port of Our Father San Francisco, and that the arm of the sea which they told us about was certainly the estuary of which the pilot Cabrera Bueno spoke, the mouth of which we had not seen because we went down to the harbor through a ravine. That pilot, speaking of it, uses these words: "Through the opening in the center enters an estuary of salt water without any breaking of the waves at all, and by going in one will find friendly Indians and can easily take on water and wood." We conjectured also from these reports that the explorers could not have crossed to the opposite shore which was seen to the north, and consequently, would not succeed in exploring the point which we judge to be that of Los Reyes, for it would be impossible in the three days that they were to be gone to make the detour that they would unavoidably have to make to round the estuary, whose extent the hunters represented as being very great.

Friday, November 3.—To-day we had a feast on the good and very large mussels that are to be found in such abundance in this harbor. At night the explorers returned, firing loud salutes, thus letting us know in advance that they were bringing some good news. They told us what they had learned or inferred from the uncertain signs made by the heathen; that is, that two days' march from the place which they had reached, which was the end or head of the estuary, there was a harbor and a ship in it. As a result of this many now believed that we were at Monterey, and that the packet *San José* or the *San Carlos* was awaiting us. And certainly our necessities made us wish, even if we did not believe, that we were in Monterey instead of San Francisco. In consequence of these reports the commander decided to continue the journey in search of the port and ship of which the heathen had given information to our explorers.

Saturday, November 4.—We celebrated this day in honor of San Carlos, the patron of the royal presidio and mission to be founded at the port of Monterey, and also in honor of our king, Don Carlos III (whom God keep) by performing the holy sacrifice of Mass in this little valley, on the beach of the harbor, without the least doubt, of my Father San Francisco. About one in the afternoon we set out to continue the journey, following the beach to the north. We then entered the mountains, directing our course to the northeast and from the summit of a peak [Sweeny Ridge] we beheld the great estuary or arm of the sea, which must have a width of four or five leagues, and extends to the southeast and south-southeast. Keeping it always on the left hand, and, turning our backs to the bay, we took a valley open to the south and southwest. After three hours' travel in which we made two leagues, we halted in a valley at the foot of a mountain range covered with low, very green woods, and having near the camp a grove of live oaks on the west slope of the mountains. . . .

3. Juan Bautista de Anza Guides Soldiers and Families from Arizona to California, 1775

. . . Sunday, November 19.—At two o'clock in the morning a soldier reported that his wife, Dolores, had been taken with violent parturition pains. I got up immediately to arrange that she be given assistance, wherewith she successfully gave birth to a boy, for which reason I suspended the march for today. At a suitable hour the child was baptized.

Monday, November 20.—The mother not being in a fit condition to travel, it was necessary to remain here today.

Tuesday, November 21.—The patient being taken with severe pains and other troubles following upon the childbirth, it was not possible to march today. In the days just past, especially yesterday and today, the cold has been so severe that as a result of it and of the ice, six of our saddle animals have died during the last four days. In the course of [going back and forth], which it has been necessary to [do] at this place, there has been found in an estuary of the river a great quantity of salt that is both white and hard, from which the necessary supply has been obtained.

Wednesday, November 22.—At half past eleven we set forth on the march, continuing west-southwest along the bottom lands of the Gila by a road that was sandy in part, for in the stretch from this place to the junction with the Colorado begin the little sand hills which we commonly call médanos. They very badly crippled the riding animals because of their natural difficulty, as we experienced today, and now especially with the horned cattle. But having accomplished the passage and covered five leagues in as many hours, we halted for the night at the foot of a lone hill which we called Santa Cicilia [Antelope Hill], where the first pasturage was found. From Tubac to Santa Cicilia, 88 leagues.

Thursday, November 23.—Having loaded the packs, and even begun the march, the men who were driving the cattle reported that many beeves were lacking and had gone into the brush along the river, from which they could not extract them. On hearing this news, which required some delay and caused some trouble, I went back with men and also ordered those who were already on the way to return, since as a result of the occurrence there was not time enough now to get to the camp site, which it was necessary to reach in the daytime, for otherwise we should expose ourselves to still greater delays. The work of extracting the cattle from the brush was completed at the end of the afternoon, after imponderable labor, because the animals obstinately refused to travel and in order to escape it refused to come out of their hiding places, where they became so enraged that they attacked as if they were wild cattle. At nightfall a woman who is near parturition was taken with pains which continued the whole night long.

Friday, November 24.—Because this woman was suffering with most severe pains it was necessary to suspend the march today. Later in the day it was seen that the pains were not those most appropriate for the complete result, and for this reason measures were taken to prevent the miscarriage with which she was threatened, by means of such medicines as it was possible to give her, and as a result she improved during the night.

Saturday, November 25.—At half past nine we moved our train and set forth on the march to the west-southwest. In this direction we traveled four leagues in as many hours, along the bottom lands of the river, over ground that was as soft as it was full of thick brush, and as a result of which one of our horses died. At half past one we halted in order to pass the night at a place where pasturage was found and which we called Laguna Salada [west of Welton, Arizona]. Shortly after twelve o'clock I was met by a messenger from Palma, captain of the Yumas, who was sent to welcome me and to tell me that for four days he had been awaiting me about eight leagues this side of his house, but since I did not come he had returned to assemble provisions and prepare lodgings for me there, and to ask if I would please inform him just when I should arrive, in order that he might return to meet me, as he desired to see me and all my people. From Tubac to Laguna Salada, 92 leagues.

Sunday, November 26.—At ten o'clock we began our march, continuing along the same bottom lands and over the same kind of country, going west-northwest with some turns to the west. In this direction we traveled until nearly two o'clock, covering about four leagues, at the end of which we halted for the night at a place with some pasturage near some hills called Cerros del Cajón. From Tubac to the Cerros del Cajón, 96 leagues.

Monday, November 27.—At half past nine we continued our march, skirting some hills on the left and going toward the west with some turns to the west-northwest, until, at the end of three leagues, and having traveled a little more than three hours, we came to the end of the hills which we were skirting, when I was obliged to halt for the night at a place called Los Cerritos, because there was pasturage here, which is lacking all the way to the junction of the rivers, a stretch which is difficult to cover because the ground is of pure sand. From Tubac to Los Cerritos, 99 leagues. . . .

4. Father Junípero Serra Asks Viceroy Antonio Bucareli for Leniency for the Indians, 1775

Monterey, December 15, 1775

+

Hail Jesus, Mary, Joseph!

Most Excellent Lord.

My most revered and most excellent Sir:

As we are in the vale of tears, not all the news I have to relate can be pleasant. And so I make no excuses for announcing to Your Excellency the tragic news I have just received of the total destruction of the San Diego Mission, and of the death of the senior of its two religious ministers, called Father Fray Luis Jayme, at the hand of the rebellious gentiles and of the Christian neophytes. All this happened, November 5th, about one or two o'clock at night. The gentiles came together from forty rancherías, according to information given me, and set fire to the church, after sacking it. Then they went on to the storehouse, the house where the Fathers lived, the soldiers' barracks, and all the rest of the buildings.

They killed a carpenter from Guadalaxara and a blacksmith from Tepic. They wounded with their arrows the four soldiers, who alone were on guard at the said mission. Even though two of them were badly wounded, they have already recovered.

The other religious, whose name is Father Fray Vicente Fuster, over and above the fright he got, received no further injuries than a wound in the shoulder, caused by a stone. He suffered pain from it for several days. On the morning following that sad night, he withdrew, in company with the handful still surviving, to the presidio. They carried on the shoulders of those Christian Indians who had remained loyal the dead, and the badly wounded. From there he writes to me asking me to tell him what he is to do.

. . . On the subject of the loss of San Diego Mission, various thoughts have come to my mind. But since complaining about the past remedies nothing, I will change the subject. But, while I think of it, I might suggest again to Your Excellency what I proposed in one of my earlier letters: that in conquests of this kind the place where soldiers are most important is in the missions. The presidios, in many places, may be most suitable and very necessary; but for the situation here, I describe only what is before my eyes.

The San Diego Mission is about two leagues from the presidio, but it is in such a position that, throughout the day, they can see the mission from the presidio; and the gunshot that is fired each morning at dawn in the presidio, to change the watchword of the night guard, can generally be heard in the Mission. Yet while the mission was all on fire, the flames leaping up to a great height from one or two o'clock in the morning until dawn, and during all that time shooting was going on, they saw and heard nothing at the presidio; and the wind, they say, was favorable.

Although there were only two men who fired shots during all that time, many lives were saved which would have been lost without the said defense. And now, after the Father has been killed, the Mission burned, its many and valuable furnishings destroyed, together with the sacred vessels, its paintings, its baptismal, marriage and funeral records, and all the furnishings for the sacristy, the house, and the farm implements—now, the forces of both presidios come together to set things right.

While the circumstances leading up to the outbreak seem very much like the case of San Sabá Mission—which I was appointed to, and all in readiness to set out for, from our College, having been summoned in great haste for that purpose from the Sierra Gorda—may God not permit the results to be the same.

What happened was that before they set about re-establishing the Mission, they wanted to join the various presidios together, and lay hands on the guilty ones who were responsible for the burning of the Mission, and the death of the Fathers, and chastise them. The harassed Indians rebelled anew and became more enraged. I had to stay home and not set out for the Mission and I do not know whether, up to the present time, the Mission has been re-established or not.

And so the soldiers there are gathered together in the presidios, and the Indians in their state of heathenism.

Most Excellent Lord, one [of] the most important requests I made of the Most Illustrious Inspector General, at the beginning of these conquests was: if ever the Indians, whether they be gentile or Christian, killed me, they should be forgiven. The same request I make of Your Excellency. It has been my own fault I did not make this request before. To see a formal statement drawn up by Your Excellency to that effect, in so far as it concerns me, and the other religious who at present are subject to me or will be in the future, would be for me a special consolation during the time Our Lord God will be pleased to add to my advancing years.

While the missionary is alive, let the soldiers guard him, and watch over him, like the pupils of God's very eyes. That is as it should be. Nor do I disdain such a favor for myself. But after the missionary has been killed, what can be gained by campaigns?

Some will say to frighten them and prevent them from killing others.

What I say is that, in order to prevent them from killing others, keep better guard over them than they did over the one who has been killed; and, as to the murderer, let him live, in order that he should be saved—which is the very purpose of our coming here, and the reason which justifies it. Give him to understand, after a moderate amount of punishment, that he is being pardoned in accordance with our law, which commands us to forgive injuries; and let us prepare him, not for death, but for eternal life.

Most Excellent Lord, may Your Excellency pardon me for my interference, who knows for what result.

The details of all that has occurred, Your Excellency will see in the Officers' reports.

In the statements are suggested some discouraging news from the Colorado River. The fact is that Señor Anza has not yet put in his appearance, and we do not know what may have happened to him.

I have no time to say more, and I ask Your Excellency to overlook my deficiencies and indiscretions, because this letter has been written in great haste.

May God keep Your Excellency many years, and, in the interest of souls in these regions, may He extend the period in which you are to rule over these territories, as you now do with so much conscientious care, for the length of time I so devoutly wish. And may He ever keep you increasingly in His holy grace.

From this Mission, totally dependent on Your Excellency, of San Carlos de Monterey, December 15, 1775.

Most Excellent Lord,

Kissing the hand of Your Excellency,

Your most affectionate and devoted servant and chaplain, who holds you in the highest affection,

Fray Junípero Serra

5. The Los Angeles Census of 1781 Shows a Diverse Ethnic Mix

Census of the population of the Pueblo of the Queen of the Angeles (Reyna de los Angeles), founded on September 4, 1781, on the bank of the Porciuncula River, distant 45 leagues from the Presidio of San Diego, 27 leagues from the site selected for the establishment of the Presidio of Santa Barbara, and about a league and a half from Mission San Gabriel; including the names and ages of the residents, their wives, sons and daughters, and also showing the number of animals and their kind which have been distributed to them, with a note on those that are to be held in common as sires of the different kinds, the implements for smithing and for field work, for carpentry, and the others that have been received.

Names	***Men***	***Women***	***Sons***	***Daughters***	***Ages***
Josef de Lara, Spaniard	*				50
Maria Antonia Campos, light-skinned Indian		*			23
Josef Julian			*		4
Juana de Jesus				*	6
Maria Faustina				*	2
Josef Antonio Navarro, mestizo	*				42
Maria Regina Dorotea, mulata		*			47
Josef Maria			*		10
Josef Clemente			*		2
Maria Josefa				*	4
Bacilio Rosas, Indian	*				67
Maria Manuela Calistra, mulata		*			43
Josefa Maximo			*		15
Carlos			*		12
Anto. Rosalino			*		7
Josef Marcelino			*		4
Juan Estevan			*		2
Maria Josefa				*	8
Antonio Mesa, Negro	*				38
Ana Gertrudis Lopez, mulata		*			27
Antonio Maria			*		8
Maria Paula				*	10
Antonio Villavicencio, Spaniard	*				30
Maria de los Santos Soberina, Indian		*			26
Maria Antonia Josefa				*	8
Josef Vanegas, Indian	*				28
Maria Maxima Aguilar, Indian		*			20
Cosme Damien			*		1
Alejandro Rosas, Indian	*				19
Juana Rodriguez, native of the country		*			20
Pablo Rodriguez, Indian	*				25
Maria Rosalia Noriega, Indian		*			26
Maria Antonia				*	1
Manuel Camero, mulato	*				30
Maria Tomasa, mulata		*			24
Luis Quintero, Negro	*				55

Names	Men	Women	Sons	Daughters	Ages
Maria Petra Ruvio, mulata		*			40
Josef Clemente			*		3
Maria Gertrudes				*	16
Maria Concepcion				*	9
Tomasa				*	7
Rafaela				*	6
Josef Moreno, mulato	*				22
Maria Guadalupe Gertrudis, mulata		*			19
Antonio Miranda Rodriguez, Chino widower	*				50
Juana Maria				*	11
Totals	12	11	11	12	

Note

That in addition to the cattle, horses, and mules, distributed to the first eleven settlers, as set forth, they were granted building lots on which they have constructed their houses, which for the present are built of palisades, roofed with earth; also two irrigated fields to each settler for the cultivation of two fanegas of corn; in addition, a plow share, a hoe, and an axe; and for the community, the necessary tools for making carretas, as also the breeding animals as specified, for which the settlers must account to the royal treasury at the prices fixed; with the corresponding charges made against their accounts, as found in the Book of the Population (Población), wherein are also to be found the building lots, planting fields, farming equipment, and animals belonging to settler Antonio Miranda Rodriguez, who is at the Presidio of Loreto, and which will be granted to him as soon as he presents himself at the said Pueblo.

San Gabriel, November 19, 1781.

6. The French Count of La Pérouse Comments on Monterey, California, 1786

. . . The church is very clean, although thatched with straw. It is dedicated to Saint-Charles [San Carlos] and decorated with good enough pictures copied from Italian originals. There was a picture of Hell in which the painter seemed to have borrowed somewhat from the imagination of Calot, but as it is absolutely necessary to appeal to the senses of these recent converts, I am convinced that such a representation has never been more useful in any country, and it would be impossible for the Protestant cult, which proscribes images and almost all the other ceremonial features of our Church, to make any progress with these people. I doubt that the picture of Paradise which hangs facing that of Hell produces as good an effect on them. The quiet scene it represents and the sweet satisfaction of the blest who surround the throne of the Supreme Being are concepts too sublime for men like brutes, but there must be rewards alongside of the punishments and it was a bounden duty not to permit any change in the kinds of delights that the Catholic religion promises.

On leaving the church we passed the same rank of Indian men and women. They had not left their stations during the *Te Deum,* only the children had gone a little way off and stood in groups near the house of the missionaries, which is opposite the church, as are the several storehouses.

On the right is the Indian village, made up of about fifty huts which serve as lodging for the seven hundred and forty persons of both sexes, including children, who make up the mission of Saint-Charles or Monterey. . . .

This general architectural type of the two Californias[1] has never been changed by the exhortations of the missionaries. The Indians say that they love the open air, that it is convenient to set fire to the house when one is eaten up by too many fleas, and build another, which takes less than two hours. The independent Indians who change their dwelling place frequently, as hunting peoples, have one more reason.

The color of these Indians which is that of negroes, the house of the friars, their storehouses which are built of bricks and plastered with mortar, the threshing floor where they trample out the grain, the cattle, the horses, everything, in fact, reminds us of a plantation in Santo Domingo or any other colony. Men and women are assembled at the sound of the bell. A friar conducts them to work, to church, or to other activities. It hurts us to say it but the resemblance [to Santa Domingo] is so great that we have seen men and women loaded with irons, others in the *bloc*,[2] and, finally, the blows of the whip might have reached our ears, this punishment being also admitted but carried out with little severity.

. . . We wanted to witness the distributions which are made at each meal-time, and since one day is like another for this kind of friars, by sketching the history of a single day the reader is given to know that of the entire year.

Like the missionaries, the Indians rise with the sun and go to prayers and mass, which last for an hour. During this time in three great cauldrons in the middle of the plaza they cook the barley-meal, the grain of which has been roasted before it is ground. This sort of soup, which the Indians call *atole* and of which they are very fond, is not seasoned with butter or salt and for us would be a very flat-tasting dish.

Each hut sends to get the ration for all its inhabitants, in a bowl made of bark. There is no confusion nor disorder and when the cauldrons are empty the scrapings are distributed to the children who have best remembered the lessons of the catechism.

This meal takes three quarters of an hour, after which they all go to their labor. Some work the soil with the cattle, others cultivate the garden; in fact each is employed at the different needs of the settlement and always under the surveillance of one of the friars.

The women are charged with hardly more than the care of their homes and their children, and roasting and grinding the grain. . . .

7. *George Vancouver Describes Spanish Settlements, 1794*

. . . The Presidio of San Diego seemed to be the least of the Spanish establishments with which we were acquainted. It is irregularly built, on very uneven ground, which makes it liable to some inconveniences, without the obvious appearance of any object for selecting such a spot. The situation of it is dreary and lonesome, in the midst of a barren uncultivated country, producing so little herbage, that, excepting in the spring months, their cattle are sent to the distance of twenty or thirty miles for pasturage. During that season, and as long as the rainy weather may continue, a sufficient number are then brought nearer for the use of the Presidio and mission; and such as have not been wanted are again sent back to the interior country when the dry weather commences; which, although more productive in point of grass, is not very prolific in grain, pulse, fruits, roots, or other culinary vegetables. I understood that they are frequently obliged to resort for a supply of these articles to the mission of San Juan Capistrano, which abounded in vegetables and animal productions, consisting of great herds of cattle, flocks of sheep, and goats; and I was

[1]The two Californias are Lower (or Baja) California and Upper (or Alta) California.

[2]A *bloc* is a hinged piece of wood fit around a person's leg to prevent movement.

assured it was one of the most fertile establishments in the country.

The pueblos differ materially from either the missions or the Presidios, and may be better expressed by the name of villages, being unsupported by any other protection, than that of the persons who are resident in them. These are principally old Spanish, or creole,[1] Soldiers; who, having served their respective turns of duty in the missions or in the Presidios, become entitled to exemption from any further military services, and have permission either to return to their native country, or to pass the remainder of their lives in these villages. Most of these soldiers are married, and have families; and when the retirement of the pueblos is preferred, grants of land, with some necessary articles, are given them to commence their new occupation of husbandry, as a reward for their former services, and as an incitement to a life of industry; which, with the assistance of a few of the friendly and well disposed natives, they carry into effect with great advantage to their families. Fertile spots are always chosen for planting these colonies; by cultivating which, they are soon enabled to raise corn and cattle sufficient, not only for their own support, but for the supply of the wants of the missions and Presidios in their neighbourhood. Being trained to arms, they early instruct the rising generation, and bring them up to the obedience of military authority; under the laws of which they themselves continue to be governed. There is no superior person or officer residing amongst them for the purpose of officiating as governor, or as chief magistrate; but the pueblos are occasionally visited by the ensign of the Presidio, within whose particular jurisdiction they are situated. This officer is authorized to take cognizance of, and in a certain degree to redress, such grievances or complaints as may be brought before him; or to represent them, together with any crimes or misdemeanors, to his commanding officer; and also to report such improvements, regulations, or other matters arising in these little societies, as may either demand his permission or assent; from whose decision there is no appeal, but to the governor of the province; whose powers, I understood, were very extensive, though I remained ignorant concerning the particular nature of his jurisdiction.

These pueblos generally consist of about thirty or forty old soldiers with their families, who may be considered as a sort of militia of the country, and as assisting in the increase of its population, which, as far as it respects the Spaniards, is yet in a very humble state. . . .

8. Nikolai P. Rezanov Tells of His Meeting with the Argüello Family in California, 1806

. . . Embracing at once the opportunity offered by a favoring wind and tide to enter the puerto [Port of San Francisco] on the following morning [March 28, 1806, o.s. (Julian calendar): April 8, 1806, n.s. (Gregorian calendar)], and the suspicious nature of the Spanish government being known to me, I thought it best to go straight through the gate and by the fort, in view of our desperate situation. I deemed it useless to send in and ask for permission to enter, since, in the event of refusal, we should necessarily perish at sea, and decided that two or three cannon-balls would make less difference to us than refusal.

With all sails full, we ran for the puerto. As we neared the fort a great commotion was observed among the soldiers, and when abreast of it one of them asked, through a speaking trumpet, "What ship is that?" "Russian," we replied. They shouted to us several times to anchor, but we merely replied, "Si, señor; si, señor," and simulated an active effort to comply with their demand, but in the mean time we had passed the fort and were running up the puerto, and at a cannon-shot's distance complied. . . .

Associating daily with and paying my addresses to the beautiful Spanish señorita [Concepción

[1]A *creole* is a person born in the New World of pure Spanish parents.

Argüello] I could not fail to perceive her active, venturesome disposition and character, her unlimited and overweening desire for rank and honors, which, with her age of fifteen years, made her, alone among her family, dissatisfied with the land of her birth. She always referred to it jokingly; thus, as "a beautiful country, a warm climate, an abundance of grain and cattle,—and nothing else."

I described Russia to her as a colder country, but still abounding in everything, and she was willing to live there, and at length I imperceptibly created in her an impatient desire to hear something more explicit from me, and when I proffered my hand, she accepted.

My proposal was a shock to her parents, whose religious upbringing was fanatical. The difference in religion, besides the prospective separation from their daughter, was, in contemplation, a dreadful blow to them.

They sought the counsel of the misioneros, who did not know what to do. The parents forced their daughter to church and had her confessed. They urged her to refuse me, but her brave front finally quieted them all. The holy padres decided to leave the final decision to the throne of Rome.

Not being able to bring about the marriage, I had a written conditional agreement made, and forced a betrothal. Consent was given on condition that the agreement be kept secret pending the decision of the pope. Thereafter my deportment in the house of Comandante Argüello was that of a near relative, and I managed this puerto of his Catholic majesty as my interests called for. . . .

9. Gabriel Franchere Describes the Royal Family of Hawaii, 1811

There is no good anchorage in the Bay of Uhytiti,[1] inside the bar or coral reef: the holding-ground is bad: so that in case of a storm the safety of the ship would have been endangered. Moreover, with a contrary wind it would have been difficult to get out of the inner harbor; for which reasons, our Captain preferred to remain in the road. For the rest, the country surrounding the bay is even more lovely in aspect than that of Karaka-koua; the mountains rise to a less elevation in the back-ground, and the soil has an appearance of greater fertility.

Taméaméa,[2] whom all the Sandwich Isles obeyed when we were there in 1811, was neither the son nor the relative of Tierroboo, who reigned in Owyhee (Hawaii) in 1779, when Captain Cook and some of his people were massacred. He was at that date but a chief of moderate power; but being skilful, intriguing, and full of ambition, he succeeded in gaining a numerous party and finally possessed himself of the sovereignty. As soon as he saw himself master of Owyhee, his native island, he meditated the conquest of the leeward islands, and in a few years he accomplished it. He even passed into Atouay, the most remote of all, and vanquished the ruler of it, but contented himself with imposing on him an annual tribute. He had fixed his residence at Owahou [Oahu] because of all the Sandwich Isles it was the most fertile, the most picturesque—in a word, the most worthy of the residence of the sovereign. . . .

Taméaméa was above the middle height, well made, robust and inclined to corpulency, and had a majestic carriage. He appeared to me from fifty to sixty years old. He was clothed in the European style and wore a sword. He walked a long time on the deck, asking explanations in regard to those things which he had not seen on other vessels, and which were found on ours. A thing which appeared to surprise him was to see that we could render the water of the sea fresh by means of the still attached to our caboose; he could not imagine how that could be done. We invited him into the cabin, and having regaled him with some glasses of wine, began to talk of business matters: we offered him merchandise in exchange for hogs, but were not able to conclude

[1]Honolulu Harbor.

[2]Also spelled Kameamea.

the bargain that day. His Majesty re-embarked in his double pirogue at about six o'clock in the evening. It was manned by twenty-four men. A great chest containing firearms was lashed over the center of the two canoes forming the pirogue; and it was there that Taméaméa sat, with his prime-minister at his side.

In the morning, on the 22d, we sent our water-casks ashore and filled them with excellent water. At about noon His Sable Majesty paid us another visit, accompanied by his three wives and his favorite minister. These females were of an extraordinary corpulence and of unmeasured size. They were dressed in the fashion of the country, having nothing but a piece of tappa, or bark-cloth, about two yards long, passed round the hips and falling to the knees. We resumed the negotiations of the day before and were more successful. I remarked that when the bargain was concluded he insisted with great pertinacity that part of the payment should be in Spanish dollars. We asked the reason, and he made answer that he wished to buy a frigate of his brother, King George, meaning the King of England. The bargain concluded, we prayed His Majesty and his suite to dine with us; they consented, and toward evening retired, apparently well satisfied with their visit and our reception of them.

In the meantime, the natives surrounded the ship in great numbers with hundreds of canoes, offering us their goods, in the shape of eatables and the rude manufactures of the island, in exchange for merchandise; but as they had also brought intoxicating liquors in gourds, some of the crew got drunk; the Captain was, consequently, obliged to suspend the trade, and forbade any one to traffic with the Islanders except through the first mate, who was intrusted with that business. . . .

Uhytiti [Honolulu], where Taméaméa resides, and which, consequently, may be regarded as the capital of his kingdom, is—or at least was at that time—a moderate-sized city, or rather a large village. Besides the private houses, of which there were perhaps two hundred, constructed of poles planted in the ground and covered over with matting, there were the royal palace, which was not magnificent by any means: a public store, of two stories, one of stone and the other of wood; two *morais,* or idol temples, and a wharf. At the latter we found an old vessel, the *Lilly Bird* [Lelia Byrd], which some American nagivators had given in exchange for a schooner; it was the only large vessel which King Taméaméa possessed; and, besides, was worth nothing. As for schooners, he had forty of them, of from twenty to thirty tons burden: these vessels served to transport the tributes in kind paid by his vassals in the other islands. Before the Europeans arrived among these savages, the latter had no means of communication between one isle and another but their canoes, and as some of the islands are not in sight of each other, these voyages must have been dangerous. Near the palace I found an Indian from Bombay, occupied in making a twelve-inch cable, for the use of the ship which I have described.

Taméaméa kept constantly round his house a guard of twenty-four men. These soldiers wore, by way of uniform, a long blue coat with yellow; and each was armed with a musket. In front of the house, on an open square, were placed fourteen four-pounders, mounted on their carriages. . . .

References

1. Pedro Fages Writes a Letter to José de Gálvez Reporting on Alta California, 1769
Iris Engstrand, trans. and ed., "Pedro Fages and Miguel Costansó: Two Early Letters from San Diego in 1769," *Journal of San Diego History,* Vol. 21 (Spring 1975): 1–7.

2. Father Juan Crespí Reports the Discovery of San Francisco Bay, 1769
Herbert E. Bolton, trans. and ed., *Fray Juan Crespí: Missionary Explorer on the Pacific Coast 1769–1774* (Berkeley: University of California Press, 1927), pp. 229–231.

3. Juan Bautista de Anza Guides Soldiers and Families from Arizona to California, 1775
   Herbert E. Bolton, trans. and ed., *Anza's California Expeditions* (New York: Russell & Russell, 1966), 3: 33–37.
4. Father Junípero Serra Asks Viceroy Antonio Bucareli for Leniency for the Indians, 1775
   Antonine Tibesar, O.F.M., trans. and ed., *Writings of Junípero Serra* (Washington, D.C.: American Academy of Franciscan History, 1955–1966), 2: 401–407.
5. The Los Angeles Census of 1781 Shows a Diverse Ethnic Mix
   California Archives, Bancroft Library (Berkeley), 420–421.
6. The French Count of La Pérouse Comments on Monterey, California, 1786
   Charles N. Rudkin, trans. and ed., *The First French Expedition to California: Lapérouse in 1786* (Los Angeles: Glen Dawson, 1959), pp. 61–67.
7. George Vancouver Describes Spanish Settlements, 1794
   Marguerite Eyer Wilbur, ed., *Vancouver in California, 1792–1794: The Original Account of George Vancouver* (Los Angeles: Glen Dawson, 1954), pp. 230–233.
8. Nikolai P. Rezanov Tells of His Meeting with the Argüello Family in California, 1806
   T. C. Russell, ed., *The Rezanov Voyage to Nueva California in 1806* (San Francisco, 1926), pp. 11, 36–37, 97–99, quoted by John and LaRee Caughey, *California Heritage: An Anthology of History and Literature* (Los Angeles: Ward Ritchie Press, 1962), pp. 109–111.
9. Gabriel Franchere Describes the Royal Family of Hawaii, 1811
   A Voyage to the Northwest Coast of America, ed. Milo Milton Quaife (Chicago: Lakeside Press, 1954), pp. 35–40.

Document Set 3

Mexico Maintains Its Tenuous Hold on California and the Southwest, 1821–1846

The newly established Mexican government sent an official representative to California in 1822 to inform the people that they were no longer under the flag of Spain. Most residents took the news calmly, for they had experienced little contact with Spanish officials, and few felt any strong ties to Fernando VII, the Spanish king who had opposed colonial representation in 1815. They had not received needed supplies for twelve years, the soldiers' pay was in arrears, the missions had become self-supporting, and smuggling had grown common.

Mexico struggled throughout the next twenty-five years to govern its distant provinces, but pressures from home and abroad made proper administration difficult. Nevertheless, life in California continued much as it had under Spanish control, with the exception that foreigners, especially Americans, began to enter the area in ever-increasing numbers.

In Document 1, Juana Machado Wrightington reminisces about the day that Father Agustin Fernández de San Vicente told the soldiers to take down the Spanish flag and put up the new tricolored Mexican *bandera*. She and her family soon moved from Presidio Hill and settled in the pueblo of San Diego. The missions continued to expand, and one more was founded under Mexico in 1823. Twenty-one missions then stretched from San Diego northward to San Francisco Solano at Sonoma.

Frederick W. Beechey, a British captain sailing on the H.M.S. *Blossom,* visited California in the late fall of 1826 and analyzed the mission system (Document 2). He had spent the summer in the Bering Strait searching for an ocean passage through the Northwest. William Smyth, senior admiralty mate on the *Blossom,* had sketched the *bidarkas* (boats) of the native peoples in Alaska in August (Document 3). As ships sailed up and down the Pacific coast, families moved westward across the Mississippi River into Missouri. Some of the more restless young men left their parents' farms and headed for Santa Fe and Taos to participate in the great western fur trade.

The Mexican government faced a most difficult challenge in California: removing the missions from under church control. Officials issued a decree to this effect in Mexico (Document 4) and then gave a local order on August 9, 1834, that distributed land to Indians but that left abundant acreage available for private land grants. Soldiers and settlers alike coveted the valuable agricultural lands for their own ranchos, and more than six hundred grants were made before 1846. Document 5 illustrates some of the brands used to identify cattle in San Diego County.

In Oregon by the mid-1830s, American Methodists had answered a call to minister to the needs of their countrymen who had settled there. Marcus Whitman and his wife, Narcissa, along with the Reverend Henry H. Spalding and his wife, left St. Louis in March 1836 and traveled to the Pacific coast in the company of fur traders of the American Fur Company and the Hudson's Bay Company. The wives became the first American women to cross the continental divide. Narcissa Whitman (Document 6) describes Fort Walla Walla in her diary upon their arrival on September 1, 1836.

In the meantime, the Mexican government lost Texas when Texans won their independence in 1836, and factionalism in Mexico City had widened the gap between centralists who wanted strict control over the states, and federalists, who believed in more local control. Clashes arose in California over the office of governor, location of the capital, trade restrictions, and municipal government. This tension gradually weakened Mexico's position on its far northern frontier. The Frenchman Abel du Petit-Thouars commented rather harshly on those in charge of California (Document 7). Soon, too, the steady trickle of foreigners into the West would become a flood. The days of Mexican control were numbered.

While Mexico was unable to keep a careful watch on California, the Russians also let their influence over their distant settlement slip away. In 1836, responding to the decline in sea otter pelts, they considered abandoning Fort Ross. The Russians also suffered a serious smallpox epidemic that year and saw little future for their settlement in California.

John Sutter, known mainly for his role in the gold rush of 1849, purchased the Russian fort in 1841 (Document 8) and moved the buildings to his property at the junction of the American and Sacramento rivers. Sutter's Fort became the first stopping place for overland travelers arriving in California from the East during the 1840s. These people would bring their American ideals with them and continue to look eastward to Washington, D.C., rather than to Mexico for government loyalties.

Questions for Analysis

1. In your opinion, did the change from Spanish to Mexican rule cause much of a problem in California?
2. In view of today's life-style in California, do you think that the Indians should have been taught agriculture and other useful arts? Were Native Americans in the West better prepared to meet newcomers than Indians in the East or Midwest when other Europeans and Americans arrived?
3. Were the Alaskan *bidarkas* as practical and durable as small boats built by Europeans?
4. Do you think that it was time for control of Indians and their lands by the missionaries to end? Did the Mexican government watch out for the welfare of the Indians?
5. If you were going to create a cattle brand, what would it look like?
6. What motivated people to emigrate from their homes to try living in a distant land?
7. Was the French captain of the *Venus* promoting the idea of U.S. ownership of California?
8. How did John Sutter benefit from his purchase of Fort Ross from the Russians?

1. Juana Machado Wrightington Discusses the Changeover from Spanish to Mexican Rule, 1822

. . . The change of flag in 1822 was as follows:

There came from the north (I do not recall whether by sea or land) a prebendary called Don Valentin [Agustín] Fernandez de San Vicente, who brought with him a chaplain or secretary, I do not know what he was. I do not remember ever having seen him dressed as a priest. The prebendary wore a garment of a color resembling red. This gentleman was the agent of the Mexican empire to establish here the new order of things. I well recall that when some woman or girl, excited by the richness and the colors of his dress, which were really very showy and handsome would ask, "Who is this gentleman?" someone would answer, "The prebendary."

Such a person never had been seen before in California. He and his companion stayed above in the house of the comandante. The comandante was Captain Francisco María Ruiz, who had been in office for many years.

The troops of infantry, cavalry and some few artillery were ordered to form in the plaza of the presidio; the cannons were put outside the plaza to the door of the guard room, looking toward the ocean. There was as yet no flag. A corporal or soldier had the Spanish flag on a little stick, and another the Mexican flag. When Comandante Ruiz, in the presence of the official, Don José María Estudillo, cried out "Long live the Mexican Empire!" the Spanish flag was lowered and the Mexican flag raised in the midst of salvos of artillerymen and musketeers. After this the troops did nothing.

On the following day an order was given to cut off the braids of the soldiers. This produced in everyone, men and women, a very disagreeable reaction. The former were accustomed to wear their hair long and braided with a knot of ribbon or silk at the end; on some it came below the waist; it was somewhat like the manner of the Chinese with the exception that they did not shave any part of the head.

This order was carried out. I remember that when papa came home with his braid in his hand and gave it to mama his face was very sad and that of mama no less so; she looked at the braid and cried.

The manner in which men dressed during my childhood until Echeandia arrived was as follows:

Undershirt of cotton or other material; waistcoat without facings which came down to the waist; of different colors; but the troops wore blue. Over the waistcoat was the doublet which was a coat with lapels on the sides; with red borders on all the edges; and with a red collar. That is what the troops wore, and the countrymen who were very few and the retired soldiers wore more or less the same, the color being varied by each according to his likes.

Short trousers of cloth, nankeen,[1] drill,[2] or whatever each one had; the troops wore cloth. These short trousers reached to the knees where they had openings on the outside with flaps which fell on each side and six buttons on each side.

Then came the chamois legging; it was a piece of chamois about three-quarters long, which went around the leg and was tied with ribbons or tapes. This chamois was ornamented with tooling; underneath on the feet were shoes and stockings.

On his head the man wore his hat of felt, straw, [or] vicuna,[3] and the fine ones that came from Spain were carefully treated. For common use the men wore hats of palm which the Indians made. . . .

2. Frederick W. Beechey Gives His Analysis of the California Mission System, 1826

The object of the missions is to convert as many of the wild Indians as possible, and to train them up within the walls of the establishment in the exercise of a good life, and of some trade, so that they may in time be able to provide for themselves and become useful members of civilized society. As to the various methods employed for the purpose of bringing proselytes to the mission, there are several reports, of which some were not very creditable to the institution: nevertheless, on the whole I am of opinion that the priests are innocent, from a conviction that they are ignorant of the means employed by those who are under them. Whatever may be the system, and whether the Indians be really dragged from their homes and families by armed parties, as some assert, or not, and forced to exchange their life of freedom and wandering for one of confinement and restraint in the missions, the change according to our ideas of happiness would seem advantageous to them, as they lead a far better life in the missions than in their forests,

[1]A light-colored cotton cloth originally imported from Nankin, China.

[2]A coarse linen or cotton cloth.

[3]A soft fur from a South American animal of the camel family used in making hats and coats.

where they are in a state of nudity, and are frequently obliged to depend solely upon wild acorns for their subsistence.

Immediately the Indians are brought to the mission they are placed under the tuition of some of the most enlightened of their countrymen, who teach them to repeat in Spanish the Lord's Prayer and certain passages in the Romish litany; and also to cross themselves properly on entering the church. In a few days a willing Indian becomes a proficient in these Mysteries, and suffers himself to be baptized, and duly initiated into the church. If, however, as it not unfrequently happens, any of the captured Indians show a repugnance to conversion, it is the practice to imprison them for a few days, and then to allow them to breathe a little fresh air in a walk round the mission, to observe the happy mode of life of their converted countrymen; after while they are again shut up, and thus continue to be incarcerated until they declare their readiness to renounce the religion of their forefathers.

I do not suppose that this apparently unjustifiable conduct would be pursued for any length of time; and I had never an opportunity of ascertaining the fact, as the Indians are so averse to confinement that they very soon become impressed with the manifestly superior and more comfortable mode of life of those who are at liberty, and in a very few days declare their readiness to have the new religion explained to them. A person acquainted with the language of the parties, of which there are sometimes several dialects in the same mission, is then selected to train them, and having duly prepared them takes his pupils to the padre to be baptized, and to receive the sacrament. Having become Christians they are put to trades, or if they have good voices they are taught music, and form part of the choir of the church. Thus there are in almost every mission weavers, tanners, shoemakers, bricklayers, carpenters, blacksmiths, and other artificers. Others again are taught husbandry, to rear cattle and horses; and some to cook for the mission: while the females card, clean, and spin wool, weave, and sew; and those who are married attend to their domestic concerns.

In requital of these benefits, the services of the Indian, for life, belong to the mission, and if any neophyte should repent of his apostacy from the religion of his ancestors and desert, an armed force is sent in pursuit of him, and drags him back to punishment apportioned to the degree of aggravation attached to his crime. It does not often happen that a voluntary convert succeeds in his attempt to escape, as the wild Indians have a great contempt and dislike for those who have entered the missions, and they will frequently not only refuse to re-admit them to their tribe, but will sometimes even discover their retreat to their pursuers. This animosity between the wild and converted Indians is of great importance to the missions, as it checks desertion, and is at the same time a powerful defence against the wild tribes, who consider their territory invaded, and have other just causes of complaint. The Indians, besides, from political motives, are, I fear, frequently encouraged in a contemptuous feeling towards their unconverted countrymen, by hearing them constantly held up to them in the degrading light of *béstias!* and in hearing the Spaniards distinguished by the appellation of *génte de razón*. . . .

At some of the missions they pursue a custom said to be of great antiquity among the aborigines and which appears to afford them much enjoyment. A mud house, or rather a large oven, called *temeschal* by the Spaniards, is built in a circular form, with a small entrance, and an aperture in the top for the smoke to escape through. Several persons enter this place quite naked and make a fire near the door, which they continue to feed with wood as long as they can bear the heat. In a short time they are thrown into a most profuse perspiration, they wring their hair, and scrape their skin with a sharp piece of wood or an iron hoop, in the same manner as coach horses are sometimes treated when they come in heated; and then plunge into a river or pond of cold water, which they always take care shall be near the temeschal.

A similar practice to this is mentioned by Shelekoff as being in use among the Konaghi, a tribe of Indians near Cook's River, who have a method of heating the oven with hot stones, by which they avoid the discomfort occasioned by the wood smoke; and, instead of scraping their skin with iron or bone, rub themselves with grass and twigs. . . .

3. William Smyth of the H.M.S. Blossom *Sketches Native* Bidarkas *in Alaska, 1826*

"From two of these they landed fourteen persons, eight tent poles, forty deer skins, two kyacks, many hundred weight of fish, numerous skins of oil, earthen jars for cooking, two living foxes, ten large dogs, bundles of lances, harpoons, bows and arrows, a quantity of whalebone, skins full of clothing, some immense nets, made of hide, for taking small whales and porpoises, eight broad planks, masts, sails, paddles, etc., beside sea-horse hides and teeth, and a variety of nameless articles."

From Frederick W. Beechey, *Narrative of a Voyage to the Pacific and Beering's Strait to Cooperate with the Polar Expeditions* (London, 1831), 1: 405.

4. The Mexican Congress Decrees Secularization of the Missions, 1833

Article 1. The Government will proceed to secularize the Missions of Upper and Lower California.

Art. 2. In each of said Missions shall be established a parish, served by a secular clergyman, with a stipend of from two thousand to two thousand five hundred dollars a year, as the Government shall decide.

Art. 3. These Parochial Curates shall not recover or receive any fees, for marriages, baptisms, or under any other name. As regards fees for processions, they shall be entitled to receive such as may be specifically named in the list made out for that object, as concisely as possible, by the Reverend Bishop of the Diocese, and approved by the Supreme Government.

Art. 4. The churches which have served in each Mission shall serve as parish churches, with the sacred vases, ornaments, and other articles, which each possesses at present, and such additional furniture belonging to said church as the Government may deem necessary for the more decent use of said parish.

Art. 5. The Government shall cause to be laid out a *campo santo* [cemetery] for each parish out of the way of the population.

Art. 6. Five hundred dollars a year are appropriated for the service and worship of each parish church.

Art. 7. Of the houses belonging to each Mission, the most suitable shall be selected as the residence of the Curate, the land appropriated to him not to exceed two hundred yards square, and the rest shall be specially devoted to a town house, primary school, and public establishments and offices.

Art. 8. In order to provide promptly and effectively for the spiritual wants of both the Californias, there is established in the capital of the Upper a vicarship, which shall have jurisdiction over the two Territories, and the Reverend Diocesan shall endow it with the most ample powers.

Art. 9. Three thousand dollars are appropriated as an endowment to this vicarship, the Vicar being required to discharge his duties free of charge under any pretext or name, not even for paper.

Art. 10. If for any other cause whatever the Parochial Curate of the capital, or any other parish in the district, shall act as Vicar, there shall be paid to him one thousand five hundred dollars, besides the stipend of his curacy.

Art. 11. There shall not be introduced any custom which shall require the inhabitants of California to make offerings, however pious they may be, although they may be termed *necessary*; and neither time nor the will of the said inhabitants shall give them any force or weight whatever.

Art. 12. The Government shall take effectual care that the Reverend Diocesan shall contribute, so far as he is concerned, to fulfill the objects of this law.

Art. 13. The Supreme Government shall provide for the gratuitous transportation by sea, of the new Curates that may be appointed and their families, and besides may give to each one, for his traveling by land, from four to eight hundred dollars, according to the distance and the number of his family which he brings.

Art. 14. Government shall pay the traveling expenses of the religious [regulars] Missionaries who move; and that they may be accommodated on land as far as their colleges or convents, may give to each from two to three hundred dollars, and, at discretion, so much as may be necessary to such as have not sworn to support the indepedence, that they may leave the Republic.

Art. 15. The Supreme Government shall pay the expenses arising under this law out of the products of the securities, capitals, and rents, which are regarded as the pious fund in the Missions of California.

August 17th, 1833.

5. Brands from San Diego County Indicate Cattle Ownership

Pedro Carrillo,
Península de San Diego

Cave Couts,
Rancho Guajome

Pío Pico,
Rancho Jamul

Francisco Ruiz,
Rancho de los Peñasquitos

Juan Osuna,
Rancho San Dieguito

José Joaquin Ortega,
Rancho Santa María

Miguel de Pedrorena,
Rancho El Cajon

Joseph Snook,
Rancho San Bernardo

Ex-Mission San Diego

Juan José Marron,
Rancho Agua Hedionda

Juan José Warner,
San José del Valle

Pío Pico,
Rancho Santa Margarita

6. *Narcissa Whitman Meets Pierre Pambrun and Praises Fort Walla Walla, 1836*

. . . After breakfast we were shown the novelties of the place, they are so to us. While at breakfast, however, a young cock placed himself upon the cell [sill] of the door and crowed. Now whether it was the sight of the first white females or out of compliment to the company I know not, this much for him. I was pleased with his appearance. You may think me simple for speaking of such a small circumstance as this. . . . The dooryard was filled with hens turkeys pigeons & in another place we saw cows hogs & goats in abundance, & I think the largest & fattest cattle & swine I ever saw. We were soon shown a room, which Mr Pambrun said he had prepared for us by making two bedsteads . . . bunks, on hearing of our approach. . . . Having arranged our things, we were soon called to a feast of mellons, the finest I think I ever saw or tasted. The mushmelon was the largest measuring eighteen inches in length, fifteen arround the small end and nineteen around the largest end. You may be assured we were not any of us satisfied or willing to leave the table untill we had filled our plates with chips. . . .

7. *Abel du Petit-Thouars Describes California in His Journal on Board the* Venus, *1836*

. . . Shortly after the fort is seen the end of the cove comes in sight, where the bell tower of the presidio chapel in the easterly quarter will be the first thing observed, as well as the buildings which serve it and which are all contained in the same walled enclosure. Then in succession as the ship advances, to the west of the presidio some houses are to be seen, scattered here and there in no kind of order. Taken all together they form what is called the "town of Monterey," no doubt in deference to the seat of government. It seems worth while to add that there are no public buildings except the presidio church. Among the houses which may amount to thirty or forty several are whitewashed, some have a second story and a certain appearance of comfort, but the greater part are miserable boxes roofed with reeds or the branches of trees. Almost none have courtyards or gardens and on the slopes of the hills by which this establishment is surrounded there is not the slightest trace of cultivation to be seen. It looks as if the colony had just been founded, everything around it appears just as it did in the days of the first disembarkation. This uncared for and abandoned condition is the more astonishing since the mountains that stand near Monterey are fertile and wooded right up to their summits, which gives a decidedly picturesque aspect to the countryside.

As we rounded the northward projection of Point Pinos, which we have named "Point Venus" in commemoration of our visit, we recognized the Mexican flag floating over the little battery of which we have spoken. The sight of this flag seemed to give the lie to the news we had gotten at the Sandwich Islands about a revolution which had happened in 1836, as a result of which Upper California was to become independent of Mexico. In spite of this deceitful appearance the news was correct, the revolution had taken place but the political results had not been what the instigators might have desired. The proclamation of the independence of Upper California from Mexico was not definitive, it was still only conditional. For the purpose of explaining more clearly the political situation of Upper California at the time of our visit to Monterey it seems necessary to go back at least to 1823, the date of the emancipation of this country [from Spain]. Thereby it will be made easier to understand the lack of social institutions and the tendency of the minds of the people toward a new political order, a tendency which has already shown itself more than once. . . .

The Californians have made little advance in civilization. Education is almost wholly lacking. They are dominated by a mass of prejudices and in spite of the multiple relations which they have had with the Americans of the United States, relations which should, it would seem, have established bonds of friendship between these two peoples, they still evidence a sort of estrangement toward them. No doubt one need seek for the cause no further than in their customs and religion. Thus it is that after the revolution of 1836, so strongly seconded by the United States Americans, the Californians drew away from them as soon as they recognized the motives which had brought them the support they had received, and modified their first plans for emancipation.

If one can judge from some words let slip by some highly placed officers, the Russians, shut up in their farming establishment at Bodega (today in the most flourishing condition), covet the possession of the fine port of San Francisco, the fertile shores of its two basins and the magnificent river Sacramento which is navigable for vessels of two to three hundred tons up to 50 leagues from its mouth. Today it would be difficult to say to which nation this excellent port will some day belong, but the power which has the fortunate boldness to seize it by a *de facto* occupation will not be disturbed in its possession. . . .

8. John Sutter Buys Fort Ross from the Russians, 1841

. . . Captain Ringgold visited me again on his return trip and while he was in his camp near my Fort, Governor Alexander Rotchev arrived aboard a Russian schooner. He had come to offer the Russian colonies in California for sale. The vicinity of Fort Ross had not proved to be a good wheat country, furs were getting scarce, and the expenses were greater than the income. This was the first time that I had heard that the Russians intended to sell their settlements, and I was surprised that they had come to me. The Russians were not on good terms with the Californians at that time, and the Governor at Sitka had instructed Rotchev to offer the colonies to me first. An agent, Peter Kostromitinov, had been sent to complete arrangements. . . .

. . . [The Governor] requested me to accompany him to Bodega [Bay] at once. We sailed down the river together with Captain Ringgold's boats; so it was quite an impressive fleet that arrived at the Bay. We landed at San Rafael, where we found Russian servants with horses ready to convey us to Bodega. Kostromitinov, as well as the captain of the ship *Helena,* which was lying at anchor at the port of Bodega, were present.

After supper Kostromitinov made a formal offer on behalf of the Russian Government. He offered me the Russian establishment at Bodega and Fort Ross, together with the farms and the stores, as well as all the cattle and implements, and the schooner, aboard which the Governor had come to my Fort. The price for all this was extremely low—thirty thousand dollars with a down payment of two thousand dollars. The rest I was to pay in produce, chiefly in wheat at two dollars the *fanega* [1.6 bushel]. No time was specified; every year the Russians would send down a vessel from Alaska and receive from me whatever quantity of wheat I could give them. . . .

I did not hesitate to accept this favorable offer. The deed was drawn up immediately, written in French and containing the sentence, "With the consent of the Emperor of all Russians." . . .

Even before the document was signed, I was the acknowledged owner of all the Russian possessions in California. The Russians began to abandon their places before I started for Yerba Buena [San Francisco], some taking passage on board the *Helena,* and some on the *Alexander.* I wanted some of the Russians to remain with me as hired men, but the officers told me that they could hardly manage them and that I should not be able to do anything with them, because I was not severe enough.

We then embarked in a small boat for Yerba Buena. The boat was manned by four powerful Russian sailors. The tide was against us, the sea ran high, and we narrowly escaped being drowned. I said to Rotchev, who accompanied me to Yerba Buena: "Your control over these men is so complete that they would carry you straight to hell if your ordered them to." However, we finally crossed the Golden Gate, landed safely at Yerba Buena and proceeded to the office of the

Hudson's Bay Company. Here the *alcalde* joined us and the papers were executed. The Russians did not demand a note or any other document from me, and they continued to treat me very liberally in later years. With every vessel that came down the coast to fetch my instalment they sent supplies which were very necessary to me: iron, steel, ammunition, etc. At times I had more ammunition stored up than the whole California Government possessed. After the deed was signed by both parties, I paid over the two thousand dollars in money, and the transfer was complete.

On September the twenty-eighth I sent a clerk, a young Englishman by the name of Robert Ridley, with a number of men to Bodega in order to receive the live stock. In crossing the Sacramento River about one hundred of the two thousand head of cattle were drowned. Fortunately we were able to save most of the hides, at that time the real banknotes of California. Some of the horses and cattle were left at Fort Ross. The schooner *Sacramento,* which kept up communication between New Helvetia and Fort Ross, brought several shiploads of lumber to my settlement with which I was enabled to finish my Fort.

After I had bought Fort Ross, I informed the Mexican Government of my purchase and asked for a title. I was informed, however, that the Russians had no title to the land and hence no right to sell it to me. If I had had a few thousand dollars of ready cash, I could have easily secured a legal title. Money made the Mexican authorities see anything. Now I regret that I did not abandon Fort Sutter at once in order to settle at Fort Ross. The location was beautiful and healthy, there was good soil and plenty of timber, and by far more improvements than at New Helvetia. There would have been no gold hunters to rob me; indeed, gold might never have been discovered.

In the fall of 1841 and the spring of 1842, I gradually removed everything which I could carry away from Fort Ross and Bodega to Fort Sutter, dismantled the fort, tore down the buildings, and shipped it all up on my schooner. This vessel of mine did me good service, and the Indians had become expert seamen. It was at least two years before I had transferred everything from the Russian settlements to my place, and during this time the schooner made numerous trips back and forth.

The government not only refused to give me a title, but sold titles to other settlers who went to Ross and Bodega and took possession of my property. . . . I never received a cent for all the property I was obliged to leave there. Yet I had made a good bargain, especially since the payments were easy; but, as I have stated before, I should have left the Sacramento Valley and settled at Fort Ross. . . .

References

1. Juana Machado Wrightington Discusses the Changeover from Spanish to Mexican Rule, 1822
Raymond S. Brandes, trans. and ed., "Times Gone By in Alta California: Recollections of Señora Doña Juana Machado Alipaz de Ridington (Wrightington)," Historical Society of Southern California *Quarterly* (September 1959): 201–203.

2. Frederick W. Beechey Gives His Analysis of the California Mission System, 1826
Msgr. Francis J. Weber, ed., *Prominent Visitors to the California Missions* (Los Angeles: Dawson's Book Shop, 1991), pp. 74–77, 83.

3. William Smyth of the H.M.S. *Blossom* Sketches Native *Bidarkas* in Alaska, 1826
John Frazier Henry, *Early Maritime Artists of the Pacific Northwest Coast, 1741–1841* (Seattle: University of Washington Press, 1984), p. 126.

4. The Mexican Congress Decrees Secularization of the Missions, 1833
John W. Dwinelle, *The Colonial History of California* (San Francisco, 1863) addenda XV, pp. 26–27.
5. Brands from San Diego County Indicate Cattle Ownership
Philip S. Rush, *Some Old Ranchos and Adobes* (San Diego: Neyenesch Printers, 1965).
6. Narcissa Whitman Meets Pierre Pambrun and Praises Fort Walla Walla, 1836
Clifford Merrill Drury, *First White Women over the Rockies* (Glendale: Arthur H. Clark Company, 1963), 1: 94–95.
7. Abel du Petit-Thouars Describes California in His Journal on Board the *Venus,* 1836
Abel du Petit-Thouars, *Voyage of the* Venus: *Sojourn in California,* trans. Charles N. Rudkin (Los Angeles: Glen Dawson, 1956), pp. 10–12, 36–37.
8. John Sutter Buys Fort Ross from the Russians, 1841
"Reminiscences of John Sutter," in Erwin G. Gudde, *Sutter's Own Story* (New York: G. P. Putnam's Sons, 1936), pp. 74–80.

Document Set 4

Mountain Men Lead the Way West, 1824–1848

From the earliest days of settlement by the British and the French, the fur trade provided a motive for exploration westward across the continent. Independent trappers and members of the Hudson's Bay Company and Northwest Company had penetrated farther and farther west until their isolated trails reached the Pacific. The demand for furs encouraged participants from all countries. Beaver pelts, a main item of trade, were coveted by Indians and Europeans alike. Vitus Bering opened the trade for the Russians. The British, as a result of Captain James Cook's expedition to Vancouver Island in 1778, profited from the sale of sea otter pelts in China.

Mountain men roamed the Rockies, the Southwest, and California in search of furs until the late 1840s, when poor markets and a scarcity of furs signaled the end of an economic boom. The rendezvous system, a unique contribution of Americans to the fur trade, allowed trappers to remain in the mountains and to meet company representatives at designated places to trade pelts for supplies. In 1825 General William Ashley, businessman and fur trader, inaugurated the rendezvous at the mouth of Henry's Fork on the Green River near today's Wyoming-Utah border.

In the first document, Ashley and James Beckwourth, a well-known black trapper, talk about their experiences on the Platte River in 1824. Because Beckwourth was often accused of exaggeration, California historian Hubert Howe Bancroft claimed in 1886 that no one could have "the slightest faith" in Beckwourth's statements. It is fascinating and instructive to compare his and Ashley's accounts of the same event.

Documents 2 and 3 illustrate the attempt by the Governor José María Echeandía of California to prevent the entry of American mountain men overland into Mexico's most northerly province. Nevertheless, Jedediah Smith entered California without permission and did not leave by the appropriate route. Argüello's letter shows the clash of cultures and provides insight into one Mexican's thoughts about Smith's actions. Mountain men and fur traders continued to enter California steadily after 1829.

Document 4 reveals why the majority of mountain men were young and single. Some, for religious reasons, shunned drinking, but most happily relaxed with some whiskey. Ewing Young, a former mountain man who settled in Oregon, tried to build a still but met with opposition from the Oregon Temperance Society and from Dr. John McLoughlin of the Hudson's Bay Company. McLoughlin sold supplies, including whiskey, at Fort Vancouver. Finally, William Slacum, a representative from the United States, asked Young to desist (Document 5).

Rufus B. Sage, in the sixth document, describes the fort on the Uintah River run by a French Canadian, Antoine Robidoux, that supplied mountain men in the Rocky Mountain region. Robidoux later lived in St. Joseph, Missouri, and accompanied General Stephen Watts Kearny's campaign as an interpreter during the Mexican War. Other mountain men had already settled in California and taken Mexican citizenship.

Jean Baptiste Charbonneau, the son of the Shoshone woman Sacajawea and French trader Toussaint Charbonneau, who guided the Lewis and Clark expedition to the Pacific coast, proved one of the most interesting traders. Well educated and multilingual, he also traveled with Jim Beckwourth and engaged in mining in California and Montana. Document 7 summarizes his many activities.

George Nidever, another famous trapper from Tennessee, spent time in California and earned admiration as an excellent marksman and a fearless hunter of grizzly bear. His reputation reached as far east as New England and the pen of Ralph Waldo Emerson. Document 8 is Emerson's tribute to Nidever in his essay "Courage."

Today mountain men live on in stories of daring and adventure about the American West.

Questions for Analysis

1. What was the rendezvous system? What do you feel were the most important characteristics of the mountain men?
2. Could people today survive in the wilderness as the mountain men did in the 1830s and 1840s?
3. Do you believe that Jedediah Smith made an honest effort to leave California?
4. Were Argüello's opinions about the American trappers justified?
5. Why was there opposition to Ewing Young's distillery?
6. What were the major articles of trade at Robidoux's fort?
7. How would you compare the life of Jean Baptiste Charbonneau with other mountain men of the time?
8. Why do you think people in the East glorified the mountain men?

1. General William Ashley and James Beckwourth Describe Their Experiences on the Platte River, 1824

General William Ashley: . . . [O]n the afternoon of the 5th, I overtook my party of mountaineers (twenty-five in number), who had in charge fifty pack horses, a wagon and teams, etc. On the 6th we had advanced within ——— miles of the Grand Pawney's when it commenced snowing and continued with but little intermission until the morning of the 8th. During this time my men and horses were suffering for the want of food, which, combined with the severity of the weather, presented rather a gloomy prospect. . . . On the 22nd of the same month we found ourselves encamped on the Loup fork of the river Platt within three miles of the Pawney towns. Cold and hunger had by this time killed several of my horses, and many others were much reduced from the same cause. On the day last named we crossed the country southwardly about fifteen miles to the main fork of the Platt, where we were so fortunate as to find rushes and game in abundance, whence we set out on the 24th and advanced up the Platt. . . .

James Beckwourth: On our arrival at the upper camp . . . we found the men, twenty-six in number, reduced to short rations, in weakly condition, and in discouraged state of mind. They had been expecting the arrival of a large company with abundant supplies, and when we rejoined them without any provisions, they were greatly disappointed. . . . We numbered thirty-four men, all told, and a duller encampment, I suppose, never was witnessed. No jokes, no fire-side stories, no fun; each man rose in the morning with the gloom of the preceding night filling his mind; we built our fires and partook of our scanty repast without saying a word. At last our general gave order for the best hunters to sally out and try their fortune. I seized my rifle and issued from the camp alone. . . .

Ashley: [The men] had undergone an intense suffering from the inclemency of the weather, which also bore so severely on the horses as to cause the death of many of them.

This, together with a desire to purchase a few horses from the [Pawnee] Loups and to prepare my party for the privations which we had reason to anticipate in traveling the next two hundred miles (described as being almost wholly destitute of wood) induced me to remain at the Forks until the 23d December, the greater part of which time we were favoured with fine weather, and notwithstanding the uplands were still covered with from 18 to 24 inches of snow, the Valleys were generally bare and afforded a good range for my horses, furnishing plenty of dry grass and some small rushes, from the use of which they daily increased in strength and spirits.

Beckwourth: A severe storm setting in about this time, had it not been for our excellent store of provisions [the deer and elk killed previously by Jim?] we should most probably have perished of starvation. There was no game to be procured and our only resource was the flesh of horses which died of starvation and exposure to the storm. It was not such nutritious food as our fat buffalo and venison, but in our present circumstances it relished tolerably well. . . . When the storm was expended we moved up the river, hoping to fall in with game. . . . It was midwinter, and every thing around us bore a gloomy aspect. We were without provisions, and we saw no means of obtaining any. At this crisis, six or seven Indians of the Pawnee Loup band came into our camp. . . . They invited us to their lodges. . . . The Indians . . . spread a feast. . . . Our horses, too, were well cared for, and soon assumed a more rotund appearance. . . .

2. Jedediah Smith Explains His Actions to Governor Echeandía, 1827

Mission of St. Joseph [San Jose]
Oct. 26th 1827

[To:] His excellency the Governor General of the Callifornias

Dear Sir it will undoutedly surprise you to hear that Jedediah S. Smith is at this place, but I will endeavor to remove all suspicion by relating the simple truth—

when I left St Gabriel [in January 1827], I endeavored to go back by the same route which I had come, according to your orders, but the Mountains hung covered with snow, [and] were impassable and I was obliged to go northwardly—

when I had got about one hundred fifty miles above this place, I fell in with some Indians which proved to be enemies, they shot some arrows at some of my men and I killed some of them, but they were so numerous that I concluded it impracticable to pass with so small a Party (for I had now but eleven Men, one of My Men (Daniel Furguson), having deserted at St Gabriel, and another (John Wilson), I had disengaged at a place called the Flag Lake (in consequence of his cursing my self and every thing else) I engaged an Indian to pilot him to the nearest Mission and should be glad to see him no more

having got a little respite from the Indians I endeavored again to cross the Mountains but found it impossible, lost several Horses suffered a good deal from hunger & returned, I then came back opposite to this place, and concluded that the only method by which I could save the lives of my Men would be to take two men and endeavor to slip through the Indians undiscovered—succeeded in avoiding the Indians, reached Camp Defiance, on the Deposit, took such an equipment as I thought expedient, consisting of eighteen Men and what suplies I wood [be] in kneed of, to return to my company & fight our way through

I then came by the same bad route which I had first came, as I knew of no better way—
but in crossing the Colorado River, the Amuc-ha-bas [Mojave] Indians attacked & defeated my Party killing ten men (& two women half breeds) which I had ommitted mentioning, belonging to the Party, I lost my Horses and every thing that I had—I then had but eight men left, with which I

came direct to St Bernardino, I here left two of my men—Thomas Virgin, who was not able to travel, in consequence of wounds which he had received by the Indians, & Isaac Gilbreth, to accompany him—

I got some Horses & some provision at this place & in fifteen days reached my company with my remaining six men

My party now con[sisted?] of fifteen Men, almost destute of all kind of necessaries, the only resource I had left, I thought would be to go to the nearest Mission and let the Gen know my situation and endeavor to get permission to remain here untill some Vessel should arrive or some other opportunity should offer of getting such supplies as I stood in kneed of

I then took three men and came to St Joseph, where I was received as a man suspected, the Lieutenant was sent for, and I stated to him my situation—he will be more particular in mentioning the articles I stand in kneed of—

should I get permission to stay, to get the necessaries I stand in kneed of, I wish to get permission to hire two or three Men and to Purchase some Horses & Mules—I request beg of the Gen to have those two men, Virgin (if he is able) and Gilbreth, forwarded to me

Mission of St Joseph
October 26th 1827

your servant

J. S. Smith

3. San Francisco Presidio Commandant Luis Argüello Complains About Smith's Actions to Governor Echeandía, 1828

Port of San Francisco Jan. 2, 1828

Señor don Jose Maria Echeandia,

My esteemed friend and companion: Captain Smith of the foreign trappers appeared before me on the 25th of last December. He let me know that he was ready to attempt his retreat. He revealed his intention to me, should I desire to verify it, that he was to return by way of the Cosames [Consumnes] (the route by which second lieutenant don Jose Sanches brought them), and other ways contrary to those that your excellency commanded. It is not the route that you ordered them to follow. Having before me your order to escort Smith with the troops from my company, there was no way I could agree to his plans, notwithstanding his assertions and insistence upon his ideas.[1] To the contrary, I did not content myself with explaining your order to him verbally, but I showed it to him officially, for his information. And in light of this, under no circumstances should he disobey it. Moreover, it would put at great risk the troops that must accompany him. The route by way of the Cosames and open plains would, by my reckoning, make them go around Ft. Ross—a great mistake that would triple the distance to be covered by the party of troops that must accompany them. Ultimately, I could not fulfill my orders.[2]

In spite of all this prior consultation, without waiting for further action or your excellency's approval, he has left with only the presumption of approval. As I see it, he mocks your excellency's high orders and even tramples upon sacred national laws. He cannot claim ignorance in this affair, because I, far from agreeing with his ideas, could barely bring myself to agree with his contention that crossing the Straits of the Karquines [Carquinez] (the mouth of the rivers at this port)

---

[1]Echeandía ordered that a military escort of "ten men, more or less, appointed by you under the command of Alferez D. Jose Sanchez" accompany Smith's party as far as the mission at Sonoma.

[2]In other words, if Smith insisted on taking this route, Argüello could not comply with his orders to send a military escort to accompany him.

and from there, turning to the north, they would continue by the same route to a place where they consider themselves in their own territory.

I have not the least doubt that these foreigners have illegal plans to upset the harmonious purposes of our nation. They only care for themselves. They have convinced me of their designs, because they are not grateful for the favors given to them. Abusing those favors, they mock the authorities.

After having been treated with the kindness characteristic of our nation, they have left owing debts against the sale of their furs (which, if I am not mistaken, they usurped), import duties and other taxes that they should have paid for goods purchased from the frigate *Franklin,* and other private debts including one to me—they owe me some forty pesos. The worst is that I fear that after all these deceits they will not leave our territory and that they will return by the same routes that they wished, concealing themselves among the treasures that attract them (as I understand it), and again will gather as many furs as possible and will remove them from our territory, in which they are abundant. In the meantime, we repose in our confidence.

I have considerable evidence to convince me of this point. I believe, however, it is more prudent to restrain myself in order not to overwhelm your excellency [with information]. I will conclude only by saying that Smith's farewell was to send me a letter from San Jose that I could not understand because it is in his language and because I do not have an official interpreter to translate it. Smith sent another letter for your excellency that I believe will treat the permit that you agreed to. But be that as it may, I do not wish to be anything other than a loyal executor of commands and higher orders in everything that concerns the best interest of the nation and the fulfillment of my obligations.

Perhaps this is a point of honor. On various occasions Captain Smith and other foreigners have insulted me, threatening [to report me] to your excellency only because I have upheld higher orders. Perhaps because I communicate them verbally, the foreigners believe that they are promulgated by me. So, too, the English expeditionary frigate *Blossom* tried to intimidate me, but they miscalculated because my character is not that of one who surrenders, except in justice and in reason to the voice of legitimate authorities.

I certainly hope that my suspicions, based on my limited knowledge, will not come back to haunt me after a few days. I say this in respect to *Caudillo* Smith and his party based on their conduct, and I do not know if my suspicions can be deduced from [the behavior of] his countrymen or fellow countrymen who live among us in the guise of mediators. They alone know their motives, while we [remain] full of the utmost trust in their actions and conduct, contracts, arrangements, and friendships. Only experience itself and knowledge of their language (allowing oneself to understand), can remove doubts. We overlook their not infrequent deceits, and in no way would I, and much less your excellency, want anyone to treat our nation, and the authorities that represent her, with such contempt.

Things experienced first-hand make, no doubt, a greater impression than those heard from afar. Perhaps since your excellency has to listen from afar to my version, this will convince one who vacilates between whether it could or could not be as I tell it. But I am confident of your broad grasp and I have no doubt that your excellency will treat the matter with the urgency that its seriousness deserves.

Meanwhile, whether or not the deception occurs, I remain wishing your excellency all happiness. With the truest expressions of high solidarity, your loyal *compañero* who appreciates you, respects you, and kisses your hand.

Luis Antonio Argüello

Received in the mail that arrived on the 29th of January at this place.

A. V. Zamorano

4. John Rogers Advertises for Young Men of Enterprise, 1829

To Young Men of Enterprise

The undersigned will start, on the 15th of Sept. next, from Fort Smith, on a Trapping Expedition to the Rocky Mountains. He wishes to raise about 100 men for the trip, to be absent two years. The company will choose their own officers, and be subject to such regulations for their government as may be adopted by them. The articles of association are already drawn up and signed by a number of persons. The outfit will be furnished by me, (with the exception of the horses and guns,) to such as may desire it. It is confidently believed, that this enterprise affords a prospect of great profit to all who may engage in it.

Ft. Smith, July 20th, 1829 John Rogers

5. William A. Slacum Asks Ewing Young Not to Distill Whiskey, 1837

. . . After duly considering the great benefit that would result to this thriving country if the distillery of Ewing Young could be prevented from being put into operation, and inasmuch as he candidly admitted it was nothing but sheer necessity that compelled him to adopt the measure, I told him (Young) that I thought he had gained his point without adopting the expedient that produced it, as I was authorized by Mr. Finlayson to say, "if he would abandon his enterprise of distilling whiskey, he could be permitted to get his necessary supplies from Fort Vancouver, on the same terms as other men." . . .

6. Rufus B. Sage Describes the Fort of Antoine Robidoux, 1842

A small party from a trading establishment on the waters of Green river, who had visited Taos for the procurement of a fresh supply of goods, were about to return, and I availed myself of the occasion to make one of their number.

On the 7th of October we were under way. Our party consisted of three Frenchmen and five Spaniards, under the direction of a man named Roubideau, formerly from St. Louis, Mo. Some eight pack mules, laden at the rate of two hundred and fifty pounds each, conveyed a quantity of goods;—these headed by a guide followed in Indian file, and the remainder of the company, mounted on horseback, brought up the rear.

Crossing the Del Norte, we soon after struck into a large trail bearing a westerly course; following which, on the 13th inst. we crossed the main ridge of the Rocky Mountains by a feasible pass at the southern extremity of the Sierra de Anahuac range [an old name for the La Plata Mountains], and found ourselves upon the waters of the Pacific.

Six days subsequent, we reached Roubideau's Fort, at the forks of the Uintah, having passed several large streams in our course, as well as the two principal branches which unite to form the Colorado. . . .

The trade of this post is conducted principally with the trapping parties frequenting the Big Bear, Green, Grand, and the Colorado Rivers, with their numerous tributaries, in search of fur-bearing game.

A small business is also carried on with the Snake and Utah Indians, living in the neighborhood of this establishment. The common articles of dealing are horses, with beaver, otter, deer, sheep, and elk skins, in barter for ammunition, firearms, knives, tobacco, beads, awls, etc.

The Utahs and Snakes afford some of the largest and best finished sheep and deer skins I ever beheld,—a single skin sometimes being amply sufficient for common sized pantaloons. These skins are dressed so neatly as frequently to attain a snowy whiteness, and possess the softness of velvet.

They may be purchased for the trifling consideration of eight or ten charges of ammunition each, or two or three awls. . . . Skins are very abundant in these parts, as the natives, owing to the scarcity of buffalo, subsist entirely upon small game, which is found in immense quantities. The trade is quite profitable. The articles procured so cheaply, when taken to Santa Fe and the neighboring towns, find a ready cash market at prices ranging from one to two dollars each.

7. *Three Obituaries Summarize the Life of Jean Baptiste Charbonneau, 1866*

a.

Death of a California Pioneer.—We are informed by Mr. Dana Perkins, that he has received a letter announcing the death of J. B. Charbonneau, who left this country some weeks ago, with two companions, for Montana Territory. The letter is from one of the party, who says Mr. C., was taken sick with mountain fever, on the Owyhee, and died after a short illness.

Mr. Charbonneau was known to most of the pioneer citizens of this region of country, being himself one the first adventurers (into the territory now known as Placer county) upon the discovery of gold; where he has remained with little intermission until his recent departure for the new gold field, Montana, which, strangely enough, was the land of his birth, whither he was returning in the evening of life, to spend the few remaining days that he felt was in store for him.

Mr. Charbonneau was born in the western wilds, and grew up a hunter, trapper, and pioneer, among that class of men of which Bridger, Beckwourth, and other noted trappers of the woods were the representatives. He was born in the country of the Crow Indians—his father being a Canadian Frenchman, and his mother a half breed of the Crow tribe. He had, however, better opportunities than most of the rough spirits, who followed the calling of trapper, as when a young man he went to Europe and spent several years, where he learned to speak, as well as write several languages. At the breaking out of the Mexican War he was on the frontiers, and upon the organization of the Mormon Battalion he was engaged as a guide and came with them to California.

Subsequently upon the discovery of gold, he, in company with Jim Beckwourth, came upon the North Fork of the American river, and for a time it is said were mining partners.

Our acquaintance with Charbonneau dates back to '52, when we found him a resident of this country, where he has continued to reside almost continuously since—having given up frontier life. The reported discoveries of gold in Montana, and the rapid peopling of the Territory, excited the imagination of the old trapper, and he determined to return to the scenes of his youth.—Though strong of purpose, the weight of years was too much for the hardships of the trip undertaken, and he now sleeps alone by the bright waters of the Owyhee.

Our information is very meager of the history of the deceased—a fact we much regret, as he was of a class that for years lived among stirring and eventful scenes.

The old man, on departing for Montana, gave us a call, and said he was going to leave California, probably for good, as he was about returning to familiar scenes. We felt then as if we met him for the last time.

Mr. Charbonneau was of pleasant manners, intelligent, well read in the topics of the day, and was generally esteemed in the community in which he lived, as a good meaning and inoffensive man.

b.

J. B. Charbonneau died recently on his way from this country to Owyhee. Strangely enough, Montana was the land of his birth. He was by nature and occupation a hunter, trapper, and pioneer with Bridger and Beckwourth—his father a Canadian Frenchman, his mother a half-breed Crow squaw.

c.

Died.—We have received a note (don't know who from) dated May 16, '66, requesting the publication of the following:

"At Inskip's Ranche, Cow Creek, in Jordan Valley, J. B. Charbouneau aged sixty-three years—of pneumonia. Was born at St. Louis, Mo.; one of the oldest trappers and pioneers; he piloted the Mormon Brigade through from Lower Mexico in '46; came to California in '49, and has resided since that time mostly in Placer County; was en route to Montana."

8. Ralph Waldo Emerson Immortalizes George Nidever at the End of His Essay "Courage," 1870

George Nidiver [sic]

Men have done brave deeds,
And bards have sung them well,
I of good George Nidiver
Now the tale will tell.

In California mountains
A hunter bold was he:
Keen his eye and sure his aim
As any you should see.

A little Indian boy
Followed him everywhere,
Eager to share the hunter's joy
The hunter's meal to share.

And when the bird or deer
Fell by the hunter's skill,
The boy was always near
To help with right good will.

One day as through the cleft
Between two mountains steep,
Shut in both right and left,
Their questing way they keep,

They see two grizzly bears
With hunger fierce and fell
Rush at them unawares
Right down the narrow dell.

The boy turned round with screams,
And ran with terror wild;
One of the pair of savage beasts
Pursued the shrieking child.

The hunter raised his gun,—
He knew *one* charge was all,—
And through the boy's pursuing foe
He sent his only ball.

The other on George Nidiver
Came on with dreadful pace:
The hunter stood unarmed,
And met him face to face.

I say *unarmed* he stood,
Against those dreadful paws
The rifle butt, or club of wood,
Could stand no more than straws.

George Nidiver stood still
And looked him in the face;
The wild beast stopped amazed,
The came with slackening pace.

Still firm the hunter stood,
Although his heart beat high;
Again the creature stopped,
And gazed with wondering eye.

The hunter met his gaze,
  Nor yet an inch gave way;
The bear turned slowly round,
  And slowly moved away.

What thoughts were in his mind
  It would be hard to spell:
What thoughts were in George Nidiver
  I rather guess than tell.

But sure that rifle's aim,
  Swift choice of generous part,
Showed in its passing gleam
  The depth of a brave heart.

References

1. General William Ashley and James Beckwourth Describe Their Experiences on the Platte River, 1824
   Elinor Wilson, *Jim Beckwourth: Black Mountain Man and War Chief of the Crows* (Norman: University of Oklahoma Press, 1972), pp. 34–35.
2. Jedediah Smith Explains His Actions to Governor Echeandía, 1827
   David J. Weber, *The* Californios *versus Jedediah Smith, 1826–1827: A New Cache of Documents* (Spokane: Arthur H. Clark Company, 1990), pp. 44–46.
3. San Francisco Presidio Commandant Luis Argüello Complains About Smith's Actions to Governor Echeandía, 1828
   David J. Weber, *The* Californios *Versus Jedediah Smith, 1826–1827* (Spokane: Arthur H. Clark Company, 1990), pp. 51–55.
4. John Rogers Advertises for Young Men of Enterprise, 1829
   LeRoy Hafen, "Alexander Sinclair," in *The Mountain Men and the Fur Trade of the Far West* (Glendale: Arthur H. Clark Company, 1966), 4: 300.
5. William A. Slacum Asks Ewing Young Not to Distill Whiskey, 1837
   Kenneth L. Holmes, *Ewing Young: Master Trapper* (Portland: Binfords & Mort, 1967), pp. 117–118.
6. Rufus B. Sage Describes the Fort of Antoine Robidoux, 1842
   William Wallace, "Antoine Robidoux," in LeRoy Hafen, ed., *The Mountain Men and the Fur Trade of the Far West* (Glendale: Arthur H. Clark Company, 1966), 4: 267–269.
7. Three Obituaries Summarize the Life of Jean Baptiste Charbonneau, 1866
   Ann W. Hafen, "Jean Baptiste Charbonneau," in LeRoy Hafen, ed., *The Mountain Men and the Fur Trade of the Far West* (Glendale: Arthur H. Clark Company, 1965), 1: 222–223.
8. Ralph Waldo Emerson Immortalizes George Nidever at the End of His Essay "Courage," 1870
   Margaret E. Beckman and William H. Ellison, "George Nidever," in LeRoy Hafen, ed., *The Mountain Men and the Fur Trade of the Far West* (Glendale: Arthur H. Clark Company, 1965), 1: 338–339.

Document Set 5

Americans Look to the West: The Era of the Mexican War, 1843–1848

Although many Americans and other foreigners criticized California's progress under the Mexican regime, they appreciated certain aspects of the area's slower-paced life-style and its *rancho* economy. The abundance of land gave rise to a pattern of activity that differed markedly from that of the bustling Northeast, and the temperate climate contrasted sharply with the harsh winters and hot summers of the Midwest, where pioneers struggled to build homes and cultivate the soil. The dominant Catholic faith also called forth a prejudiced view from many Protestants who came in contact with former Spanish lands. Traveler William Thomes from Boston gives a glimpse of California life during the 1840s in Document 1.

After 1841 individual American travelers as well as wagon trains followed the trails to California. The Mexican government allowed foreigners to apply for land grants, and opportunities for settlement near Sutter's Fort became well known. Edwin Bryant, a visitor in 1846 and 1847, describes a buffalo hunt on the Platte River in Document 2. Although nine wagon trains successfully crossed the Great Plains and Sierra Nevadas into California between 1841 and 1845, the tenth became disorganized, lagged behind schedule, wandered into uncharted territory through faulty directions, and hit an early and harsh winter in the high mountains. The Donner party experienced the worst conditions faced by emigrants to the West and lost thirty-four members of their group. Patrick Breen recorded their hardships in his diary (Document 3).

The Oregon Country, north of California and stretching nearly to Alaska, had long been the domain of the British Hudson's Bay Company. Since the 1830s it had attracted missionaries and settlers, who had created a farming community in the Willamette Valley and wanted the land to become a part of the United States. The question of ownership with Great Britain was settled by treaty after the election of President James Knox Polk, an expansionist. The forty-ninth parallel, with some adjustments, became the dividing line between the United States and western Canada.

International questions to the south were not solved so easily. As diplomatic relations between Mexico and the United States deteriorated over the States' annexation of Texas and the location of Texas's southern boundary, troops from both countries moved into the disputed area. Hostilities broke out in late April 1846, and on May 9 President Polk called for a declaration of war against Mexico. The war's immediate cause proved less important than the feeling among many Americans that the United States' "manifest destiny" demanded occupation of the entire continent from coast to coast. Lieutenant John Frémont happened to be traveling in California on a mapping expedition, and his presence near Sutter's Fort afforded him a pivotal role in the United States' takeover of California (Document 4). Frémont supported Americans known as the Bears, who led an uprising in northern California against Mexican officials and who declared the independence of the "Bear Flag Republic" in June 1846 (Document 5).

Across the continent during the pre–Mexican War period, the Mormons, members of the Church of Jesus Christ of Latter-Day Saints, which had been founded in New York in 1830, faced persecution in several cities in the East. They received a devastating blow in Nauvoo, Illinois, when founder Joseph Smith in 1843 sanctioned polygyny (a marriage form in which a man has two or more wives at the same time). Anti-Mormon feeling ran so high that Smith and his brother were brutally killed. Church members chose Brigham Young to lead them safely to the

West to settle beyond the jurisdiction of the United States. A small party reached the area of today's Salt Lake City on July 22, 1847 (Document 6), and Young's well-organized Pioneer Band arrived two days later. Soon some 1,800 Saints, as the Mormons were called, settled around the southern tip of the Great Salt Lake. Another group traveled by sea under Sam Brannan and reached California just as the U.S. Navy took over Monterey and San Francisco as a result of the Mexican War. The Mormons sent a battalion to California to aid their countrymen in defending themselves against the Mexicans, but because hostilities had ceased for the most part, these forces helped residents of San Diego to repair buildings instead.

Fighting in California was sporadic, and the Mexicans did their best to defend the province against combined forces of the U.S. Navy, Army, and Marine Corps. After a seemingly easy victory over the Californios (the descendants of California's original Spanish colonists), Kit Carson carried the news to General Stephen Watts Kearny's Army of the West on its thousand-mile march overland to California from Fort Leavenworth, Kansas. Kearny sent two hundred of his three hundred dragoons back to Santa Fe and proceeded optimistically along the southern route. Near Escondido, California, he met the native California soldiers armed with lances who exerted a final effort to defend their ground at the Battle of San Pascual on December 6, 1846 (Document 7). The war in California ended with the Capitulation of Cahuenga, signed on January 13, 1847.

The Treaty of Guadalupe Hidalgo (Document 8), signed on February 2, 1848, promised perpetual peace between the United States and Mexico. Article V set the boundary line between the two countries, and Article VIII guaranteed the Mexican residents of California and other conquered territories the right to become U.S. citizens and to retain title over their land. Many of these people became citizens, but because of complicated and costly legal proceedings, not all obtained clear title to their land.

Questions for Analysis

1. Why do you think that New Englanders considered Californians lazy? What did Thomes believe were the advantages of California?
2. What were the benefits of the buffalo?
3. What would you have done if you were a member of the Donner party?
4. Should John Frémont have remained in California with his men after Castro asked him to leave?
5. The Bear Flaggers had been in California for about four years. Do you think they were justified in declaring independence?
6. Why did the Mormons go West?
7. What advantages did the Californios have over the Americans under General Kearny? What were their disadvantages?
8. What were the overall effects of the Treaty of Guadalupe Hidalgo?

1. William Henry Thomes Recalls Life in California Under Mexico, 1843

. . . With the Bay of Santa Barbara full of fish which could be obtained by simply dropping a line overboard; with shellfish off the Castle Point which could be obtained by hundreds by simply dropping a bone overboard with a line attached to it when the shellfish would cling to it and you could haul them up. There was not a single boat owned in the place. They never had a mess of fish unless it was caught for them by some of the Merchant ships and sent on shore as a present. They were too lazy, too indolent to care for vegetables except in beans and chillis to give piquancy to their stews. With a soil that would produce anything that grows they had managed to have a few apple and pear trees and a few straggling grape vines that were never trimmed and no care taken of them whatever. Orange trees, except in Los Angeles and Santa Barbara were unknown and yet by a little labor and a little foresight they could have produced any kind of crops that they needed and abundance of them but no one cared to take the trouble. They lived for today and let mañana take care of itself and such was the case all up and down the Coast with the exception of Los Angeles where some Americans and Germans had settled and had planted vineyards and cultivated crops, and at the Mission of San Gabriel the fathers were more ambitious than they were in other parts of the State, for they had planted oranges, limes, figs, and nut trees, and raised very nice crops, and also manufactured a rude species of California wine, and also aguardiente which they shipped to all parts of the Coast and sold for a large profit. It was a fiery strong liquor something like our raw whiskey, and half a tumbler full would make a man fighting drunk.

At that time any man who announced his intention of becoming a Mexican citizen could receive a grant of land equal to three square leagues of any land owned by the state and if he wanted more he could have it on application or paying a very small sum. Some of our American people in the South and also in the North of California took advantage of this, and preempted thousands and thousands of acres of land, which they held, and some of them disposed of at a mere nominal rate. Some Americans held as many as two or three hundred thousand acres of land at the time of the Mexican war and owned thousands of cattle and horses. The horses, however, were regarded as an annoyance of no value whatever as you could neither sell them nor give them away and they consumed the pasturage; they rendered no adequate return; but they were the best horses to be found in the world, untiring; ride them in a gallop from sunrise to sunset without water and without feed and they were apparently as fresh after a 90 mile ride as they were when they started; but the race of all those mustangs has all died out and we have now a different breed. To show you how easy it was then, you could start from San Diego on horseback, with your saddle and blanket, and you could ride from San Diego to San Francisco, and you need not have one single dollar in your pocket. When it came night you would stop at a ranch, you were welcome to the best that the house afforded; with your saddle for your pillow and your blanket to wrap around you, you occupied any place in the house that you were disposed to. Beds they had none; furniture they had none; of the conveniences of life they had none. Towels and sheets were luxuries only used by the very richest of people, and then only in one or two of the guest chambers for distinguished guests, for show and not for use. When you got ready to start in the morning, if your horse was lame or his hoofs were worn a little, your host would send a vaquero to the fields to lasso a fresh horse and you would leave your own in exchange and ride on to the next ranch; you were bid to come again when you pleased and in an hour after you left you were forgotten.

Such was life in California in those early days, a simple Arcadian sort of life with a happy contented people who were rich in lands and cattle, cared nothing for wealth, firm in their friendships, bitter and deadly in their hostilities, not always truthful and the lower class not always honest, but the upper classes gentlemanly, polished with a natural born courtesy that seemed to be innate. On the whole you could not help liking them in spite of their procrastinations and as for the women, it was utterly impossible for a susceptible American to be in their society without loving them and you can hardly blame them that to obtain possession they renounced their own religion and embraced Catholicism.

The people of the present day have but little idea of the grandeur of the old Spanish Mexican families, of their generous hospitality, of the number of retainers which each family possessed and the little trouble which they took to entertain you, yet of the hearty manner in which they received you and the fervent manner in which they bid you "God speed" on your journey and to come again when you were disposed, though if you remained with them a week, a month or six months and had offered to recompense them for their trouble, it would have been looked upon as an insult almost unpardonable. . . .

2. *Edwin Bryant Describes a Buffalo Hunt on the Platte River, 1846*

. . . We saw large herds of buffalo during our march, some of which approached us so nearly that there was danger of their mingling with our loose cattle. The buffalo-hunt is a most exciting sport to the spectator as well as to those engaged in it. Their action when running is awkward and clumsy, but their speed and endurance are such, that a good horse is required to overtake them or break them down in a fair race. Although the uninitiated in this sport may without much difficulty wound one of these animals with his rifle or pistol, it requires the skill and practice of a good hunter to place the ball in those parts which are fatal, or which so much disable the strong and shaggy quadruped as to prostrate him or force him to stop running. I have known a buffalo to be perforated with twenty balls, and yet be able to maintain a distance between himself and his pursuers. Experienced hunters aim to shoot them in the lungs or the spine. From the skull the ball rebounds, flattened as from a rock or a surface of iron, and has usually no other effect upon the animal than to increase his speed. A wound in the spine brings them to the ground instantly, and after a wound in the lungs their career is soon suspended from difficulty of breathing. They usually sink, rather than fall, upon their knees and haunches, and in that position remain until they are dead, rarely rolling upon their backs.

The flesh of the bull is coarse, dry, tough, and generally poor. The beef from a young fat heifer or cow, (and many of them are very fat,) is superior to our best beef. The unctuous and juicy substances of the flesh are distributed through all the muscular fibres and membranes in a manner and an abundance highly agreeable to the eye and delightful to the palate of the epicure. The choice pieces of a fat cow, are a strip of flesh along each side of the spine from the shoulders to the rump; the tender-loin; the liver; the heart; the tongue; the hump-ribs; and an intestinal vessel or organ, commonly called by hunters the "marrow-gut," which, anatomically speaking, is the chylo-poetic duct. This vessel contains an unctuous matter resembling marrow, and hence its vulgar name. No delicacy which I have ever tasted of the flesh kind can surpass this when properly prepared. All parts of the buffalo are correspondingly palatable with those of tame cattle; but when they are abundant, the principal part of the carcass is left by the hunter to feast the beasts and birds of prey. . . .

3. Patrick Breen Records the Hardships of the Donner Party, 1846

. . . Friday Nov. 20th 1846 came to this place on the 31st of last month that it snowed we went on to the pass the snow so deep we were unable to find the road, when within 3 miles of the summit then turned back to this shanty on the Lake, Stanton came one day after we arriveed here we again took our teams & waggons & made another unsuccessful attempt to cross in company with Stanton we returned to the shanty it continueing to snow all the time we were here we now have killed most part of our cattle having to stay here untill next spring & live on poor beef without bread or salt it snowed during the space of eight days with little intermission, after our arrival here, the remainder of time up to this day was clear & pleasant frezeing at night the snow nearly gone from the valleys.

sat. 21st fine morning wind N:W 22 of our company are about starting across the mountain this mor[n]ing including Stanton & his indians, some clouds flying thawed to day wnd E

Sunday 22nd froze hard last night this a fine clear morning, wind E.S.E no account from those on the mountains

monday 23rd Same weather wind W the Expedition across the mountains returned after an unsuccessful attempt

tuesday 24th fine in the morning towards eve[ni]ng Cloudy & windy wind W looks like snow freezeing hard

wendsday 25th wind about WNW Cloudy looks like the eve of a snow storm our mountainers intend trying to cross the Mountain tomorrow if fair froze hard last night

Thurssday the 26th began to snow yesterday in the evening now rains or sleet the mountaniers dont start to day the wind about W. wet & muddy

Friday 27 Continues to snow, the ground not covered, wind W dull prospect for crossing the mountains

Saturday 28th Snowing fast now about 10 o clock snow 8 or 10 inches deep soft wet snow, weather not cold wind W

Sunday 29th still snowing now about 3 feet deep, wind W killed my last oxen today will skin them tomorrow gave another yoke to Fosters hard to get wood

Monday 30th Snowing fast wind W about 4 or 5 feet deep, no drifts looks as likely to continue as when it commenced no liveing thing without wings can get about

December 1st Tuesday Still snowing wind W snow about 5 1/2 feet or 6 deep difficult to get wood no going from the house completely housed up looks as likely for snow as when it commenced, our cattle all killed But three or four [of] them, the horses & Stantons mules gone & cattle suppose lost in the Snow no hopes of finding them alive

wedns. 2nd. Continues to snow wind W sun shineing hazily thro the clouds dont snow quite as fast as it has done snow must be over six feet deep bad fire this morning . . .

Sunday 13th Snows faster than any previous day wind N:W Stanton & Graves with several others makeing preperations to cross the Mountains on snow shoes, snow 8 feet deep on the level dull

monday 14 fine morning sunshine cleared off last night about 12 o clock wind E:S:E dont thaw much but fair for a continueance of fair weather

Tuesday 15th Still continues fine wind W: S: W

Wed'd 16th fair & pleasant froeze hard last night & the Company started on snow shoes to cross the mountains wind S.E looks pleasant

Thursd. 17th Pleasant sunshine today wind about S.E bill Murp[hy] returned from the mountain party last evening Bealis [Williams] died night before last Milt. [Elliott] & Noah [James] went to Donnos [Donners] 8 days since not returned yet, thinks they got lost in the snow. J Denton here to day

Frid'd 18 beautiful day sky clear it would be delightful were it not for the snow lying so deep thaws but little on the south side of shanty saw no strangers today from any of the shantys

Satd. 19 Snowed last night commenced about 11 Oclock. squalls of wind with snow at intervals this morning thawing wind. N by W a little

Singular for a thaw may continue, it continues to Snow Sun Shining cleared off towards evening

Sund. 20 night clear froze a little now clear & pleasant wind N W thawing a little Mrs Reid here. no account of Milt. yet Dutch Charley [Burger] started for Donnghs turned back not able to proceed tough times, but not discouraged our hopes are in God. Amen

Mond. 21 Milt. got back last night from Donos camp sad news. Jake Donno[,] Sam Shoemaker[,] Rinehart, & Smith are dead the rest of them in a low situation snowed all night with a strong S-W wind to day Cloudy wind continues but not snowing, thawing sun shineing dimly in hopes it will clear off

Tuesd. 22nd Snowed all last night Continued to snow all day with some few intermissions had a severe fit of the gravel yesterday I am well to day, Praise *be to the God of Heaven*

Wend. 23rd Snowed a little last night clear to day & thawing a little. Milt took some of his meat to day all well at their camp began this day to read the Thirty days prayer, may Almighty God grant the request of an unworthy sinner that I am. *Amen*

Thursd. 24th rained all night & still continues to rain poor prospect for any kind of Comfort Spiritual or temporal, wind S: may God help us to spend the Christmass as we ought considering circumstances

Friday 25th began to snow yesterday about 12 o clock snowed all night & snows yet rapidly wind about E by N Great difficulty in getting wood John & Edwd. has to get [it] I am not able offered our prayers to God this Cherimass morning the prospect is apalling but hope in God *Amen*

Satd. 26th Cleared off in the night to day clear & pleasant Snowed about 20 inches or two feet deep yesterday. the old snow was nearly run soft before it began to snow now it is all soft the top dry & the under wet wind S.E

Sun 27 Continues clear froze hard last night Snow very deep say 9 feet thawing a little in the sun scarce of wood to day chopt a tree dow[n] it sinks in the snow & is hard to be got

Monday 28th Snowed last night Cleared off this morning snowed a little now Clear & pleasant

Tuesday 29th fine clear day froze hard last night. Charley sick. Keysburg has Wolfing[er]s Rifle gun

Wedsd. 30th fine clear morning froze hard last night Charley died last night about 10 Oclock had with him in money $1.50 two good loking silver watches one razor 3 boxes caps Keysburg tok them into his possession Spitzer took his coat & waistcoat Keysburg all his other little effects gold pin one shirt and tools for shaveing.

Thursday 31st last of the year, may we with Gods help spend the comeing year better than the past which we purpose to do if Almighty God will deliver us from our present dredful situation which is our prayer if the will of God sees it fiting for us Amen—morning fair now Cloudy wind E by S for three days past freezeing hard every night looks like another snow storm Snow Storms are dredful to us snow very deep crust on the snow

Jany. 1st 1847 we pray the God of mercy to deliver us from our present Calamity if it be his Holy will Amen. Commenced snowing last night does not snow fast wind S.E sun peeps out at times provisions geting scant dug up a hide from under the snow yesterday for Milt. did not take it yet . . .

4. *John Bidwell Blames John Frémont for Precipitating the War in California, 1846*

. . . After several weeks Frémont and his entire party became united in the San Joaquin Valley.[1] While at Monterey he had obtained permission from José Castro, the commandant-general, to winter in the San Joaquin Valley, away from the settlements, where the men would not be likely to annoy the people. He had in all in the exploring party about sixty well-armed men. He also had permission to extend his explorations in the spring as far south as the Colorado River.

Accordingly early in the spring (1846) Frémont started south with his party. When Castro gave him permission to explore towards the Colorado River he no doubt supposed he would go south or southeast from where he was camped in the San Joaquin Valley, and on through the Tejon Pass and the Mojave Desert; but, instead, Frémont with his sixty armed men started to go west and southwest through the most thickly settled parts of California, namely, the Santa Clara, Pajaro, and Salinas valleys. As he was approaching the last valley Castro sent an official order by an officer warning Frémont that he must leave, as his action was illegal. The order was delivered March 5. Frémont took possession of an eminence called Gavilan Peak, and continued to fortify himself for several days, perhaps a week or more, Castro meantime remaining in sight and evidently increasing his force day by day. Frémont, enraged against Castro, finally abandoned his position in the night of March 9, and, gaining the San Joaquin Valley, made his way rapidly northward up the Sacramento Valley and into Oregon, leaving Sutter's about March 24.

A little over four weeks after Frémont left I happened to be fishing four or five miles down the river, having then left Sutter's service with the view of trying to put up two or three hundred barrels of salmon, thinking the venture would be profitable. An officer of the United States, Lieutenant A. H. Gillespie, of the marines, bearing messages to the explorer, came up the river in a small boat and at once inquired about Frémont. I told him he had gone to Oregon. Said he: "I want to overhaul him. How far is it to the fort?" And receiving my reply, he pushed rapidly on. He overtook Frémont near the Oregon line. Frémont, still indignant against Castro, who had compelled him to abandon his explorations south, returned at once to California. It so happened that Castro had sent Lieutenant Arce to the north side of the bay of San Francisco to collect scattered Government horses. Arce had secured about one hundred and fifty and was taking them to the south side of the bay, *via* Sutter's Fort and the San Joaquin Valley. This was the only way to transfer cattle or horses from one side of the bay to the other, except at the Straits of Carquinez by the slow process of swimming one at a time, or of taking one or two, tied by all four feet, in a small boat or launch. Arce, with the horses and seven or eight soldiers, arrived at Sutter's Fort, staid overnight as the guest of Sutter, and went on his way to the Cosumne River (about sixteen or eighteen miles) and camped for the night.

Frémont's hasty departure for Oregon and Gillespie's pursuit of him had been the occasion of many surmises. Frémont's sudden return excited increased curiosity. People flocked to his camp: some were settlers, some hunters; some were good men, and some about as rough specimens of humanity as it would be possible to find anywhere. Frémont, hearing that the horses were passing, sent a party of these promiscuous

---

[1]His men in the mountains had suffered considerably. Frémont had given positive orders for them to wait at a certain gap or low divide till he should meet them with supplies, but the place could not be found. The men got out of provisions and bought from the Indians. The kind they most relished was a sort of brown meal, which was rich and spicy, and came so much into favor that they wanted no other. After a while the Indians became careless in the preparation of this wonderful meal, when it was discovered to be full of the broken wings and legs of grasshoppers! It was simply dried grasshoppers pounded into a meal. The men said it was rich and would stick to the mouth like gingerbread, and that they were becoming sleek and fat. But after the discovery they lost their appetites. How hard it is sometimes to overcome prejudice!

people and captured them. This of course was done before he had orders or any positive news that war had been declared. When Gillespie left the United States, as the bearer of a despatch to Larkin and Frémont and of letters to the latter, war had not been declared. The letters included one from Senator Benton, who had the confidence and knew the purposes of the Administration. As Gillespie had to make his way through Mexico, he committed the despatch and his orders to memory, destroyed them, and rewrote them on the vessel which took him, *via* the Sandwich Islands, to the coast of California. There had been no later arrival, and therefore no later despatches to Frémont were possible. Though Frémont was reticent, whatever he did was supposed to be done with the sanction of the United States. Thus, without giving the least notice even to Sutter, the great friend of Americans, or to Americans in general, scattered and exposed as they were all over California, he precipitated the war. . . .

5. William B. Ide Proclaims Independence for California as the Bear Flag Republic, 1846

To all persons, Citizens of Sonoma, requesting them to remain at peace, and to follow their rightful occupations without fear of Mollestation.

The Commander in Chief of the Troops assembled at the Fortress of Sonoma give his inviolable pledge to all persons in California not found under arms that they shall not be disturbed in their persons, their property or social relations one to another by men under his command.

He also solemnly declares his object to be First, to defend himself and companions in arms who were invited to this country by a promise of Lands on which to settle themselves and families who were also promised a "Republican Government," who, when having arrived in California were denied even the privilege of buying or renting Lands of their friends, who instead of being allowed to participate in or being protected by a "Republican Government" were oppressed by a "Military Despotism," who were even threatened, by "proclamation" from the Chief officer of the aforesaid Despotism, with extermination if they would not depart out of the Country; leaving all their property, their arms and beasts of burden, and thus deprived of the means of flight or defence. We were to be driven through deserts, inhabited by hostile Indians to certain destruction. To overthrow a "Government" which had seized upon the property of the Missions for its individual aggrandizement; which has ruined and shamefully oppressed the labouring people of California, by their enormous exactions on goods imported into this country; is the determined purpose of the brave men who are associated under his command.

He also solemnly declares his object in the Second place to be to invite all peaceable and good Citizens of California who are friendly to the maintenance of good order and equal rights (and I do hereby invite them to repair to my camp at Sonoma without delay) to assist us in establishing and perpetuating a "Republican Government" which shall secure to all; civil and religious liberty; which shall detect and punish crime; which shall encourage industry virtue and literature; which shall leave unshackled by Fetters, Commerce, Agriculture, and Mechanism.

He further declares that he relies upon the rectitude of our intentions; the favor of Heaven and the bravery of those who are bound to, and associated with him, by the principle of self preservation; by the love of truth; and by the hatred of tyranny—for his hopes of success.

He further declares that he believes that a Government to be prosperous and happifying in its tendency must originate with its people who are friendly to its existence. That its Citizens, are its Guardians, its officers are its Servants, and its Glory their reward.

Signed *William B. Ide*

Head Quarters Sonoma June 15th 1846.

6. William Clayton Catches a Glimpse of the Great Salt Lake Slightly Ahead of Brigham Young, 1846

. . . While the brethren were cutting the road, I followed the old one to the top of the hill and on arriving there was much cheered by a handsome view of the Great Salt Lake lying, as I should judge, from twenty-five to thirty miles to the west of us; and at eleven o'clock I sat down to contemplate and view the surrounding scenery. There is an extensive, beautiful, level looking valley from here to the lake which I should judge from the numerous deep green patches must be fertile and rich. The valley extends to the south probably fifty miles where it is again surrounded by high mountains. To the southwest across the valley at about twenty to twenty-five miles distance is a high mountain, extending from the south end of the valley to about opposite this place where it ceases abruptly leaving a pleasant view of the dark waters of the lake. Standing on the lake and about due west there are two mountains and far in the distance another one which I suppose is on the other side of the lake, probably from sixty to eighty miles distance. To the northwest is another mountain at the base of which is a lone ridge of what I should consider to be rock salt from its white and shining appearance. The lake does not show at this distance a very extensive surface, but its dark blue shade resembling the calm sea looks very handsome. The intervening valley appears to be well supplied with streams, creeks and lakes, some of the latter are evidently salt. There is but little timber in sight anywhere, and that is mostly on the banks of creeks and streams of water which is about the only objection which could be raised in my estimation to this being one of the most beautiful valleys and pleasant places for a home for the Saints which could be found. Timber is evidently lacking but we have not expected to find a timbered country. . . . For my own part I am happily disappointed in the appearance of the valley of the Salt Lake, but if the land be as rich as it has the appearance of being, I have no fears but the Saints can live here and do well while we will do right. When I commune with my own heart and ask myself whether I would choose to dwell here in this wild looking country amongst the Saints surrounded by friends, though poor, enjoying the privileges and blessings of the everlasting priesthood, with God for our King and Father; or dwell amongst the gentiles with all their wealth and good things of the earth, to be eternally mobbed, harassed, hunted, our best men murdered and every good man's life continually in danger, the soft whisper echoes loud and reverberates back in tones of stern determination; give me the quiet wilderness and my family to associate with, surrounded by the Saints and adieu to the gentile world till God says return and avenge you of your enemies.

7. Henry Smith Turner Describes Conditions at the Battle of San Pascual, 1846

San Diego U. California
Dec. 21, 1846

My own dear wife:

We have arrived at the close of our long laborious and hazardous march at last—have encountered many difficulties on the route, from now have nothing to look forward to but a continuation of campaigns against an enemy that surpasses the Florida Indians far in subtlety. Labor and fatigue is the order of the day and we lie down at night but to rise again at early dawn to recommence our labors. Before we left New Mexico, as I have already informed you, we met the express from California to Washington City, bearing the intelligence that this country was in the hands of the Americans, that the people were reconciled, indeed pleased at the changes, and that the new government was in full operation. We had then a force of 300 active efficient Dragoons; on the receipt of this information the General determined to leave in New Mexico the greater part of this force, and proceed to California with a force just sufficient to protect him from the Indians—100 Dragoons accompanied us commanded by Captain Moore. . . . On the evening of December 5th, when within about 50 miles of this place, we learned that about 160 of the enemy [Californians] were encamped six miles from us; Lt. Hammond with a few Dragoons was sent to make a reconnoisance; they returned about one o'clock on the morning of the 6th, and reported that the enemy were in considerable force, and that the information in relation to their numbers and whereabouts was correct; It was immediately determined to attack them; and saddling up we reached their camp just at dawn of day: Captain Abraham Robinson Johnston who had command of the advance guard made a furious charge on them when within a quarter of a mile of them; the enemy having discovered Lt. Thomas C. Hammond's reconnoitering party a few hours before, were all in the saddle and ready to receive us. Capt. Johnston's guards were followed by Capt. Benjamin D. Moore's Dragoons with the General and his staff at their head. The enemy fired into us several vollies as we approached; Capt. Johnston was shot in the head at the first volley and fell dead from his horse. After firing a few vollies into us the enemy fled and was pursued by Capt. Moore and about 40 Dragoons, accompanied by the General and staff, the major portion of the Dragoons being mounted on the broken down mules which we had brought in from New Mexico, were scarcely able to do more than keep in sight of the party headed by Capt. Moore. After pursuing the enemy about half a mile at full speed and becoming separated from the body of our command, he discovered the small force who were in pursuit, and about 150 charged upon us, and did terrible execution with their lances; this struggle lasted about 15 minutes, fighting each man hand to hand with his antagonist. We finally beat them off the second time; they fled leaving us in possession of the field. Then came the painful task of collecting our dead and wounded, 18 of the former, among them Capt. Johnston and Lt. Hammond (Lt. H. survived a few hours,) and 14 or 15 wounded, among them Gen. Kearny and Lt. Warner quite badly, myself very slightly. Capt. Moore and Lt. Hammond being killed the command of the Dragoons devolved upon me, and the duty of disposing of the dead and providing for the wounded had to be performed and I am unable to describe to you what were my sensations as I superintended the arrangements for the burial of the poor fellows, who but a few hours before had been in our midst without a presentiment of what so soon was to be their fate. A large grave was dug and all deposited in it, officers and men together there to remain until an opportunity is presented of paying them proper funeral honors. After constructing during the night rude ambulances for our wounded men, we continued our march the following morning in the direction of San Diego. The enemy in considerable force showing themselves at short distances from our route throughout the day. Before reaching camp, and near sunset, it became necessary to pass near the base of a hill, which we discovered to be in possession of the enemy, from which an incessant galling fire might have been poured into us as we passed. So it became necessary to drive the enemy from this position: the men being dismounted the order was given to charge up the hill on foot: the order was nobly executed notwithstanding we were in open field and the enemy were protected from our fire by large rocks on the crest of the hill, from behind which they fired upon us continually—they stood their ground until we approached them within gun shot when they abandoned their secure position and fled precipitately: as they stepped from behind the rocks to make their escape we fired at them and killed and wounded several—they made their escape so rapidly that many of them dropped their arms in their flight. Finding ourselves again in possession of the field and in a commanding position secure from attack, at the same time that we could subsist ourselves and animals, on the recommendation of the surgeon it was determined that we should remain here for several days for the purpose of resting the wounded men. On the night of the third day a reinforcement reached us from this place, San

Diego, having been sent out by Commodore Stockton, who having heard of our fight very wisely considered that such assistance would be acceptable to us. It was well for us that such a step was taken, for we have since learned that during our stay on the hill the enemy had been reinforced to quadruple our strength, and that all arrangements were made by them to charge upon us the moment we descended into the plain, and in our encumbered and reduced condition it is altogether probable that they would not have left one of us to tell the tale. The day after our reinforcement arrived we marched for San Diego, and arrived here on the second day. It was reported but a few months ago that this country had been conquered by Col. Frémont and Com. Stockton. This report has reached the U.S. and the minds of the people in authority are doubtless at rest on this subject; but never was there a more untrue, or rather, a more unfounded impression—the people of this country are now in arms and in possession of the greater portion of the Territory. There is no telling where this matter will end, or what are the sacrifices yet to be made; not only in heavy expenditures but also in human life, for we have a most subtle and formidable enemy to contend with. They have control of the resources of the country which consist of cattle and horses; the former we require for subsistence, the latter for transportation; we can prosecute a war against them no better without the one than without the other—we can whip these people wherever they will meet us in a pitched battle; or anything like a regular fight; but this they know as well as we do, therefore we need not expect to have another fight with them; but there is no telling how long the guerilla warfare, which from this time will no doubt be their policy, will continue. . . .

This letter goes via the Sandwich Islands and cannot reach you for six months and indeed may never reach you—of course, you will use the proceeds of house rent as you may require money—I require little or no money out here and will be able to lay up a portion of the pay which I have reserved for myself.

Your ever fond husband
H.S. Turner

General Kearny sends his regards to you and our kind Mother, so do I to everybody including Mrs. K.

8. The Treaty of Guadalupe Hidalgo Guarantees Certain Rights to Mexicans, 1848

In the name of Almighty God:

The United States of America, and the United Mexican States, animated by a sincere desire to put an end to the calamities of the war which unhappily exists between the two Republics, and to establish upon a solid basis relations of peace and friendship, which shall confer reciprocal benefits upon the citizens of both, and assure the concord, harmony and mutual confidence, wherin the two Peoples should live, as good Neighbours, have for that purpose appointed their respective Plenipotentiaries: that is to say, the President of the United States has appointed Nicholas P. Trist, a citizen of the United States, and the President of the Mexican Republic has appointed Don Luis Gonzaga Cuevas, Don Bernardo Couto, and Don Miguel Atristain, citizens of the said Republic; who, after a reciprocal communication of their respective full powers, have, under the protection of Almighty God, the author of Peace, arranged, agreed upon, and signed the following

Treaty of Peace, Friendship, Limits and Settlement Between the United States of America and the Mexican Republic

Article I

There shall be firm and universal peace between the United States of America and the Mexican Republic, and between their respective Countries, territories, cities, towns and people, without exception of places or persons. . . .

Article V

The Boundary line between the two Republics shall commence in the Gulf of Mexico, three leagues from land, opposite the mouth of the Rio Grande, otherwise called Rio Bravo del Norte, or opposite the mouth of its deepest branch, if it should have more than one branch emptying directly into the sea; from thence, up the middle of that river, following the deepest channel, where it has more than one to the point where it strikes the Southern boundary of New Mexico; thence, westwardly along the whole Southern Boundary of New Mexico (which runs north of the town called *Paso*) to its western termination; thence, northward, along the western line of New Mexico, until it intersects the first branch of the river Gila; (or if it should not intersect any branch of that river, then, to the point on the said line nearest to such branch, and thence in a direct line to the same;) thence down the middle of the said branch and of the said river, until it empties into the Rio Colorado; thence, across the Rio Colorado, following the division line between Upper and Lower California, to the Pacific Ocean.

The southern and western limits of New Mexico, mentioned in this Article, are those laid down in the Map, entitled *"Map of the United Mexican States, as organized and defined by various acts of the Congress of said Republic, and constructed according to the best authorities. Revised edition. Published at New York in 1847 by J. Disturnell:"* Of which Map a Copy is added to this Treaty, bearing the signatures and seals of the Undersigned Plenipotentiaries. And, in order to preclude all difficulty in tracing upon the ground the limit separating Upper from Lower California, it is agreed that the said limit shall consist of a straight line, drawn from the middle of the Rio Gila, where it unites with the Colorado, to a point on the Coast of the Pacific Ocean, distant one marine league due south of the southernmost point of the Port of San Diego, according to the plan of said port, made in the year 1782, by Don Juan Pantoja, second sailing-Master of the Spanish fleet, and published at Madrid in the year 1802, in the Atlas to the voyage of the schooners *Sutil* and *Mexicana:* of which plan a Copy is hereunto added, signed and sealed by the respective Plenipotentiaries.

In order to designate the Boundary line with due precision, upon authoritative maps, and to establish upon the ground landmarks which shall show the limits of both Republics, as described in the present Article, the two Governments shall each appoint a Commissioner and a Surveyor, who, before the expiration of one year from the date of the exchange of ratifications of this treaty, shall meet at the Port of San Diego, and proceed to run and mark the said Boundary in its whole course to the mouth of the Rio Bravo del Norte. They shall keep journals and make out plans of their operations; and the result, agreed upon by them, shall be deemed a part of this treaty, and shall have the same force as if it were inserted therein. The two Governments will amicably agree regarding what may be necessary to these persons, and also as to their respective escorts, should such be necessary.

The Boundary line established by this Article shall be religiously respected by each of the two Republics, and no change shall ever be made therein, except by the express and free consent of both nations, lawfully given by the General Government of each, in conformity with it's own constitution. . . .

Article VIII

Mexicans now established in territories previously belonging to Mexico, and which remain for the future within the limits of the United States, as defined by the present Treaty, shall be free to continue where they now reside, or to remove at any time to the Mexican Republic, retaining the property which they possess in the said territories, or disposing thereof and removing the proceeds wherever they please; without their being subjected, on this account, to any contribution, tax or charge whatever.

Those who shall prefer to remain in the said territories, may either retain the title and rights of Mexican citizens, or acquire those of citizens of the United States. But, they shall be under the obligation to make their election within one year from the date of the exchange of ratifications of this treaty: and those who shall remain in the said territories, after the expiration of that year, without having declared their intention to retain the character of Mexicans, shall be considered to have elected to become citizens of the United States.

In the said territories, property of every kind, now belonging to Mexicans not established there, shall be inviolably respected. The present owners, the heirs of these, and all Mexicans who may hereafter acquire said property by contract, shall enjoy with respect to it, guaranties equally ample as if the same belonged to citizens of the United States. . . .

References

1. William Henry Thomes Recalls Life in California Under Mexico, 1843
   William Henry Thomes, *Recollections of Old Times in California,* George R. Stewart, ed. (Berkeley: Friends of the Bancroft Library, 1974), pp. 22–25. (Thomes's original 1887 manuscript is in the Bancroft Library.)
2. Edwin Bryant Describes a Buffalo Hunt on the Platte River, 1846
   Edwin Bryant, *What I Saw in California: Being the Journal of a Tour . . . in the Years 1846, 1847* (Minneapolis: Ross & Haines, Inc., 1967), pp. 95–96.
3. Patrick Breen Records the Hardships of the Donner Party, 1846
   "The Diary of Patrick Breen," in George R. Stewart, *Ordeal by Hunger: The Story of the Donner Party* (Boston: Houghton Mifflin, 1960), pp. 323–328.
4. John Bidwell Blames John Frémont for Precipitating the War in California, 1846
   John Bidwell, *In California Before the Gold Rush* (Los Angeles: Ward Ritchie Press, 1948), pp. 96–99.
5. William B. Ide Proclaims Independence for California as the Bear Flag Republic, 1846
   Manuscript HM 4116, Huntington Library, San Marino, California.
6. William Clayton Catches a Glimpse of the Great Salt Lake Slightly Ahead of Brigham Young, 1846
   William Mulder and A. Russell Mortensen, eds., *Among the Mormons: Historic Accounts by Contemporary Observers* (New York: Alfred A. Knopf, 1958), pp. 225–226.
7. Henry Smith Turner Describes Conditions at the Battle of San Pascual, 1846
   Dwight L. Clarke, ed., *The Original Journals of Henry Smith Turner with Stephen Watts Kearny to New Mexico and California, 1846–1847* (Norman: University of Oklahoma Press, 1966), pp. 144–148.
8. The Treaty of Guadalupe Hidalgo Guarantees Certain Rights to Mexicans, 1848
   Richard Griswold del Castillo, *The Treaty of Guadalupe Hidalgo: A Legacy of Conflict* (Norman: University of Oklahoma Press, 1990), appendix 2, pp. 183–190.

Document Set 6

The Mining Frontier from California to Colorado, 1848–1859

In any country's history, only a few events are of such significance that we can call them turning points. James Marshall's discovery of gold in California on January 24, 1848, is just such an event. Because of California's relative isolation, the gold rush did not take place until 1849. But once the word spread, fortune seekers arrived from Mexico, the East Coast, the Midwest, Hawaii, and South America, and finally from Europe, China, and Australia. California's population skyrocketed from about 14,000 in 1848, excluding Indians, to nearly 100,000 by the end of 1849. More than half of the newcomers had come from the United States; many of them were single young men looking to make their fortune and then return home.

The rugged journey to California required a long overland trek or an equally long sea voyage, both trips under difficult and crowded conditions. When the gold became scarce, many Americans set out eastward to recross the continent. En route, some discovered lodes in Nevada and Colorado, igniting mining booms across the country.

Marshall, an employee of Swiss immigrant and California colonist John Sutter whom Sutter charged with building a sawmill at Coloma on the American River, first noticed the yellow flakes. Aided by his crew, he gave the metal some preliminary tests. Sutter confirmed the discovery and asked the group to keep their findings a secret. The news soon leaked, but owing to slow communication, more than a month passed before prospectors began their rush to the site. The first report of the discovery appeared in the *Californian*, a San Francisco newspaper, on March 15, 1848 (Document 1), and by June almost everyone in northern California seemed to be flocking to the mines (Document 2). By 1850 many Anglo-Americans working in the area, among them Charles W. Churchill of Ohio (Document 3), reported their activities to relatives back home. For successful miners, freight and banking operations such as Wells-Fargo & Co. began to protect and transport gold. Less fortunate prospectors were immortalized in the song "The Lousy Miner" (Document 4).

Coincidentally, some Mormons who had reached California with Sam Brannan obtained jobs at Sutter's Mill and sent word of the discovery to Salt Lake City, where Brigham Young's followers had laid out a well-organized municipality (Document 5). The Mormons profited from the gold rush by acquiring gold and by selling supplies, for their settlement was located on a main wagon route to the West. In this same period, San Francisco underwent explosive growth. As its population increased from a mere few hundred in 1845 to many thousands in 1853, the booming city suffered from a lack of organized law enforcement. New England Yankees accused San Francisco officials, some of them southerners, of corruption, fraud, and failure to protect citizens, and insisted that vigilante committees were necessary to enforce the law. The sixth document describes some of the uneasy conditions in San Francisco.

Toward the middle of the 1850s, California gold had become difficult to find, and few individuals could make a living by prospecting. Large companies had taken over and used methods such as hydraulic mining to get to less accessible areas. When news came of gold strikes in other locations, it set off little booms. Occasionally, camps such as those along the Fraser River in British Columbia, Bannack and Last Chance in Idaho, Gila City in Arizona, Gold Hill in Utah, and Conconully and Ruby in Washington Territory prospered only briefly and then were abandoned.

Some prospectors who had not fared well in California discovered silver in Nevada, although at first they did not recognize the ore. They were looking for gold and failed to realize that the heavy, bluish sand that clogged their sifting equipment was actually a rich silver sulfide mixed with gold, assaying at nearly $4,000 a ton. Peter O'Riley and Patrick McLaughlin made the initial discovery in 1859, but it was Henry Comstock who took advantage of the find; he relates the story of his success in Document 7. Other lucky individuals found gold in Colorado, and a rush began to Pike's Peak (Document 8). New fortunes were made, and the wealth of the mining frontier became an important consideration in the growing split between the North and the South on the eve of the Civil War. Both Union and Confederate sympathizers would try to gain control of gold and silver to finance military operations.

Questions for Analysis

1. What motivated people to head west and search for gold in California?
2. What were the living conditions for miners in the West?
3. Why were the Mormons able to organize a tightly run community in Salt Lake City?
4. Are committees of vigilance a good idea? What are the alternatives?
5. How did people uncover gold and silver in other parts of the United States?

1. *The* Californian *Modestly Announces the Discovery of Gold, 1848*

CALIFORNIAN.

EVILS FROM IGNORANCE—REMEDIES FROM KNOWLEDGE.

Vol. II. SAN FRANCISCO, WEDNESDAY, MARCH 15, 1848. No. 44.

WM. H. D...

Wholesale and Retail Merchant.
San Francisco, Alta California.

KILBORN, LAWTON & CO.
General Commission Merchants,
AND DEALERS IN
OREGON PRODUCE.

Consignments respectfully solicited.—Refer to

C. L. ROSS,
San Francisco.
S. H. WILLIAMS, & Co.,
Honolulu, S. I.

Oregon City, Nov. 1st, 1847. 28-tf

L. EVERHART,
FASHIONABE TAILOR,
Montgomery Street, San Francisco, U. C.

L. W. HASTINGS.
Attorney and Counsellor at Law, and Solicitor in Chancery.
San Francisco, Upper California. y-5

EVERETT & CO.,
General Commission Merchants,

E. P. Everett, J. Jarves. } Honolulu, Oahu, H. I.

☞Money advanced, on favorable terms, for Bills of Exchange on the United States, England and France.

Honolulu, 1847. tf-33

S. H. WILLIAMS, & CO.
General Commission Merchants,
Honolulu, Oahu,

S. H. Williams, J. F. B. Marshall, Wm. Baker, Jr. } Hawaiian Islands.

Exchange on the United States & Europe, taken on the most favorable terms. 26-3m.

JASPER O'FARRELL.
Civil Engineer and Land Surveyor,
By appointment of Col. R. B. Mason, Gov. of California.
(Office Portsmouth Square, San Francisco.)

J. B. ...LORG, y Co.
Los Angeles y 8 de Enero de 1848. 37-tf

KNOW ALL MEN BY THESE PRESENTS, that I, Richard B. Mason, Col. 1st Regiment of Dragoons, United States Army, and Governor of California, by virtue of authority in me vested, do hereby appoint Jacob R. Snyder, Land Surveyor, in the Middle Department of Upper California.

Done at Monterey, the Capital of California, this the 22d day of July 1847, and the 72d of the Independence of the United States.

R. B. MASON, Col. 1st Drag's.
12-tf Gov. of California.

JUST LANDED.

1 case superior Ladies Hosiery, to be sold low by the dozen, at the
40 BEE HIVE.

IRON POTS.

100 three-leg'd Iron Pots for sale, a bargain, at the
40 BEE HIVE.

TO INVALIDS & OTHERS.

Messrs DICKSON & HAY have just received, and now on hand 100,000 lbs. superior ARROW ROOT and 500 lbs. COCOA, recommended by the faculty, well worthy the attention of Invalids, &c.

Gold Mine Found.—In the newly made raceway of the Saw Mill recently erected by Captain Sutter, on the American Fork, gold has been found in considerable quantities. One person brought thirty dollars worth to New Helvetia, gathered there in a short time. California, no doubt, is rich in mineral wealth; great chances here for scientific capitalists. Gold has been found in almost every part of the country.

2. Walter Colton Describes the Effects of the Gold Rush, 1848

. . . The excitement produced was intense; and many were soon busy in their hasty preparations for a departure to the mines. The family who had kept house for me caught the moving infection. Husband and wife were both packing up; the blacksmith dropped his hammer, the carpenter his plane, the mason his trowel, the farmer his sickle, the baker his loaf, and the tapster his bottle. All were off for the mines, some on horses, some on carts, and some on crutches, and one went in a litter. An American woman, who had recently established a boarding-house here, pulled up stakes, and was off before her lodgers had even time to pay their bills. Debtors ran, of course. I have only a community of women left, and a gang of prisoners, with here and there a soldier, who will give his captain the slip at the first chance. I don't blame the fellow a whit; seven dollars a month, while others are making two or three hundred a day! that is too much for human nature to stand.

Saturday, July 15. The gold fever has reached every servant in Monterey; none are to be trusted in their engagement beyond a week, and as for compulsion, it is like attempting to drive fish into a net with the ocean before them. Gen. Mason, Lieut. Lanman, and myself, form a mess; we have a house, and all the table furniture and culinary apparatus requisite; but our servants have run, one after another, till we are almost in despair: even Sambo, who we thought would stick by from laziness, if no other cause, ran last night; and this morning, for the fortieth time, we had to take to the kitchen, and cook our own breakfast. A general of the United States Army, the commander of a man-of-war, and the Alcalde of Monterey, in a smoking kitchen, grinding coffee, toasting a herring, and pealing onions! These gold mines are going to upset all the domestic arrangements of society, turning the head to the tail, and the tail to the head. . . .

Thursday, Aug. 16. Four citizens of Monterey are just in from the gold mines on Feather River, where they worked in company with three others. They employed about thirty wild Indians, who are attached to the rancho owned by one of the party. They worked precisely seven weeks and three days, and have divided seventy-six thousand eight hundred and forty-four dollars,—nearly eleven thousand dollars to each. Make a dot there, and let me introduce a man, well known to me, who has worked on the Yuba river sixty-four days, and brought back, as the result of his individual labor, five thousand three hundred and fifty-six dollars. Make a dot there, and let me introduce another townsman, who has worked on the North Fork fifty-seven days, and brought back four thousand five hundred and thirty-four dollars. Make a dot there, and let me introduce a boy, fourteen years of age, who has worked on the Mokelumne fifty-four days, and brought back three thousand four hundred and sixty-seven dollars. Make another dot there, and let me introduce a woman, of Sonoranian birth, who has worked in the dry diggings forty-six days, and brought back two thousand one hundred and twenty-five dollars. Is not this enough to make a man throw down his leger and shoulder a pick? But the deposits which yielded these harvests were now opened for the first time; they were the accumulation of ages; only the foot-prints of the elk and wild savage had passed over them. Their slumber was broken for the first time by the sturdy arms of the American emigrant.

Tuesday, Aug. 28. The gold mines have upset all social and domestic arrangements in Monterey; the master has become his own servant, and the servant his own lord. The millionaire is obliged to groom his own horse, and roll his wheelbarrow. . . .

3. Charles W. Churchill Reports from the Mines, 1850

Nevada City 7th Nov. 1850

Mr. Mendall Churchill

My Dear Brother

I wrote you from Sacramento City last Feb when I was on my way to the Yuba river. Since leaving their I have not received a letter from you, in fact but one letter has reached me and that was from Cousin Wm announcing the melancholy intelligence of his Mother's death. I feel now considerable anxiety to hear from you, and it would afford me unspeakable pleasure to know that you were all in the enjoyment of good health. I trust however such is the case. After leaving Sacramento I went to Marysville, and from their to Fosters Bar on the North Fork of the Yuba, distant 40 miles. I started from Marysville with my blankets on my back leaving my baggage to follow in a wagon, but it soon commenced raining and I was obliged to sleep out two nights in no very comfortable plight. I remained at Foster's until April when I started up the river prospecting. At that time the North Fork of the Yuba was considered the richest stream in California. Thousands of miners were hurrying up the river to secure claims to work when the river fell, for you must bear in mind the water was too high to admit of much work being done on the bars and it was not untill June that the river was low enough to be worked to advantage. I accordingly travelled up to the "Fork" 35 miles from Foster's. The diggings about the Fork were know to be good, but it was a very difficult matter to locate a claim that would warrant a man in laying by for two or three months before we would be able to prospect it, and ascertain whether it was good for anything. The river about the Forks proved to be very *rich* in *spots*. Finally I located on the South Fork of the North Fork—10 miles from the "Fork." I found gold in the bank and on the bars when I could find one that was not covered with water. I remained their until the latter part of July when the claim which my partner and I had taken up were worked out. We were on a large bar that paid us from one to two ounces per day when the water allowed us to work which was very seldom, and by throwing out a wing dam promised us a seasons work. The "bed rock" was slate. We found no gold in the gravel on the slate, but the slate was full of creavase, and in the creavases we found the gold. We built our dam but with no very sanguine hopes as the river had been turned in several places in our immediate vicinity, and proved an entire failure, their being no gold in the bed of the stream. And such we found to be the case with our claims when we got the water off them. I started on a prospecting tour but found nothing to suit me until I reached this place. The only diggings here of any note are the Coyota Diggings. They are from 10 to 100 feet below the surface and are worked by sinking wells or shafts, and then drift from the shaft until all the gravel is taken out from the face of the bed rock. It is rather dangerous looking to one not accustomed to working under ground. I commenced sinking wells when I reached here and was fortunate enough to find one that would pay me small wages. My partner and I took in two lead miners from Galena as we were not acquainted with this kind of mining. We have the claims drifted out and the gravel on top of the ground, and are anxiously waiting for the rains to commence to wash up. We have also bought some gravel which we design to wash, and laid in our stock of winter provisions and have a comfortable log cabin to live in. The Coyota diggings have been unquestionably the richest diggings in California. Some claims have paid as high as $100,000, and it is not uncommon for a claim to pay $10,000, but at the same time they are the most uncertain. A man might dig wells for six months and never see the color of gold. These diggings will now soon be over with for this season as they cannot be worked after the rain sets in. A great number of men will be employed on them next season, but I think the richest Coyota leads have been worked out.

I do not design remaining here after the spring opens. I think it probable I will go up between the Yuba and Feather Rivers in search of dry diggings. Soon after the rain commences and we have got a part of our gravel washed up, I will remit Cousin Wm 25 ounces of dust, a part of which I shall direct him to forward to you for Mother. I think next spring will bring me out about $1000. ahead of the game. I have enjoyed excellent health. The cholera is at Sacramento City, (80 miles from here) but I have no fear of its coming here.

A "claim" in this country is 30 square feet. Flour is worth here now 20c per lb. Pork 40c—Coffee, Sugar and Beans 50c per lb. When I first went on the Yuba I paid $1.00 per lb for Flour and for Pork, Sugar and Coffee $1.50 per lb. I would have made money their if I could have lived without eating, or had not been compelled to lay idle so long waiting for the river to fall. I have given up the idea of seeing home for two or three years. It is of no use for me to return unless my fortunes are mended. I like the country and a miners life. I have since last spring (untill a few weeks back) slept in a hammock slung between two trees out in the open air.

We have now a P.O. in this place, and if you write soon after the receipt of this please direct to "Nevada City," but as my stay in this place is rather uncertain, when you write a second time you had better direct to San Francisco.

The letter which I made mention of as coming from Cousin Wm was dated 12th April and made no mention of your designing to come to California, therefore I trust that you have made up your mind to remain at home. Mining is a good business provided you are successful, but if you are unfortunate it is the most discouraging business a man ever followed. However I hope to soon peruse a sheet from you and please give me your views on the subject.

I believe a majority [of] those who came through this season will return home as soon as they can make money enough to carry them their, and a large part of them will barely be able to make their living this winter.

Do not delay writing. You will hear from me again soon. I sincerely hope you are all in the enjoyment of good health. I feel particularly anxious about Mother. With Love to all.

Your Aff Brother
C. W. Churchill

4. *A Miner's Song Laments His Difficult Life, c. 1854*

The Lousy Miner

It's four long years since I reached this land,
In search of gold among the rocks and sand;
And yet I'm poor when the truth is told,
I'm a lousy miner,
I'm a lousy miner in search of shining gold.

I've lived on swine 'till I grunt and squeal,
No one can tell how my bowels feel,
With slapjacks swimming round in bacon grease.
I'm a lousy miner,
I'm a lousy miner; when will my troubles cease?

I was covered with lice coming on the boat,
I threw away my fancy swallow-tailed coat,
And now they crawl up and down my back;
I'm a lousy miner,
I'm a lousy miner; a pile is all I lack.

My sweetheart vowed she'd wait for me
'Till I returned; but don't you see
She's married now, sure, so I am told,
Left her lousy miner,
Left her lousy miner, in search of shining gold.

Oh, land of gold, you did me deceive,
And I intend in thee my bones to leave;
So farewell, home, now my friends grow cold,
I'm a lousy miner,
I'm a lousy miner in search of shining gold.

5. Calvin Taylor Praises the Mormon City on the Great Salt Lake, 1850

. . . The Great Salt Lake City is handsomely laid out—situated on the north side of the valley at the foot of a high bluff or bench of the Utah range of mountains, the ground falling gradually toward the river Jordan between one and two miles distant. The streets are of great breadth and cross each other at right angles, forming large squares which are cut at regular distances by streets of a smaller size, dividing the square into equal parts. . . . The city is not compactly built, being unlike all other cities in this respect. To each house is allowed one and a quarter acre of ground which is enclosed and sufficient to produce all the necessary garden vegetables in the greatest profusion, besides a considerable quantity of wheat and corn, quite adequate to the wants of each family. This arrangement of houses and lots gives to the city quite a pleasant and rural appearance, and might with propriety be called an agricultural city. The city is watered from the mountains by means of ditches which convey the water through every part of the city; each principal street having a stream upon each side, from which are sluice ways to conduct the water into the gardens for irrigation and other purposes whenever required.

The houses are built of adobes or sundried bricks which are much larger than the ordinary brick, being 12 inches long, 6 inches wide, and 21 inches thick. They are of a lead color and have the appearance at a distance of being painted. There are no bricks burned here owing to the great scarcity of wood. . . . The houses are generally moderate sized and from one to one and a half storys high and built in modern style. There is a large public building called the State House now being finished [the Council House, located on the corner of South Temple and Main streets]. It is a square building two storys high. The first story is built of a reddish sandstone with sills and caps of the same material. The second story is built of adobes. It is altogether quite a respectable building and situated upon the corner of one of the principal streets. Besides there are several stores—a post and printing office, and mechanic shops of various kinds, and a large number of buildings now in the process of erection. Opposite the state house is the church, an immense building of a temporary character designed only for present use, it being the intention of the Mormons to build a magnificent temple far surpassing in splendor and magnitude the far famed temple of Nauvoo, of which no doubt they have the energy and ability to accomplish, judging from what they have already achieved during the short time which has elapsed since their arrival and settlement in this valley.

6. *The Committee of Vigilance Issues a Proclamation, 1856*

PROCLAMATION

OF THE

VIGILANCE COMMITTEE

OF SAN FRANCISCO.

JUNE 9th, 1856.

TO THE PEOPLE OF CALIFORNIA

The Committee of Vigilance, placed in the position they now occupy by the voice and countenance of the vast majority of their fellow-citizens, as executors of their will, desire to define the necessity which has forced this people into their present organization.

Great public emergencies demand prompt and vigorous remedies. The People—long suffering under an organized despotism which has invaded their liberties—squandered their property—usurped their offices of trust and emolument—endangered their lives—prevented the expression of their will through the ballot-box, and corrupted the channels of justice—have now arisen in virtue of their inherent right and power. All political, religious and sectional differences and issues have given way to the paramount necessity of a thorough and fundamental reform and purification of the social and political body. The voice of a whole people has demanded union and organization as the only means of making our laws effective and regaining the rights of free speech, free vote, and public safety.

For years they have patiently waited and striven, in a peaceable manner, and in accordance with the forms of Law, to reform the abuses which have made our city a by-word, fraud and violence have foiled every effort, and the laws to which the people looked for protection, while distorted and rendered effete in practice, so as to shield the vile, have been used as a powerful engine to fasten upon us tyranny and misrule.

As Republicans, we looked to the ballot-box as our safe-guard and sure remedy. But so effectually and so long was its voice smothered, the votes deposited in it by freemen so entirely outnumbered by ballots thrust in through fraud at midnight, or nullified by the false counts of judges and inspectors of elections at noon day, that many doubted whether the majority of the people were not utterly corrupt.

Organized gangs of bad men, of all political parties, or who assumed any particular creed from mercenary and corrupt motives, have parcelled out our offices among themselves, or sold them to the highest bidders;

Have provided themselves with convenient tools to obey their nod, as Clerks, Inspectors and Judges of election;

Have employed bullies and professional fighters to destroy tally-lists by force, and prevent peaceable citizens from ascertaining, in a lawful manner, the true number of votes polled at our elections;

And have used cunningly contrived ballot boxes, with false sides and bottoms, so prepared that by means of a spring or slide, spurious tickets, concealed there previous to the election, could be mingled with genuine votes. . . .

Embodied in the principles of republican governments are the truths that the majority should rule, and when corrupt officials, who have fraudulently seized the reins of authority, designedly thwart the execution of the laws and avert punishment from the notoriously guilty, the power they usurp reverts back to the people from whom it was wrested.

Realizing these truths, and confident that they were carrying out the will of the vast majority of the citizens of this country, the Committee of Vigilance, under a solemn sense of the responsibility that rested upon them, have calmly and dispassionately weighed the evidences before them, and decreed the death of some and banishment of others, who by their crimes and villainies, had stained our fair land. With those that were banished this comparatively moderate punishment was chosen, not because ignominious death was not deserved, but that the error, if any, might surely be upon the side of mercy to the criminal. There are others scarcely less guilty, against whom the same punishment has been decreed, but they have been allowed further time to arrange for their final departure, and with the hope that permission to depart voluntarily might induce repentance, and repentance amendment, they have been suffered to choose within limits their own time and method of going.

Thus far, and throughout their arduous duties, they have been, and will be guided by the most conscientious convictions of imperative duty; and they earnestly hope that in endeavoring to mete out merciful justice to the guilty, their counsels may be so guided by that Power before whose tribunal we shall stand, and in the vicissitudes of after life, amid the calm reflections of old age and in the clear view of dying conscience, there may be found nothing we would regret or wish to change.

We have no friends to reward, no enemies to punish, no private ends to accomplish. . . .

The Committee of Vigilance believe that the people have entrusted to them the duty of gathering evidence, and, after due trial, expelling from the community those ruffians and assassins who have so long outraged the peace and good order of society, violated the ballot box, overridden law and thwarted justice. Beyond the duties incident to this, we do not desire to interfere with the details of government.

We have spared and shall spare no efforts to avoid bloodshed or civil war; but undeterred by threats or opposing organizations, shall continue, peaceably if we can, forcibly if we must, this work of reform, to which we have pledged our lives, our fortunes and our sacred honor.

Our labors have been arduous, our deliberations have been cautious, our determinations firm, our counsels prudent, our motives pure; and while regretting the imperious necessity which called us into action, we are anxious that this necessity should exist no longer; and when our labors shall have been accomplished, when the community shall be freed from the evils it has so long endured; when we have insured to our citizens an honest and vigorous protection of their rights, then the Committee of Vigilance will find great pleasure in resigning their power into the hands of the people, from whom it was received.

Published by order of the Committee.

No. 33 Secretary.

7. Henry Comstock Recounts His Discovery of Silver and the Naming of Virginia City in Nevada, 1859

. . . In the middle of January, 1859, I saw some queer-looking stuff in a gopher hole; I ran my hand in and took out a handful of dirt and saw silver and gold in it. At that time John Bishop and Old Virginia [the name by which another old-timer, James Finney, was known] were with me; they were sitting upon the side of a hill, Gold Hill, a couple of hundred yards from me. . . . We started rocking with my water; had only a small quantity to rock with. We made from five to ten and twelve pounds a day, and the dust was from $9 to $12 an ounce—sent that at Brewster's Bank, Placerville, California, where I did my business. . . .

Virginia City was first called Silver City. I named it at the time I gave the Ophir claim its name. Old Virginia and the other boys got on a drunk one night there, and Old Virginia fell down and broke his bottle, and when he got up he said he baptised that ground Virginia—hence Virginia City—and that is the way it got its name. At that time there were a few tents, a few little huts, and a grog-shop; that was all there was. I was camped under a cedar-tree at that time—I and my party. . . .

8. *The* Missouri Republican *Touts Pike's Peak, the Place to Go, 1859*

Those two little words, "Pike's Peak," are everywhere. The latest from Pike's Peak is eagerly devoured, no matter what it is. The quickest, safest route to Pike's Peak is what thousands want to know. Pike's Peak is in everybody's mouth and thoughts, and Pike's Peak figures in a million dreams. Every clothing store is a depot for outfits for Pike's Peak. There are Pike's Peak hats, and Pike's Peak guns, Pike's Peak boots, Pike's Peak shovels, and Pike's Peak goodness-knows-what-all, designed expressly for the use of emigrants and miners, and earnestly recommended to those contemplating a journey to the gold regions of Pike's Peak. We presume there are, or will be, Pike's Peak pills, manufactured with exclusive reference to the diseases of Cherry valley, and sold in conjunction with Pike's Peak guide books; or Pike's Peak schnapps to give tone to the stomachs of overtasked gold diggers; or Pike's Peak goggles to keep the gold dust out of the eyes of the fortune hunters; or Pike's Peak steelyards (drawing fifty pounds) with which to weigh the massive chunks of gold quarried out of Mother Earth's prolific bowels. . . .

The Pike's Peak fever, added to the usual influx of country merchants at this time of year, have served as we remarked yesterday, to fill the city with strangers. The trains of the rail-roads terminating here bring large numbers every trip; all the hotels are crowded, and St. Louis at present wears the appearance of a popular overflow. At such a time rogues find their harvest. . . .

At this moment there are hundreds of professional pick-pockets, pigeon droppers and "confidence men" here, ready to take all the cash and valuables brought by the strangers visiting the place. The levee is thronged, and the Missouri river boats particularly are beset by them from morning till night. The police force is wholly inefficient, or perhaps we ought to say insufficient, to be of much service. . . .

References

1. The *Californian* Modestly Announces the Discovery of Gold, 1848
   Californian, San Francisco, March 15, 1848.
2. Walter Colton Describes the Effects of the Gold Rush, 1848
   Rev. Walter Colton, *Three Years in California* (New York: A. S. Barnes & Co., 1854), pp. 247–253.
3. Charles W. Churchill Reports from the Mines, 1850
   Charles William Churchill, *Fortunes Are for the Few: Letters of a Forty-Niner,* Duane A. Smith and David J. Weber, eds. (San Diego: San Diego Historical Society, 1977), pp. 55–59.
4. A Miner's Song Laments His Difficult Life, c. 1854
   "The Lousy Miner," in *Put's Original California Songster* [of the 1850s] in Rodman W. Paul, *California Gold: The Beginning of Mining in the Far West* (Lincoln: University of Nebraska Press, 1974), pp. 89–90.

5. Calvin Taylor Praises the Mormon City on the Great Salt Lake, 1850
   Thomas G. Alexander and James B. Allen, *Mormons and Gentiles: A History of Salt Lake City* (Boulder, Colo.: Pruett Publishing Company, 1984), pp. 28–29.
6. The Committee of Vigilance Issues a Proclamation, 1856
   Published by Hutchings & Co., 201 Clay Street, San Francisco.
7. Henry Comstock Recounts His Discovery of Silver and the Naming of Virginia City in Nevada, 1859
   Oscar Lewis, ed., *The Autobiography of the West: Personal Narratives of the Discovery and Settlement of the American West* (New York: Henry Holt and Company, 1958), pp. 265–267.
8. The *Missouri Republican* Touts Pike's Peak, the Place to Go, 1859
   Missouri Republican, March 10, 1859, quoted in LeRoy R. Hafen, ed., *Colorado Gold Rush: Contemporary Letters and Reports, 1858–1859* (Glendale: Arthur H. Clark Company, 1941), pp. 277–279.

Document Set 7

The Civil War Era in the West, 1858–1873

Settlers along the Pacific coast sought ways to communicate with their relatives and friends back East. During the 1840s and early 1850s, the only way to travel to California was by wagon train on one of the long, overland trails or by sailing for several months around Cape Horn. Mail could take half a year to reach its destination. In 1855 a railroad line across Panama reduced some of the distance, but the trip to the West Coast remained difficult. Several stagecoach lines began to carry mail and passengers to the West; the most successful was the Butterfield Overland Mail, which traveled some twenty-eight hundred miles from Missouri to California in just under twenty-five days. Waterman Ormsby, the first through passenger on the Butterfield line, describes the journey in Document 1. Various hints were published in newspapers to ease people through the difficult trip (Document 2).

Because California joined the Union as a free state in 1850, blacks from the South could migrate into the area and find freedom. Many made money in the mines or secured jobs that enabled them to help friends and relatives to purchase their freedom and move to California. The assessed valuation of property owned by blacks in San Francisco in 1856 was estimated at $150,000. Document 3 shows how one black family made a new life in Los Angeles.

Owing to the presence of many Confederate sympathizers in California, the state's role in the Civil War has been difficult to assess. Newspapers at first took opposing stands on the war (Document 4), until those favoring the South were banned from the mails or forced to close. Californians raised money for the Union cause and supported the passage of the Pacific Railroad Act in 1862, which provided for a transcontinental line to be built along a northern route. A few Californians saw action in the war, but most served in Arizona and New Mexico against Indians.

After the Civil War, fishing rights and other considerations turned the attention of the residents of Washington toward Alaska (Document 5). Although most Americans knew little about this northern region, fishers, traders, and hunters were familiar with the area. The Russians had established the first colonies, charted the coast, and explored the interior, but they had limited their activities mainly to coastal areas. When Secretary of State William Seward found that the United States could purchase Alaska (Document 6), he worked quickly to gain Senate ratification. A few newspapers at first denounced Seward's purchase, but most influential publications rallied to his side. Charles Sumner, chairman of the Senate Foreign Relations Committee, gained enough support for the treaty to be ratified in 1867 by a vote of thirty-seven to two. From Alaska's beginnings as a U.S. territory, Americans faced the problem of governing new settlers in such a vast region.

The transcontinental railroad, authorized in 1862 and stretching from Council Bluffs, Iowa, to Sacramento, California, reached completion in record time on May 10, 1869—almost five years ahead of schedule. To gain land subsidies (based on the number of miles of track laid), company officials at both ends encouraged competition between Irish workers from the Union Pacific and Chinese crews from the Central Pacific who built tracks across the rugged Sierra Nevada and arid Great Basin region. After the railroad's completion, commemorated in an appropriate ceremony (Document 7), many thousands of Chinese laborers were laid off because of job shortages. Different in color, language, dress, and customs and willing to work for low wages, the Chinese from the start had been easy targets for discrimination and mistreatment. Problems continued for them, as well as for Native Americans, throughout the West during the next decades.

Questions for Analysis

1. How would traveling on a stagecoach for nearly a month compare with modern modes of travel?
2. Why was California so divided in its support for the Union during the Civil War? Does any evidence of a North-South controversy exist in California today?
3. Was there less discrimination than today against blacks in Los Angeles during the 1860s?
4. What were the benefits of Alaska for the United States?
5. Why did Russia want to sell Alaska?
6. What do you think happened to the stagecoach lines after the completion of the railroad?

1. *Waterman Ormsby Tells of the First Through Stage to California, 1858*

Overland to California

Special Correspondence of the New York Herald
San Francisco, Oct. 10, 1858

Safe and sound from all the threatened dangers of Indians, tropic suns, rattlesnakes, grizzly bears, stubborn mules, mustang horses, jerked beef, terrific mountain passes, fording rivers, and all the concomitants which envy, pedantry, and ignorance had predicted for all passengers by the overland mail route over which I have just passed, here am I in San Francisco, having made the passage from the St. Louis post office to the San Francisco post office in twenty-three days, twenty-three hours and a half, just one day and half an hour less than the time required by the Overland Mail Company's contract with the Post Office Department. The journey has been by no means as fatiguing to me as might be expected by a continuous ride of such duration, for I feel almost fresh enough to undertake it again.

The route is prolific in interest to the naturalist, the mineralogist, and all who love to contemplate nature in her wildest varieties, and throughout the whole 2,700 miles the interest in new objects is not allowed to flag. I have found the deserts teeming with curious plants and animal life, the mountain passes prolific in the grandest scenery, and the fruitful valleys suggestive of an earthly paradise; while, if this trip may be considered a criterion, the alleged danger from Indians is all a bugbear. . . .

The road winds over some of the steepest and stoniest hills I had yet seen, studded with inextricable rocks, each one of which seems ready to jolt the wagon into the abyss below. It is enough to make one shudder to look at the perpendicular side of the cañon and think what havoc one mischievous man could make with an emigrant train passing through the cañon.

The great peak towers as if ready any moment to fall, while huge boulders hang as if ready, with the weight of a rain drop, to be loosened from their fastenings and descend with lumbering swiftness to the bottom, carrying destruction in their paths. The water appears to have washed away the soil of the peak and its minor hills, revealing the strata like so many regularly built walls of a fortress, and the whole mass presents a scene of stupendous grandeur. Just before the bottom of the cañon is reached there stands by the roadside the grave of a Mexican guide, who had ventured in advance of his party and was murdered by the Indians—a thrilling reminder of another of the dangers of this dreadful pass.

We got through about sunset, and I never shall forget the gorgeous appearance of the clouds: tinged by the setting sun above those jagged peaks, changing like a rapid panorama, they assumed all sorts of fantastic shapes, from frantic maidens with dishevelled hair to huge monsters of fierce demeanor, chasing one another through the realms of space. We had hardly passed through before the sound of voices and the gleaming of light denoted that there was a party ahead of us. The awe inspiring scenery and the impressive sunset had almost set me dreaming as I lay listlessly in the wagon; but the possibility of meeting foes, perhaps a band of murderous Indians, in this wild and lonely spot filled me for a time with fears; but I had great faith in the captain's prowess, and felt somewhat easier when he declared it to be his opinion that the party was an American one.

In a moment we were upon them, and, to our astonishment, found that it was the overland mail which left San Francisco on the 15th [of] September, with five through passengers, and which was now eight hours ahead of time. After exchanging congratulations and telling bits of news, both parties passed on, I availing myself of the opportunity to send to the *Herald* a despatch which I had nearly written for the occasion.

2. Travel Suggestions for Stagecoach Passengers, c. 1860s

The best seat inside a stage is the one next to the driver. Even if you have a tendency to seasickness when riding backwards, you'll get over it and will get less jolts and jostling. Don't let any sly elph trade you his midseat.

In cold weather don't ride with tight fitting boots, shoes or gloves. When the driver asks you to get off and walk, do so without grumbling. He won't request it unless absolutely necessary. If the team runs away—sit still and take your chances. If you jump; nine out of ten times you will get hurt.

In very cold weather abstain entirely from liquor when on the road; because you will freeze twice as quickly when under the influence.

Don't growl at the food received at the station; stage companies generally provide the best they can get. Don't keep the stage waiting. Don't smoke a strong pipe inside the coach—spit on the leeward side. If you have anything to drink in a bottle pass it around. Procure your stimulants before starting as "ranch" (stage depot) whiskey is not "nectar."

Don't swear or lop over neighbors when sleeping. Take small change to pay expenses. Never shoot on the road as the noise might frighten the horses. Don't discuss politics or religion. Don't point out where murders have been committed if there are women passengers.

Don't lag at the wash basin. Don't grease your hair because travel is dusty. Don't imagine for a moment that you are going on a picnic. Expect annoyances, discomfort, and some hardship.

3. Biddy Mason Finds Freedom in Los Angeles, 1850s

The subject of this sketch was born in Hancock County, Georgia, and was the most remarkable pioneer of color coming to California. She came under the most trying circumstances . . .

After the Courts of Los Angeles County granted Biddy Mason and her family their freedom, she took her family to the home of Robert Owens, in Los Angeles. Then she went in search of work which she readily secured at two dollars and fifty cents per day, as confinement nurse, Dr. Griffin having engaged her services. The securing of work meant to her the great boon of acquiring not only the money for the support of her dependent family, but also an opportunity of securing a home. With the first money she could save she purchased two lots, located from Spring street to Broadway, between Third and Fourth streets in Los Angeles. There was a ditch of water on the place and a willow fence running around the plat of ground which was considered quite out of town at that date, but which today is the most valuable piece of property in all of beautiful Los Angeles.

Biddy Mason had a splendid sense of the financial value of property and such great hopes for the future of Los Angeles that she continued to buy property and retain it until after the city began to boom, when she sold a forty-foot lot for twelve thousand dollars. She then gave her sons a forty-foot lot which they sold for forty-four thousand dollars.

The world never tires of speaking of the late Hetty Green and her great financial ability. But think of this slave woman coming to California in 1851 by ox-team which consisted of three hundred wagons, and, at the end of these wagons, Biddy Mason driving the cattle across the plains, notwithstanding she had her own three little girls, Ellen, Ann and Harriett, to care for en route!

Biddy Mason was a devoted mother. Her most remarkable trait of character was her ability to teach her children and grandchildren the value of money and property. So thorough were her teachings that her vast holdings have been retained by her children and grandchildren, who have never sold a piece of property unless they were positively sure that they were making great gains by so doing. The greater part of her purchases of property in early days they have retained, and these have grown in value at least two hundred or more per cent since their first purchase by Biddy Mason. . . .

The Courts of Los Angeles County granted to her and her children their freedom January 19, 1854. . . . The doors of the home of Robert Owens were thrown open to Biddy Mason and her children. Mr. Owens was a livery-stable keeper. Two years after the Mason family came to Los Angeles, the oldest daughter, Ellen, married Mr. Robert Owen's son, Charles. She named her first son in honor of the grandfather, Robert C. Owens, and the second child, Henry L. Owens. It seems strange, but true, that Mr. Robert Owens, the father-in-law of Biddy Mason's daughter, Ellen, was the same type as the girl's mother in regard to acquiring and holding property, and he taught his son the value of both money and property and the greatest possible necessity of a good education.

Mrs. Ellen Mason-Owens, as a slave girl, had not been allowed the advantage of an education. After the birth of her second child, her husband decided that she must have an education. When his sons were old enough, he sent them and their mother to be educated in the public schools of the city of Oakland, California. After the sons had completed the course of study, he sent them to the public schools of Stockton to receive a business education under the then greatest colored educator on the coast, J. B. Sanderson. They boarded in the home of the teacher. After finishing under the instruction of J. B. Sanderson they returned to Los Angeles and, owing to the prejudice against colored persons attending the public schools, they were compelled to enter business college at night. This splendid foundation of a good education, especially the business education, has been an example to this day through the surviving son, Robert C. Owens, who is considered among the most level-headed capitalists, either white or colored, in all of Los Angeles. . . .

4. California's Newspapers Debate the War, 1861–1863

Confederates

Sonora Democrat, January, 1861, upon the formation of the Confederacy:

> We are for a Pacific Republic. . . . We believe it to be the true policy of California . . . to cut loose from both sections, and not involve herself in the general ruin. . . . We shall never consent to pay taxes for the coercion of a sovereign State; neither do we desire to see California linked on to any fragment of this Union.

San Joaquin (Stockton) *Republican*, September 10, 1861:

> . . . [T]he war is waged for the defence of Southern homes and firesides, of Southern nationality.

San Jose Tribune, December 19, 1861, on Lincoln:

> . . . [A]n illiterate backwoodsman who is not only destitute of the first requirements of a statesman, but who can scarcely write a sentence of the English language correctly!

Mariposa Free Press, March 21, 1863:

> What cares Abraham Lincoln for the good of the country? A traitor to God and humanity, his hands dripping with the blood of his countrymen.

Unionists

Stockton Argus, May, 1861:

> We are for unconditional support of the Government of the United States in its efforts to suppress rebellion and treason, and agree with Seward that "party must be forgotten in our efforts to save the Union."

San Francisco Bulletin, June 29, 1861:

> —If the government is so much in need of ready-made cavalry, let it send to California. We can raise, equip, and march across the plains, in six months, ten regiments of the best horsemen in the world. We just ask to let our vaqueros have a chance.

Los Angeles Southern News, March 19, 1862:

> We hope every leader of this iniquitous rebellion will be hung, if they fall into the hands of the Government.—Traitors who have plunged the country into a bloody and devastating civil war, to subserve their own selfish ambition, should meet with no mercy.

San Francisco Alta California, January 5, 1863, on the Proclamation of Emancipation:

> —The universal sentiment is that if slavery must die that the Republic may live, let its death-knell be sounded, no matter what the consequences.

5. Washington Territory Requests Fishing Rights in Alaska, 1866

To his Excellency Andrew Johnson,
President of the United States;

Your memorialists, the legislative assembly of Washington Territory, beg leave to show that abundance of codfish, halibut, and salmon of excellent quality have been found along the shores of the Russian possessions. Your memorialists respectfully request your excellency to obtain such rights and privileges of the government of Russia as will enable our fishing vessels to visit the ports and harbors of its possessions to the end that fuel, water, and provisions may be easily obtained, that our sick and disabled fishermen may obtain sanitary assistance, together with the privilege of curing fish and repairing vessels in need of repair. Your memorialists further request that the Treasury Department be instructed to forward to the collector of customs abstract journals, and logbooks as will enable our hardy fishermen to obtain the bounties now provided and paid to the fishermen in the Atlantic States. Your memorialists finally pray your excellency to employ such ships as may be spared from the Pacific naval fleet in exploring and surveying the fishing banks known to navigators to exist along the Pacific Coast from the Cortes bank to Behring straits; and, as in duty found, your memorialists will ever pray.

Passed the house of representatives January 10, 1866.

Edward Eldridge
Speaker of the House of Representatives.

Passed the council January 13, 1866.

Harvey K. Hines
President of the Council

6. William Seward Purchases Alaska, 1867

Department of State, Washington
March 23, 1867

Sir: With reference to the proposed convention between our respective governments for a cession by Russia of her American territory to the United States, I have the honor to acquaint you that I must insist upon that clause in the sixth article of the draught which declares the cession to be free and unencumbered by any reservations, privileges, franchises, grants, or possessions by any associated companies, whether corporate or incorporate, Russian or any other, etc., and must regard it as an ultimatum. With the President's approval, however, I will add $200,000 to the consideration money on that account.

I avail myself of this occasion to offer to you a renewed assurance of my most distinguished consideration.

William H. Seward

Mr. Edward de Stoeckl, &c., &c., &c.
(Translation)

Washington, March 17–29, 1867.

Mr. Secretary of State: I have the honor to inform you that by a telegram dated 16-28th of this month, from St. Petersburg, Prince Gortschakow informs me that his Majesty the Emperor of all the Russias gives his consent to the cession of the Russian possessions on the American continent to the United States for the stipulated sum of $7,200,000 in gold, and that his Majesty the Emperor invests me with full powers to negotiate and sign the treaty.

Please accept, Mr. Secretary of State, the assurance of my very high consideration.

Stoeckl

Hon. William H. Seward, Secretary of State
of the United States.

7. Writer Sidney Dillon Recalls the Completion of the Pacific Railroad, 1869

It was not a large crowd. In brass bands, fireworks, procession, and oratory, the demonstration, when ground was broken at Omaha, less than five years before, was much more imposing. A small excursion party, headed by Governor Stanford, had come from San Francisco; while on our side, besides our own men, there were only two or three persons present, among whom was the Rev. Dr. Todd, of Pittsfield. Not more than five or six hundred, all told, comprised the whole gathering, nearly all of whom were officials of the two companies—contractors, surveyors, and employees.

The point of junction was in a level circular valley, about three miles in diameter, surrounded by mountains. During all the morning hours the hurry and bustle of preparation went on. Two lengths of rails lay on the ground near the opening in the road-bed. At a little before eleven the Chinese laborers began levelling up the road-bed preparatory to placing the last ties in position. About a quarter past eleven the train from San Francisco, bringing Governor Stanford and party arrived and was greeted with cheers. In the enthusiasm of the occasion there were cheers for everybody, from the President of the United States to the day-laborers on the road.

The two engines moved nearer each other, and the crowd gathered round the open space. Then all fell back a little so that the view should be unobstructed. Brief remarks were made by Governor Stanford on one side, and General Dodge on the other. It was now about twelve o'clock noon, local time, or about 2 P.M. in New York. The two superintendents of construction—S. B. Reed of the Union Pacific, and S. W. Strawbridge of the Central—placed under the rails the last tie. It was of California laurel, highly polished, with a silver plate in the centre bearing the following inscription: "The last tie laid on the completion of the Pacific Railroad, May 10, 1869," with the names of the officers and directors of both companies.

Everything being then in readiness the word was given, and "Hats off" went clicking over the wires to the waiting crowds at New York, Philadelphia, San Francisco, and all the principal cities. Prayer was offered by the venerable Rev. Dr. Todd, at the conclusion of which our operator tapped out: "We have got done praying. The spike is about to be presented," to which the response came back: "We understand. All are ready in the East." The gentlemen who had been commissioned to present the four spikes, two of gold, and two of silver, from Montana, Idaho, California, and Nevada, stepped forward, and with brief appropriate remarks discharged the duty assigned them.

Governor Stanford, standing on the north, and Dr. Durant on the south side of the track, received the spikes and put them in place. Our operator tapped out: "All ready now; the spike will soon be driven. The signal will be three dots for the commencement of the blows." An instant later the silver hammers came down, and at each stroke in all the offices from San Francisco to New York, and throughout the land, the hammer of the magnet struck the bell.

The signal "Done" was received at Washington at 2.47 P.M., which was about a quarter of one at Promontory. There was not much formality in the demonstration that followed, but the enthusiasm was genuine and unmistakable. The two engines moved up until they touched each other, and a bottle of champagne was poured on the last rail, after the manner of christening a ship at the launching.

References

1. Waterman Ormsby Tells of the First Through Stage to California, 1858
   Waterman L. Ormsby, *New York Herald,* November 11, 1858, in *The Butterfield Overland Mail,* Lyle H. Wright and Josephine M. Bynum (San Marino: Huntington Library, 1942; paperback ed., 1988), pp. 58–60.
2. Travel Suggestions for Stagecoach Passengers, c. 1860s
   Omaha Herald, in Kent L. Steckmesser, *The Westward Movement: A Short History* (New York: McGraw-Hill, 1969), pp. 326–327.
3. Biddy Mason Finds Freedom in Los Angeles, 1850s
   Delilah L. Beasley, *The Negro Trail Blazers of California* (Los Angeles, 1919), pp. 108–110.
4. California's Newspapers Debate the War, 1861–1863
   Remi Nadeau, comp., *Westways* (September 1962): 17.
5. Washington Territory Requests Fishing Rights in Alaska, 1866.
   Archie W. Shiels, *The Purchase of Alaska* (College: University of Alaska Press, 1967), p. 35.
6. William Seward Purchases Alaska, 1867
   Archie W. Shiels, *The Purchase of Alaska* (College: University of Alaska Press, 1967), pp. 38–39.
7. Writer Sidney Dillon Recalls the Completion of the Pacific Railroad, 1869
   Sidney Dillon, "Historic Moment: Driving the Last Spike," *Scribner's Magazine,* vol. 12 (August 1892): 258–259.

Document Set 8

Bust and Boom Times in the West, 1871–1893

The Southern Pacific Railroad became the largest landowner and the leading employer in California and enjoyed corresponding influence over state government. Its Big Four owners—Leland Stanford, Collis P. Huntington, Mark Hopkins, and Charles Crocker—had received ample land subsidies to stretch the railroad across the continent and acquired additional land grants when they continued the line from Sacramento to Los Angeles. Leasing the land to farmers in the Central Valley, they lived in luxury on San Francisco's Nob Hill. California's initial enthusiasm for the railroad soon gave way to distrust of what had become a powerful monopoly. Prospective farmers found that the railroad had withheld millions of acres for speculation. Economist Henry George believed that profits realized from holding land were unearned and thus should be taxed for the benefit of all. He warns of the dangers of land monopoly in Document 1.

As critics levied their charges against the railroad, other writers praised the advantages of climate and beauty along the Pacific coast. "Booster" literature may have exaggerated the West's virtues, but it attracted settlers and travelers to the area. Railroads issued travel guides and supported independent writers, and chambers of commerce printed pamphlets for distribution in the East. Southern California was hailed as a cure for everything from tuberculosis to rheumatism (Document 2). Promoters began to develop the area for both residency and tourism. Farther north, the Puget Sound Business Directory (Document 3) pointed out the beauties of the verdant forests and scenic mountains awaiting hikers, botanists, and campers.

Not all was idyllic, however. The ongoing conflict between Native Americans and white settlers was reaching a climax in several areas. The Modoc War of 1873 provides one of the saddest examples of U.S. military action. The Modocs, refusing to be placed on a reservation together with their traditional enemies, the Oregon Klamaths, took a stand on the Lost River among the lava beds of northern California. Document 4 gives a firsthand glimpse of the attempt to dislodge the Modocs from their home territory. While fighting, the American army lost fifty-three soldiers plus two Indian scouts and eighteen civilians. The Indians lost only five men. The war cost half a million dollars—a high price to pay when the Modocs would have been satisfied with a two-thousand-acre reservation costing at most about $20,000.

Other vicious fighting broke out in Idaho and Montana. When three young Nez Percé warriors killed four white settlers in the Wallowa Valley of Oregon in response to the injustice of reservation policy, war inevitably followed. In 1877 chief Joseph led his people in a desperate flight across the Bitterroot Mountains to find safety in Montana or Canada. After traveling seventeen hundred miles and suffering huge losses, the Nez Percés were intercepted by Colonel Nelson Miles just forty miles from the international border, where the Indians' Chief, Joseph, surrendered (Document 5). Like the Modocs before them, the captives were exiled to Oklahoma.

Difficult economic conditions incubated unrest among other groups in California during the 1870s. Farmers who joined local granges protested high freight rates and the damage that hydraulic mining caused to streams. Laborers in San Francisco, fired up by protest leader Denis Kearney (Document 6), organized the Workingmen's party in 1877. Although some of their demands—an eight-hour workday, banking reform, a statewide public school system, and stricter control of the railroad—were reasonable planks in their platform, they targeted the Chinese and threatened to blow up the Pacific Mail

Steamship Company's dock and steamers. Their dissatisfaction with California's government, along with that of the farmers and such critics as Henry George, led to the adoption of a new California state constitution in 1879. Although correcting some wrongs, the document contained a four-part anti-Chinese article, part of which the U.S. Supreme Court declared unconstitutional in 1880. Some of the provisions were not repealed until 1952.

Despite economic hardship, the West grew and prospered. The year 1880 marked the beginning of a boom period, to which the railroads contributed, that would pull the region out of its economic doldrums, for at least a few years. Document 7 describes the rate war that reduced the cost of travel between East and West, and Document 8 shows growth in the Pacific Northwest during the 1880s. The Northern Pacific Railroad, completed in 1883, brought thousands of newcomers to Washington Territory, Oregon, and Idaho. Because fewer people traveled to Oregon than to the other two states, it most easily absorbed the new settlers.

Hawaii provided another area of conflicting forces. American diplomats had long considered the islands the key to Pacific security, and others recognized the advantages of Pearl Harbor as a coaling station. Sugar planters, who were aligned with California refiners, also saw the benefit of a reciprocal trade treaty between the United States and Hawaii. Document 9 shows how certain American interests promoted annexation of the kingdom of Hawaii and persuaded President Benjamin Harrison to ask for Senate ratification of a treaty to that effect early in 1893. But Harrison's presidential successor, Grover Cleveland, opposed annexation, and action was delayed until 1898.

Frederick Jackson Turner, a young professor of history at the University of Wisconsin, gave an address before the American Historical Association in Chicago during the summer of 1893 (Document 10). Challenging prevailing ideas that American institutions had evolved exclusively from European models, Turner pointed out that the western frontier—a vast area of free land—had exerted a powerful influence on the country's historical development. His words have been widely analyzed, criticized, and challenged but not forgotten, and they often serve as a starting point to explain United States history.

Questions for Analysis

1. Is land speculation necessarily a bad policy? Are all lands in your city or county taxed at the same rate?
2. Do you think that the southern California climate was conducive to good health? How has the weather there changed since the late 1800s?
3. How does the natural beauty of Washington compare with that of other western states?
4. Why was the U.S. Army so intolerant of Indian desires during the 1870s? What would you have done if you were an Indian?
5. Why did Denis Kearney persecute the Chinese?
6. How did the railroads contribute to the settlement of the West?
7. What was President Harrison's attitude toward Hawaii and its future?
8. Do you agree with Frederick Jackson Turner about the influence of the West?

1. Henry George Criticizes Land Monopoly, 1871

It is not we, of this generation, but our children of the next, who will fully realize the evils of the land monopolization which we have permitted and encouraged; for those evils do not begin to fully show themselves until population becomes dense.

But already, while our great State, with an area larger than that of France or Spain or Turkey—with an area equal to that of all of Great Britain, Holland, Belgium, Denmark and Greece, combined—does not contain the population of a third class modern city; already, ere we have commenced to manure our lands or to more than prospect the treasures of our hills, the evils of land monopolization are showing themselves in such unmistakable signs that he who runs may read. This is the blight that has fallen upon California, stunting her growth and mocking her golden promise, offsetting to the immigrant the richness of her soil and the beneficence of her climate.

It has already impressed its mark upon the character of our agriculture—more shiftless, perhaps, than that of any State in the Union where slavery has not reigned. For California is not a country of farms, but a country of plantations and estates. Agriculture is a speculation. The farm houses, as a class, are unpainted frame shanties, without a garden or flower or tree. The farmer raises wheat; he buys his meat, his flour, his butter, his vegetables and frequently, even his eggs. He has too much land to spare time for such little things, or for beautifying his home, or he is merely a renter, or an occupant of land menaced by some adverse title, and his interest is but to get for this season the greatest crop that can be made to grow with the least labor. He hires labor for his planting and his reaping, and his hands shift for themselves at other seasons of the year. His plow he leaves standing in the furrow, when the year's plowing is done; his mustangs he turns upon the hills, to be lassoed when again needed. He buys on credit at the nearest store, and when his crop is gathered must sell it to the Grain King's agent, at the Grain King's prices.

And there is another type of California farmer. He boards at the San Francisco hotels, and drives a spanking team over the Cliff House road; or, perhaps, he spends his time in the gayer capitals of the East or Europe. His land is rented for one-third or one-fourth of the crop, or is covered by scraggy cattle, which need to look after them only a few half-civilized vaqueros; or his great wheat fields, of from ten to twenty thousand acres, are plowed and sown and reaped by contract. And over our ill-kept, shadeless, dusty roads, where a house is an unwonted land-mark, and which run frequently for miles through the same man's land, plod the tramps, with blankets on back—the laborers of the California farmer—looking for work, in its seasons, or toiling back to the city when the plowing is ended or the wheat crop is gathered. I do not say that this picture is a universal one, but it is a characteristic one.

It is not only in agriculture, but in all other avocations, and in all the manifestations of social life, that the effect of land monopoly may be seen—in the knotting up of business into the control of little rings, in the concentration of capital into a few hands, in the reduction of wages in the mechanical trades, in the gradual decadence of that independent personal habit both of thought and action which gave to California life its greatest charm, in the palpable differentiation of our people into the classes of rich and poor. Of the "general stagnation" of which we of California have been so long complaining, this is the most efficient cause. Had the unused land of California been free, at Government terms, to those who would cultivate it, instead of this "general stagnation" of the past two years, we should have seen a growth unexampled in the history of even the American States. For with all our hyperbole, it is almost impossible to overestimate the advantages with which nature has so lavishly endowed this Empire State of ours. "God's Country," the returning prospectors used to call it, and the strong expression loses half of its irreverence as, coming over sage brush plains, from the still frost-bound East, the traveler winds, in the early Spring, down the slope of the Sierra, through interminable ranks of evergreen giants, past laughing rills and banks of wild flowers, and sees under their cloudless sky the vast fertile valleys stretching out to the dark blue Coast Range in the distance. But while nature has done her best to invite new comers, our land policy has done its best to repel them. We have said to the immigrant: "It is a fair country which God has made between the Sierra and the sea, but before you settle in it and begin to reap His bounty, you must pay a forestaller roundly for *his* permission." And the immigrant having far to come and but scanty capital, has as a general thing stayed away. . . .

2. *Charles Nordhoff Praises California as a Haven for Invalids, 1872*

A friend and neighbor of my own, consumptive for some years, and struggling for his life in a winter residence for two years at Nice and Mentone, and during a third at Aiken, in South Carolina, came last October to Southern California.

He had been "losing ground," as he said, and as his appearance showed, for two years, and last summer suffered so severely from night sweats, sleeplessness, continual coughing, and lack of appetite, that it was doubtful whether he would live through the winter anywhere; and it was rather in desperation than with much hope of a prolonged or comfortable life that he made ready for the journey across the continent with his family.

In January I was one day standing in the doorway of a hotel at Los Angeles, when I saw a wagon drive up; the driver jumped out, held out his hand to me, and sung out in a hearty voice, "How do you do?" It was my consumptive friend, but a changed man.

He had just driven sixty miles in two days, over a rough road, from San Bernardino; he walked with me several miles on the evening we met; he ate heartily and slept well, enjoyed his life, and coughed hardly at all. It was an amazing change to come about in three months, and in a man so ill as he had been.

"I shall never be a sound man, of course," he said to me when I spent some days with him, later, at San Bernardino; "but this climate has added ten years to my life; it has given me ease and comfort; and neither Nice, nor Mentone, nor Aiken are, in my opinion, to be compared with some parts of Southern California in point of climate for consumptives."

In Santa Barbara, San Diego, and San Bernardino, one may find abundant evidence corroborative of my friend's assertion. In each of these places I have met men and women who have been restored to health and strength by residence there; and though no one whom I met had had the wide experience of my friend in other winter resorts, I found not a few people of intelligence and means who bore the strongest testimony to the kindly and healing influences of the climate of Southern California.

I think I shall be doing a service, therefore, to many invalids if I give here some details concerning the places I have named, and some others, but little known as yet in the East, which are now accessible, and whose beneficial influences upon diseases of the throat and lungs are undoubtedly remarkable.

The whole of Southern California has a very mild and equable winter climate. Stockton, for instance, which lies at the head of the San Joaquin Valley, has a temperature all the year singularly like that of Naples, as is shown by observations kept for some years by one of the most eminent and careful physicians of the place. But local peculiarities cause in some places daily extremes which are not, I think, favorable for invalids; and in other points the winds are too severe for weakly persons. At Los Angeles, for instance, the days in January are warm and genial, but as soon as the sun sets the air becomes chilly, and quickly affects tender throats. San Diego, Santa Barbara, San Bernardino, with Stockton and Visalia, are the points most favorable for consumptives and persons subject to throat difficulties.

Of these, the friend of whom I spoke above found San Bernardino the most beneficial; and a physician, who had removed from an Eastern city to the new Riverside Colony near San Bernardino, told me that he lived nowhere so comfortably as there. He could not live in New York at all, being prostrated with severe throat disease; and he enjoyed, he told me, perfect health at Riverside. . . . Moreover, at all these places you will meet pleasant, intelligent, and hospitable people, who will add somewhat to your enjoyment. Santa Barbara has even a circulating library. There are good schools for children, if you have such with you; and with a little enterprise to plan excursions, your time will not hang heavily on your hands. . . .

3. The Puget Sound Business Directory Extols the Beauties of Washington Territory, 1872

The Northwest Coast has not yet become a tourist's Mecca, owing, undoubtedly, to the fact that the beauty, wild grandeur and diversified scenery of water, forest and snow-clad ranges—rivals of the Alps—which are to be found along its entire length, have not been made known, or perhaps it has been thought too distant. The latter, however, seems improbable, when we know that persons have traveled from all portions of Europe for the special purpose of beholding the grand scenery of the Yosemite Valley or the awe-inspiring Geysers. A want of knowledge, then, of our unequaled scenery, must have been the primary cause for scarcity of the seekers after the picturesque and beautiful. Though Washington may not possess a Yosemite or the Big Trees, it nevertheless has wonders of scenery which should attract any lover of the beautiful and sublime. It is scenery that is unique, and as diversified as it is peculiar. From the moment one enters Western Washington he is surrounded by towering forests of such magnitude that the evergreens of the East sink into insignificance by comparison. Many of the trees are between three and four hundred feet high, and from eight to sixteen feet in diameter. They very forcibly impress one of his diminutive form, as he gazes at their tall, straight trunks, free from branch or leaf for a distance of forty feet from the ground. These gloomy forests, which have such a weird effect, are relieved by the bright leaves of the laurel, maple, dogwood and the shrubbery and flora which grow profusely, and give them an appearance of tropical luxuriance. This flora contains many species new to botanists, hence it is very interesting to the lovers of botany. When one emerges from the forests the first objects that greet the eye are the snow-clad peaks of the Cascade and Olympic ranges, which loom in every direction. The effect of these is sublime in the highest degree. If the day is fine and the sun shining brightly, every prominent crevice in the peaks are discernible, and the play of the light upon the snow and its many and quick-changing hues become interesting to the lover of the harmony and wealth of color. This is especially the case in the morning or evening. On such occasions all the hues of the rainbow can be seen at once, sometimes fading into one color and then again transforming until all known hues are developed. Much as has been written of the beauties of the Alps, we doubt if they can excel those of the white-shrouded peaks of the Cascades. The adventurous tourist will find these worthy of all his daring and courage, and if he ascends them and happens to bear any love for the natural sciences, he will find a wealth of flora and fauna which will surprise and charm him. All these mountains show the effect of glacial action, hence possess many peculiar characteristics. The ascent of Mount Vesuvius is deemed something worth boasting of; what then must it be to ascend Mounts Rainier, St. Helens, Baker or Hood—peaks far higher and more strongly marked physically. If the volcanic displays of Vesuvius is the attraction that lures tourists, they will find Mounts Rainier and St. Helens also interesting, they being active volcanoes, though at rest since 1842; nevertheless the craters are objects of interest. Tourists will find these mountains wealthy in new species of animals and flowers. Of the former the most interesting are the mountain sheep and goat, about which extraordinary stories are told by hunters and Indians as to their swiftness, nimbleness and elasticity. Only a few of these have been killed. . . .

4. *William Henry Boyles Watches the Modoc Indians Outmaneuver the U.S. Army, 1873*

. . . Everything was soon in readiness and the day had been determined on—April 15th, 1873—to make the attack on "Captain Jack's Stronghold."[1] A consultation was held at the HdQrs and General Gillem had decided to make the attack at seven o'clock. But Colonel Mason, who had been with Wheaton in the previous fight, asked to be allowed to take his command, consisting of three companies of the 21st Infantry, two companies of the 1st Cavalry, and the Warm Springs Indians,[2] who had arrived the same day and were commanded by Captain Donald McKay, a halfbreed Indian, that very evening, so he could take up a position without loss of any of his men. He was allowed to do so and the command left camp at midnight, succeeded in getting into position and would have almost advanced to the stronghold had it not been for some of the Indians being fishing on the Lake that night.

They went into position in the following order—the Battalion, 21st Infantry, on the right, resting on the Lake; the two companies of Cavalry (dismounted) on the left of them; and the Indians on the extreme left; and a Battery of two howitzers in charge of Lieutenant Chapin, 4th Artillery, with their left in the air.

General Gillem, who remained in camp although in command, sent the troops on his side in charge of Major Green, at 8 o'clock, to take up their positions and they were met by the Indians some distance from the Lava Beds and they held the troops in check.

This shows they should have taken their position at night and not waited until daylight to make the advance. Green's command consisted of Batteries E, B and M, 4th Artillery, and E and G, 12th Infantry, (Thomas's Battalion, 4th Artillery, remaining in camp with the mortars ready-mounted for use), Captain Perry, 1st Cavalry, with Company F, 1st Cavalry, having taken up a position during the night without the loss of any men.

At about 9 o'clock, A.M., the battle became general along the whole line. Mason's command, being under cover, suffered no loss with the exception of one Warm Springs Indian, wounded. On Major Green's side of the Lava Beds, the loss was one officer, Lieutenant Eagan, wounded in the leg, three enlisted men killed and nine wounded. Major Green made one or two unsuccessful attempts to carry the enemy's position but did not succeed, and as the darkness came on, the troops remained in the position they had taken that day, General Gillem and staff in their camp, the remainder of the officers remaining at their post with the troops. Cooked rations and hot coffee were furnished the troops and they passed the night building breastworks to cover them and taking up a more advanced position. Occasional firing occurred along the line all night but no general engagement occurred.

April 16, 1873, the day broke fair and, as soon as it was light, the [Modoc] Indians discovered that the troops had advanced during the night. They commenced firing on the pickets but without doing any damage. At about 10 o'clock, a general advance was made but with little success and with a loss on our side of two killed and four wounded, these being in Colonel Green's command.

A general fusillade was kept up all day and, at evening, the firing ceased on both sides. Our troops were rationed during the night, which they passed much in the same manner as the last. The soldiers were instructed to build stone breastworks sufficient to hold five or six men and at no time to allow themselves to be surprised. So they managed to allow two or three to sleep while the others watched and you could see all the soldiers sleeping as soundly, with their heads pillowed on a rock, as if they had been in their camp.

Lieutenant Chapin took advantage of the darkness to advance his howitzers during the night on a small hill that overlooked the stronghold of Jack,

---

[1]Captain Jack (or Chief Kientepoos) had camped with about 200 Modoc Indians, including 150 women and children, in the Modoc Lava Beds near the Oregon border in northern California.

[2]These were 72 Indian allies brought in to supplement the army troops.

and in the morning he was prepared to throw his shells into the very mouth of the cave and Captain Thomas succeeded in getting his mortars in a good position to land his shells on the heads of the Modocs. Everything was in splendid condition to do execution in the morning.

The troops were in fine condition to fight and in good spirits, and as the Modocs had been cut off from water the previous evening, they thought they had them sure. But, while the preparation was going on outside the caves, Jack and his warriors were also at work, removing all of their property, women and children from the caves about two miles to a safe retreat. When the army rested the previous evening, there was a gap left open between the left of Miller's command and the right of the Warm Springs Indians, through which the Modocs carried their property, women and children, and old men.

The Warm Springs Indians reported hearing children crying during the night but did not report the fact to the Commanding Officer, so the Modocs were permitted to escape and take with them all their property, leaving sufficient men to make an appearance of their being still in position.

April 17th, 1873

This day was as fine as could be expected and as soon as it was light, the firing began on our side, seemingly with little attention from the Modocs until about 11 o'clock, when a few that were left in the caves were reinforced by a few more of the party that had assisted the women and children to escape. Then a regular engagement ensued and all the troops were brought into the field and advanced over the Lava Beds. But the Modocs had made good their escape and were again perched on top of the rocks about two miles distant. How they escaped was a miracle to the soldiers. But, when they came to examine the cave, they found a fissure in the rocks leading to the distant hills, thrown up by nature, making an avenue protected on both sides by rocks.

This pass the Modocs had carefully guarded and marked by sticks and stones piled on top of one another so that they could pass out as well by night as day. The troops marched over the dreaded caves, searching for the Modocs. In one fissure they found two squaws, more dead than alive, and, soon after, an old man who had been left behind.

The dead bodies of three Indians[3] were also found and some of the rags of plunder of the Indians, too worthless to carry so [they] were left behind. Thus ended the three day's fight under General Gillem and with the only success of having driven the Indians from their caves and to a better position in the rocky hills. . . .

---

[3]Two of these Modocs were accidentally killed while trying to open an unexploded howitzer shell.

5. *Chief Joseph Makes His Final Stand, 1877*

Tell General Howard I know his heart. What he told me before I have in my heart. I am tired of fighting. Our chiefs are killed. Looking Glass is dead. The old men are all killed. It is the young men who say yes or no. He who led the young men is dead. It is cold and we have no blankets. The little children are freezing to death. My people, some of them, have run away to the hills and have no blankets, no food; no one knows where they are, perhaps freezing to death. I want time to look for my children and see how many of them I can find. Maybe I shall find them among the dead. Hear me, my chiefs, I am tired; my heart is sick and sad. From where the sun now stands, I will fight no more forever.

6. *Denis Kearney Blames the Chinese for Low Wages, 1877*

We intend to try and vote the Chinamen out, to frighten him out, and if this won't do, to kill him out, and when the blow comes, we won't leave a fragment for the thieves to pick up. We are going to arm ourselves to the teeth, and if these land-grabbers and thieves go outside the Constitution, we will go outside the Constitution, too, and woe be to them. You must be prepared. The heathen slaves must leave this coast, if it cost 10,000 lives. We want to frighten capital and thereby starve the white men so that they will be exasperated and do their duty. This is the last chance the white slaves will ever have to gain their liberty. . . . We have the numbers to win at the ballot box, but you will be cheated out of the result, and all history shows that oppressed labor has always to get its right at the point of the sword. If the Republican robber and the Democratic thief cheat you at the election, as I know they will, shoot them down like rats. You must be ready with your bullets. We will go to Sacramento and surround the Legislature with bayonets and compel them to enact such laws as we wish. . . .

7. *The* San Diego Union *Reports on Railroad Competition, 1886*

Los Angeles, March 6. Great excitement prevailed here today over the fight between the trans-Atlantic railroads over rates to the East. Prices commenced at $15 to Kansas City at 9 A.M., rapidly falling to $4 by 11 A.M. At noon this was further reduced to $2 to Kansas City, $7 to Chicago and $20 to New York. At 12:30 tickets to Kansas City were announced at $1 by the Atchison and Southern Pacific systems. From this [time] on prices advanced again until at 2 P.M. the rate to Kansas City was again $10 for a limited first-class ticket. A great number of tickets were sold and the war was very bitter.

8. *Growth in the Pacific Northwest During the 1880s*

	1880	*1890*	*Percentage Increase*
Population			
Idaho	32,610	84,385	158.8
Oregon	174,768	313,767	79.5
Washington	75,116	349,390	365.1
Miles of railroad (single track)			
Idaho	206	945	358.7
Oregon	347	1,433	313.0
Washington	212	1,775	737.3
Total	765	4,153	442.9
True value of real and personal property	$245,000,000	$1,558,991,511	536.3
Capital in manufacturing	$ 10,191,768	$ 77,732,470	662.7
Average no. acres in farms	5,951,931	12,391,344	108.2
Agricultural production			
Bushels of wheat	9,941,921	26,760,959	169.2
Pounds of wool	7,234,796	13,658,945	88.8

9. *President Benjamin Harrison Asks the Senate to Annex Hawaii, 1893*

Executive Mansion,
Washington, February 15, 1893.

To the Senate:

I transmit herewith, with a view to its ratification, a treaty of annexation concluded on the 14th day of February, 1893, between John W. Foster, Secretary of State, who was duly empowered to act in that behalf on the part of the United States, and Lorin A. Thurston, W. R. Castle, W. C. Wilder, C. L. Carter, and Joseph Marsden, the commissioners on the part of the Government of the Hawaiian Islands. The provisional treaty, it will be observed, does not attempt to deal in detail with the questions that grow out of the annexation of the Hawaiian Islands to the United States. The commissioners representing the Hawaiian Government have consented to leave to the future and to the just and benevolent purposes of the United States the adjustment of all such questions.

I do not deem it necessary to discuss at any length the conditions which have resulted in this decisive action. It has been the policy of the Administration not only to respect but to encourage the continuance of an independent government in the Hawaiian Islands so long as it afforded suitable guaranties for the protection of life and property and maintained a stability and strength that gave adequate security against the domination of any other power. The moral support of this Government has continually manifested itself in the most friendly diplomatic relations and in many acts of courtesy to the Hawaiian rulers.

The overthrow of the monarchy was not in any way promoted by this Government, but had its origin in what seems to have been a reactionary and revolutionary policy on the part of Queen Liliuokalani, which put in serious peril not only the large and preponderating interests of the United States in the islands, but all foreign interests, and, indeed, the decent administration of civil affairs and the peace of the islands. It is quite evident that the monarchy had become effete and the Queen's Government so weak and inadequate as to be the prey of designing and unscrupulous persons. The restoration of Queen Liliuokalani to her throne is undesirable, if not impossible, and unless actively supported by the United States would be accompanied by serious disaster and the disorganization of all business interests. The influence and interest of the United States in the islands must be increased and not diminished.

Only two courses are now open—one the establishment of a protectorate by the United States, and the other annexation full and complete. I think the latter course, which has been adopted in the treaty, will be highly promotive of the best interests of the Hawaiian people, and is the only one that will adequately secure the interests of the United States. These interests are not wholly selfish. It is essential that none of the other great powers shall secure these islands. Such a possession would not consist with our safety and with the peace of the world. This view of the situation is so apparent and conclusive that no protest has been heard from any government against proceedings looking to annexation. Every foreign representative at Honolulu promptly acknowledged the Provisional Government, and I think there is a general concurrence in the opinion that the deposed Queen ought not to be restored.

Prompt action upon this treaty is very desirable. If it meets the approval of the Senate, peace and good order will be secured in the islands under existing laws until such time as Congress can provide by legislation a permanent form of government for the islands. This legislation should be, and I do not doubt will be, not only just to the natives and all other residents and citizens of the islands, but should be characterized by great liberality and a high regard to the rights of all people and of all foreigners domiciled there. The correspondence which accompanies the treaty will put the Senate in possession of all the facts known to the Executive.

Benj. Harrison.

10. Frederick Jackson Turner Characterizes the Meaning of the West in American History, 1893

In a recent bulletin of the Superintendent of the Census for 1890 appear these significant words: "Up to and including 1880 the country had a frontier of settlement, but at present the unsettled area has been so broken into by isolated bodies of settlement that there can hardly be said to be a frontier line. In the discussion of its extent, its westward movement, etc., it can not, therefore, any longer have a place in the census reports." This brief official statement marks the closing of a great historic movement. Up to our own day American history has been in a large degree the history of the colonization of the Great West. The existence of an area of free land, its continuous recession, and the advance of American settlement westward, explain American development.

Behind institutions, behind constitutional forms and modifications, lie the vital forces that call these organs into life and shape them to meet changing conditions. The peculiarity of American institutions is, the fact that they have been compelled to adapt themselves to the changes of an expanding people—to the changes involved in crossing a continent, in winning a wilderness, and in developing at each area of this progress out of the primitive economic and political conditions of the frontier into the complexity of city life. Said Calhoun in 1817, "We are great, and rapidly—I was about to say fearfully—growing!" So saying, he touched the distinguishing feature of American life. All peoples show development; the germ theory of politics has been sufficiently emphasized. In the case of most nations, however, the development has occurred in a limited area; and if the nation has expanded, it has met other growing peoples whom it has conquered. But in the case of the United States we have a different phenomenon. Limiting our attention to the Atlantic coast, we have the familiar phenomenon of the evolution of institutions in a limited area, such as the rise of representative government; the differentiation of simple colonial governments into complex organs; the progress from primitive industrial society, without division of labor, up to manufacturing civilization. But we have in addition to this a recurrence of the process of evolution in each western area reached in the process of expansion. Thus American development has exhibited not merely advance along a single line, but a return to primitive conditions on a continually advancing frontier line, and a new development for that area. American social development has been continually beginning over again on the frontier. This perennial rebirth, this fluidity of American life, this expansion westward with its new opportunities, its continuous touch with the simplicity of primitive society, furnish the forces dominating American character. The true point of view in the history of this nation is not the Atlantic coast, it is the Great West. . . .

References

1. Henry George Criticizes Land Monopoly, 1871
   Henry George, *Our Land and Land Policy, National and State* (San Francisco, 1871), pp. 24–25, quoted in John W. and LaRee Caughey, *California Heritage* (Los Angeles: The Ward Ritchie Press, 1962), pp. 331–333.
2. Charles Nordhoff Praises California as a Haven for Invalids, 1872
   Charles Nordhoff, *California for Health, Pleasure, and Residence* (New York: Harper & Bros., 1873), pp. 109–112.
3. The Puget Sound Business Directory Extols the Beauties of Washington Territory, 1872
   Charles Marvin Gates, ed., *Readings in Pacific Northwest History: Washington, 1790–1895* (Seattle: University Bookstore, 1941), pp. 278–279.
4. William Henry Boyles Watches the Modoc Indians Outmaneuver the U.S. Army, 1873
   Richard H. Dillon, ed., *William Henry Boyles's Personal Observations on the Conduct of the Modoc War* (Los Angeles: Dawson's Book Shop, 1959), pp. 40–47.
5. Chief Joseph Makes His Final Stand, 1877
   Merrill D. Beal, *"I Will Fight No More Forever": Chief Joseph and the Nez Percé War* (Seattle: University of Washington Press, 1963), pp. 229–237.
6. Denis Kearney Blames the Chinese for Low Wages, 1877
   San Francisco Bulletin, quoted in Neil Larry Shumsky, *The Evolution of Political Protest and the Workingmen's Party of California* (Columbus: Ohio State University Press, 1991), p. 178.
7. The *San Diego Union* Reports on Railroad Competition, 1886
   San Diego Union, March 7, 1886.
8. Growth in the Pacific Northwest During the 1880s
   Carlos A. Schwantes, *The Pacific Northwest: An Interpretative History* (Lincoln: University of Nebraska Press, 1989), p. 185.

9. President Benjamin Harrison Asks the Senate to Annex Hawaii, 1893
   James D. Richardson, ed., *Messages and Papers of the Presidents* (New York: Bureau of National Literature, 1897), 12: 5783–5784.
10. Frederick Jackson Turner Characterizes the Meaning of the West in American History, 1893
    Frederick Jackson Turner, "The Significance of the Frontier in American History," *American Historical Association Annual Report for the Year 1893* (Washington, D.C., 1894), pp. 199–200.

Document Set 9

The West at the Turn of the Century, 1890–1910

Despite a financial panic that began 1893, the exuberant boom of the 1880s spilled over into the following decade. Newcomers had transplanted the architectural styles of the East to the West, building magnificent Victorian mansions in Denver, Salt Lake City, Seattle, Portland, Vancouver, and throughout California, from Eureka to San Diego. Styles varied from Queen Anne to Eastlake (Document 1), and from Gothic to Second Empire. Some houses were simply eclectic. City planners followed trends set in Chicago by leaders of the City Beautiful movement. But although settlers in the West kept a sharp eye on places to the east, they also looked toward the Pacific as the United States expanded its imperial vision in these years and matured as a nation.

The Chicago Columbian Exposition of 1893, a world's fair commemorating the four hundredth anniversary of the Columbus epic, captured the imagination of people throughout the country, with all states sending products for exhibition. California, despite an economic downturn, displayed a handsome Spanish-style building at the fair and demonstrated the growth and variety of California's agricultural output. The second document is part of the state's final report on the exposition.

Whenever interest in mining waned, it seemed that another area would open up. In Colorado a rush to Cripple Creek paid dividends in 1891. Other prospectors traveled to Alaska and mined at Nome and Dawson. When news of the gold discovery in the Klondike reached the United States, thousands of Americans passed through Alaska to Canada's Yukon Territory. Many stories told of the difficult climb to the summit of Chilkoot Pass (Document 3) and of other hardships endured in the harsh weather. The U.S. government still had much to learn about the geography of Canada and Alaska.

By 1898 Henry E. Huntington, nephew of Big Four railroad magnate Collis P. Huntington, had expanded Southern Pacific's California operations while keeping costs down (Document 4). Huntington also planned an electric railway line that became known as the Pacific Electric. The new line connected southern California with the greater Los Angeles area and contributed to the development of numerous new communities. Painter William Wendt in 1898 praised the light and air of southern California (Document 5) before the smog of a later day and more modern forms of transportation left their mark.

Farther north, Washington, Oregon, and Idaho underwent growth and speculation in forest lands. Oregon had achieved statehood in 1859; Washington, in 1889; Idaho and Wyoming, in 1890. The tremendous expansion of the United States during the 1880s and 1890s had created a great market for timber products, which the Pacific Northwest supplied. The Northern Pacific Railroad, the recipient of large grants of the public domain, began to sell off its land. Legitimate and false claims made under the Homestead Act and timberland frauds in Oregon led to federal investigations.

In California, Scottish naturalist and poet John Muir tried to protect the forests and especially advocated federal government control in preserving national parks. As first president of the Sierra Club, he launched a campaign for the environment that has continued to the present day (Document 6). Muir shared many of his ideas about conservation with President Theodore Roosevelt, who incorporated these views in his messages about forest protection. Although written at the turn of the century, Muir's words carry as much impact today.

San Francisco kept its image as the cultural leader of the West. Well-known writers such as Frank

Norris, whose best-selling book *The Octopus* (1901) brought pressure to bear against unfair railroad practices, and Jack London, who returned from the Klondike to write soul-searching short stories and adventure novels, frequented the downtown Bohemian Club. Ambrose Bierce, also known as Bitter Bierce, criticized California society in the columns of the *San Francisco Examiner* with a biting sarcasm that touched all walks of life. Bierce poked fun at professionals, family values, and boosterism and penned tales of sardonic humor. His ironic definitions first appeared in *The Cynic's Word Book* in 1906. *The Devil's Dictionary* (excerpted in Document 7) followed in 1911.

At the southern end of the state, Katherine Tingley, a theosophist, appealed to the public conscience to improve humankind. The word *theosophy* comes from the Greek *theos* ("God") and *sophia* ("wisdom"); thus theosophists engaged in speculative thought about God and the universe. Tingley founded a cooperative community at Point Loma in San Diego and preached the tenets of her philosophy, which had Eastern as well as Western influences. She also valued nature and encouraged the production of organically grown vegetables for a basically vegetarian diet. After the *Los Angeles Times* report that Tingley was running a "spookery" and not giving children enough to eat, she in turn decried the press in a 1906 speech (Document 8).

The turn of the century indeed saw a new era in United States history. Large areas of unsettled open space were rapidly disappearing, and the American West had expanded to include Alaska and Hawaii, which now had territorial status. Imperialism had caught the nation's attention. The Spanish-American War had brought the Philippines and Guam under American control. Meanwhile, political and social reform within the states was long overdue, but the progressive movement of the early twentieth century soon would usher in a period of positive change.

Questions for Analysis

1. What characteristics do Victorian houses share?
2. Is California's agricultural output about the same today as it was in 1893?
3. How did the trip to the Klondike in the 1890s compare with the trek to California in 1849?
4. Henry Huntington left a fortune to establish a magnificent library in San Marino. How would you evaluate his character?
5. What attracts people to southern California today?
6. Was John Muir correct in his warnings about forest preservation?
7. How would you characterize Ambrose Bierce as a person?
8. Do you think that theosophy had a wide appeal? Explain your answer.

1. Queen Anne Style Graces California in the 1890s

Haas-Lilienthal House, San Francisco, California

1. Tower with conical roof
2. Multi-planed roof
3. Projecting attic gable with recessed porch
4. Pedimented and projecting dormer
5. Fish scale shingles
6. Upper sash with a border of small square lights
7. Horizontal siding
8. Swags
9. Board and batten

Long-Waterman House, San Diego, California

Dickinson-Boal House, National City, California

10. Roof cresting
11. Eyelid dormer
12. Domed turret with recessed porch
13. Stained glass transom
14. Flared second story with shingle siding
15. Finial
16. Pendant
17. Verge boards
18. Circular bay
19. Variant of Palladian window
20. Tall thin chimney with terra cotta panels
21. Diagonal pattern shingles
22. Polygonal turret with tent roof
23. Carved wood panels
24. Encircling porch or verandah
25. Multi-gabled roof

2. California Exhibits a Variety of Products at the Chicago Columbian Exposition, 1893

As in the Horticultural, Mining, and other departments, nearly duplicate exhibits of California's agricultural products were made in the California and in the Agricultural Buildings. In the former, the State agricultural exhibit occupied a space about 100 feet long and 18 feet wide on the west side of the lower floor, the Butte County exhibit being to the north, and that of horticulture and viticulture to the south. On a portion of the space large glass inclosures were built, reaching to the gallery. Within these were placed pyramidic forms, entirely covered with green felt cloth and with neat white shelves arranged thereon at convenient distances. Over fifteen hundred pear-shaped inverted globes and bottles of different sizes, filled with cereals and soils of various kinds, were artistically set upon the shelves, the whole presenting an attractive appearance. Running along the wall beneath the windows was a wide table stacked with sheaves of wheat, oats, rye, and barley, and with vegetables of different sizes and varieties.

The San Francisco Produce Exchange was the largest contributor to this department. Two beautiful cases, well filled with products, were furnished. One case was of polished redwood, with a base about 4 feet high, upon which rested a pyramid holding nearly every variety of cereals and fibers grown in California. This splendid collection comprised four varieties of oats, fifteen of barley, seventeen of wheat, two of buckwheat, eight of corn, ten of peas, and thirty of beans, beside Egyptian corn, broomcorn, maize, sorghum, farina, cracked wheat, rolled oats and barley, semola, graham flour, oat groats, oatmeal, hominy, split peas; canary, flax, rape, alfalfa, mustard, millet, coriander, and hemp seed; hops, ramie, silk cocoons and raw silk, grades of cotton and wool; also, a fine display of wheat, oats, and barley in sheaf from the crop of 1893. The other case was a cabinet of black walnut, within which were placed on shelves inverted globes filled with various kinds of wheat, set off by a delicate green background.

Besides this exhibit the Produce Exchange furnished seven silk banners, prettily lettered in gilt upon a dark garnet ground and bordered with long golden fringe. The largest banner was about 15 feet long, and bore this inscription: "San Francisco Produce Exchange—Products of California." The other six were smaller, but of uniform size, and contained a clear statement in brief of the agricultural products of the State. Comparative figures were given for the years 1879 and 1892, the former year being chosen, as it marked the beginning of a new era in agriculture and horticulture. The lettering upon the banners gave the following valuable information:

> Wheat—Crop 1879, 33,500,000 bushels; crop 1892, 40,000,000 bushels. Export 1879—Wheat 16,660,000 bushels; flour, 527,440 barrels. Export 1892—Wheat, 21,400,000 bushels; flour, 1,056,000 barrels.
>
> Wines—Vintage 1879, 7,000,000 gallons; 1891, 20,000,000 gallons. Brandies—Product 1879, 158,393 gallons; 1892, 1,475,525 gallons.

Barley—Largest production of any State in the Union. Crop 1879, 11,000,000 bushels; 1892, 15,000,000 bushels.

Hops—Crop 1879, 1,335,700 pounds; 1892, 7,500,000 pounds.

Wool—Production 1879, 46,903,360 pounds; 1891, 33,200,000 pounds.

Raisins—Pack 1879, 65,000 boxes; 1891, 2,150,000 boxes.

Dried fruit—Product 1884, 5,285,000 pounds; 1891, 63,710,000 pounds.

Green fruit—Shipments overland, 1879, 3,126,140 pounds; 1891, 98,680,000 pounds.

Canned fruit—Pack 1879, 298,356 cases; 1891, 1,460,000 cases.

In addition to generous contributions to this department of wheat, rye, oats, and barley from the manager of the Butte County exhibit, General John Bidwell, of Chico, furnished some very fine samples of cereals, embracing sixty-five varieties of wheat, twelve of barley, five of oats, and four of rye.

San Luis Obispo County sent a greater diversity of products than any other county, the exhibit consisting of beans, peas, corn, wheat, rye, barley, oats, onions, buckwheat flour, corn meal, cracked wheat, shorts, middlings, rolled oats and wheat, breakfast food, semola, rice, alfalfa seed, walnuts, flax, ramie, jute, yxtle, soils, and a variety of small seeds. This collection was prepared and forwarded by J. V. N. Young, of Arroyo Grande.

Los Angeles County made a fine showing of wheat, barley, corn, oats, rye, beans, walnuts, onions, squashes, potatoes, beets, etc.

Ventura County forwarded twenty-five varieties of beans, also several kinds of wheat, corn, oats, barley, nuts, and potato starch.

A very creditable exhibit was received from Merced County, including wheat, barley, rye, oats, beans, corn, cotton, tobacco, walnuts, peanuts, almonds, Egyptian corn, alfalfa, and various grasses.

Other counties contributed as follows: Sacramento—six varieties of wheat, four of barley, two of rye, and three of oats; Santa Clara—collection of two hundred varieties of seeds; Alameda—three varieties of choice barley, and the same of wheat; Sutter—choice selection of wheat, oats, and barley; El Dorado—samples of very fine rye; Orange County—walnuts and peanuts; San Diego—samples of wheat, barley, and oats; Kern—miscellaneous cereals.

The University of California, through Prof. E. W. Hilgard, loaned three hundred varieties of grains—wheat, barley, rye, oats, flax, alfalfa, clover, and numerous fine grasses. These samples were all of the best quality, and the tastily disposed sheaves of cereals and forage-plants, with a neat array of phials, to show the results of the threshing, constituted one of the finest displays in the State exhibit.

Taken as a whole, the State agricultural exhibit was a comprehensive one, and fairly represented the agricultural products of California. . . .

3. Gold Seekers Carry Supplies over Alaska's Chilkoot Pass, 1898

Miners scale Chilkoot Pass to reach Canada's Yukon Territory.

4. Henry Huntington Urges Expansion of the Southern Pacific Railroad, 1898

. . . Every foot of track built at my instigation in southern California has been through a densely populated and highly fertile territory, which yields most bountifully its share of traffic that we would otherwise not get, thereby helping to sustain the many miles of barren, desert lines that produce nothing, of which you know we have more than our share. The expense for operation of these branch lines has not increased in proportion to the mileage, as the men have been required to go in and out on them within the day's time, in addition to the ocean runs, I hardly believe any of our people today question the wisdom of reaching out and building these branches which enable us to get about 53% of the southern California traffic, when we formerly did not get 40%. . . .

Upon my advent here, as you know, I made it my business to produce every possible economy that did not interfere with the maintenance of the highest efficiency of the property, and you can well imagine that this was not a popular thing to do. . . . By analysis, you will see that we have operated 9% more miles of road, carried over the Pacific System lines 4% more revenue trains, 7% more revenue cars, and 15% more freight and passenger mileage *for 3%* less actual operating expense than it cost us in the previous period with which the comparison was made. . . .

5. William Wendt Lauds Southern California, 1898

The earth is young again. The peace, the harmony which pervades all, gives a Sabbath-like air to the day, to the environment. One feels that he is on holy ground, in Nature's temple.

The warm green of the grass, sprinkled with flowers of many hues, is a carpet whereon we walk with noiseless tread.

The perfume of the flowers and of the bay tree are wafted on high, like incense. The birds sing sweet songs of praise to their Creator. In the tops of the trees, the soughing of the wind is like the hushed prayers of the multitude in some vast cathedral. Here the heart of man becomes impressionable. Here, away from conflicting creeds and sects, away from the soul-destroying hurly-burly of life, it feels that the world is beautiful; that man is his brother; that God is good. . . .

6. John Muir Asks That Forests Be Protected, 1901

The tendency nowadays to wander in wildernesses is delightful to see. Thousands of tired, nerve-shaken, over-civilized people are beginning to find out that going to the mountains is going home; that wildness is a necessity; and that mountain parks and reservations are useful not only as fountains of timber and irrigating rivers, but as fountains of life. Awakening from the stupefying effects of the vice of over-industry and the deadly apathy of luxury, they are trying as best they can to mix and enrich their own little ongoings with those of Nature, and to get rid of rust and disease. Briskly venturing and roaming, some are washing off sins and cobweb cares of the devil's spinning in all-day storms on mountains; sauntering in rosiny pinewoods or in gentian meadows, brushing through chaparral, bending down and parting sweet, flowery sprays; tracing rivers to their sources, getting in touch with the nerves of Mother Earth; jumping from rock to rock, feeling the life of them, learning the songs of them, panting in whole-souled exercise, and rejoicing in deep, long-drawn breaths of pure wildness. This is fine and natural and full of promise. So also is the growing interest in the care and preservation of forests and wild places in general, and in the half wild parks and gardens of towns. Even the scenery habit in its most artificial forms, mixed with spectacles, silliness, and kodaks; its devotees arrayed more gorgeously than scarlet tanagers, frightening the wild game with red umbrellas,—even this is encouraging, and may well be regarded as a hopeful sign of the times.

All the Western mountains are still rich in wildness, and by means of good roads are being brought nearer civilization every year. To the sane and free it will hardly seem necessary to cross the continent in search of wild beauty, however easy the way, for they find it in abundance wherever they chance to be. Like Thoreau they see forests in orchards and patches of huckleberry brush, and oceans in ponds and drops of dew. Few in these hot, dim, strenuous times are quite sane or free; choked with care like clocks full of dust, laboriously doing so much good and making so much money,—or so little,—they are no longer good for themselves. . . .

All sorts of local laws and regulations [protecting forests] have been tried and found wanting, and the costly lessons of our own experience, as well as that of every civilized nation, show conclusively that the fate of the remnant of our forests is in the hands of the Federal

Government, and that if the remnant is to be saved at all, it must be saved quickly.

Any fool can destroy trees. They cannot run away; and if they could, they would still be destroyed,—chased and hunted down as long as fun or a dollar could be got out of their bark hides, branching horns, or magnificent bole backbones. Few that fell trees plant them; nor would planting avail much towards getting back anything like the noble primeval forests. During a man's life only saplings can be grown, in the place of the old trees—tens of centuries old—that have been destroyed. It took more than three thousand years to make some of the trees in these Western woods,—trees that are still standing in perfect strength and beauty, waving and singing in the mighty forests of the Sierra. Through all the wonderful, eventful centuries since Christ's time—and long before that—God has cared for these trees, saved them from drought, disease, avalanches, and a thousand straining, leveling tempests and floods; but he cannot save them from fools,—only Uncle Sam can do that.

7. *Ambrose Bierce Compiles a Cynical Word List, 1906*

ACQUAINTANCE, *n.*
A person whom we know well enough to borrow from, but not well enough to lend to. A degree of friendship called slight when its object is poor or obscure, and intimate when he is rich or famous.

APPEAL, *v.t.*
In law, to put the dice into the box for another throw.

ARCHITECT, *n.*
One who drafts a plan of your house, and plans a draft of your money.

BEAUTY, *n.*
The power by which a woman charms a lover and terrifies a husband.

BIGOT, *n.*
One who is obstinately and zealously attached to an opinion that you do not entertain.

CHRISTIAN, *n.*
One who believes that the New Testament is a divinely inspired book admirably suited to the spiritual needs of his neighbor. One who follows the teachings of Christ in so far as they are not inconsistent with a life of sin.

DENTIST, *n.*
A prestidigitator who, putting metal into your mouth, pulls coins out of your pocket.

FRIENDSHIP, *n.*
A ship big enough to carry two in fair weather, but only one in foul.

FUNERAL, *n.*
A pageant whereby we attest our respect for the dead by enriching the undertaker, and strengthen our grief by an expenditure that deepens our groans and doubles our tears.

HELPMATE, *n.*
A wife, or bitter half.

HISTORIAN, *n.*
A broad-gauge gossip.

HISTORY, *n.*
An account mostly false, of events mostly unimportant, which are brought about by rulers mostly knaves, and soldiers mostly fools.

HOMICIDE, *n.*
The slaying of one human being by another. There are four kinds of homicide: felonious, excusable, justifiable and praiseworthy, but it makes no great difference to the person slain whether he fell by one or another—the classification is for advantage of the lawyers.

LAWYER, *n.*
One skilled in circumvention of the law.

MISFORTUNE, *n.*
The kind of fortune that never misses.

POSITIVE, *adj.*
Mistaken at the top of one's voice.

PRESCRIPTION, *n.*
A physician's guess at what will best prolong the situation with least harm to the patient.

PUSH, *n.*
One of the two things mainly conducive to success, especially in politics. The other is Pull.

YEAR, *n.*
A period of three hundred and sixty-five disappointments. . . .

8. *Katherine Tingley Criticizes the Press, 1906*

An Appeal to Public Conscience

(Address delivered by Katherine Tingley, Sunday, July 22, 1906, at Isis Theatre, San Diego, California.)

Through my simple speech to-night, Theosophy, in seeking to touch the heart of public conscience, declares itself to be a potent factor for the betterment of humankind. It declares that man has the possibility of developing in this life the potential qualities of his Divine Nature. But in order to gain the knowledge for such a fashioning, he must first learn how to think; to understand the meaning of right action, equity and liberty.

Not having a true knowledge of the guiding principles of human life, he fails in his duty to himself, as well as to his fellows and to his country. He is but a negative apology; ignorant, without philosophy, heart or feeling; without a guiding power in life.

Realizing that America, in its great protective Constitution, declares the largest liberty of thought and action to every man, one would naturally think that this country should afford a broad field for the largest tolerance, and for the cultivation of a liberty-loving life. How seriously and exquisitely is Liberty defined in that Constitution! In no part of it is license encouraged. . . .

I wish to call your attention to some appalling pictures that darken the horizon of our beautiful America: . . .

The public press is losing its dignity and its power to serve the people justly.

No greater factor could we have to advance the true welfare of this land, if the press were the real voice of Liberty-loving people, not of tyrants, fanatics money-grabbers and persecutors.

There are exceptions to every rule, and it must be remembered that I am accentuating the injustice in yellow journalism. There are some few publications in America holding dignified positions in our work-a-day world, but they are few. . . .

Journalism to do its real work for the highest good of the country must have right and proper support; and the men who lead as editors in purifying and strengthening our national life should be financially and otherwise sustained, that they may stand free from any political obligation that does not work for the best interest of America. This surely never can be done until politics are purified, and the lovers of true Liberty are more united for our national good.

Theosophy compels much thinking, much self-analysis, much cultivation of discrimination to see men and things as they are, and not as they seem. It is this right kind of thinking that every true citizen should do. Man, once conscious of his Divine Nature and the responsibility he has assumed, will seek the path of a true and noble life; and when he sees a wrong done to one or more of his fellows, will rebuke and compel better action on the part of the transgressor by a determined stand for justice. He will count no sacrifice too great for this end: his conscience will be so aroused that he can not remain silent and see evil done to his fellows. . . .

Theosophy does not teach

a personal God, as the infinite and absolute God of the universe. As H.P.

Blavatsky says: "We reject the idea of a personal or an extra-cosmic anthropomorphic God, who is but the gigantic shadow of man, and not even of man at his best. The God of Theology, we say, —and prove it— is a bundle of contradictions and a logical impossibility."

But Theosophy does teach

belief in the Supreme,—"beyond the range of thought"—"in whom we live and move and have our being"—Infinite, beyond man's finite comprehension, the Unknowable, Absolute LIGHT.

References

1. Queen Anne Style Graces California in the 1890s
John J.-G. Blumenson, *Identifying American Architecture: A Pictorial Guide to Styles and Terms, 1600–1945* (Nashville: American Association for State and Local History, 1977, 1981), p. 63.
2. California Exhibits a Variety of Products at the Chicago Columbian Exposition, 1893
Final Report of the California World's Fair Commission, Including a Description of All Exhibits from the State of California (Sacramento: State Printing Office, 1894), pp., 32–34.
3. Gold Seekers Carry Supplies over Alaska's Chilkoot Pass, 1898
Photograph in the Anchorage Historical and Fine Arts Museum, Anchorage, Alaska, published in Claus M. Naske and Herman E. Slotnick, *Alaska: A History of the 49th State*, 2d ed. (Norman: University of Oklahoma Press, 1987), p. 78.
4. Henry Huntington Urges Expansion of the Southern Pacific Railroad, 1898
William B. Friedricks, *Henry E. Huntington and the Creation of Southern California* (Columbus: Ohio State University Press, 1992), pp. 41–42.
5. William Wendt Lauds Southern California, 1898
Joachim Smith, "The Splendid, Silent Sun: Reflections of the Light and Color of Southern California," in *California Light, 1900–1930* (Laguna Beach: Laguna Art Museum, 1990), p. 70.
6. John Muir Asks That Forests Be Protected, 1901
John Muir, *Our National Parks* (Boston and New York: Houghton Mifflin, 1917), pp. 3–5, 392–393.
7. Ambrose Bierce Compiles a Cynical Word List, 1906
Ambrose Bierce, *The Devil's Dictionary* (1911, reprint ed., New York: Thomas Y. Crowell, 1979), various selections, pp. 11, 14, 17, 22, 29, 42, 49, 68, 86, 106, 108, 154.
8. Katherine Tingley Criticizes the Press, 1906
Katherine Tingley, *An Appeal to Public Conscience* (Point Loma, Calif.: Woman's Theosophical Propaganda League, 1906), pp. 5–9, 20–21.

Document Set 10

The Progressives, World War I, and Postwar Progress, 1910–1930

The years 1910–1930 brought a wide variety of changes on the local, state, and national levels in the West. The progressives concentrated on weakening the massive influence of the railroads and other large corporations and increasing voter control over government. The election of Woodrow Wilson as president in 1912 and the outbreak of World War I in 1914, however, gave precedence for a time to international issues. Completion of the Panama Canal in 1914 brought the Pacific coast closer to the East, and war demands encouraged the material growth of the western states. By the 1920s California was in the midst of an oil boom, and the fledgling motion picture industry was flourishing in Hollywood. Mass production of the automobile began to change the local landscape forever.

Progressive politicians left their mark on California. Republican Hiram Johnson, elected governor in 1910, carried out a series of progressive reforms that Theodore Roosevelt admired as the best that any state had accomplished. The controversial initiative, referendum, and recall, giving the people of the state considerably more power over elected officials, brought forth bitter opponents, including Johnson's own father, Grove L. Johnson, a leading supporter of the Southern Pacific Railroad, and editorial writer Edward Francis Adams of the *San Francisco Chronicle* (see Document 1). But Californians, tired of the graft—real and perceived—among those holding municipal and state offices, rallied to the younger Johnson's support. Other measures provided control of public utilities, conservation of natural resources, and workmen's compensation, but poor job conditions for laborers, especially women, persisted (Document 2).

Women's suffrage also had a checkered history in the West. After Mormon leaders withdrew their public endorsement of plural marriage in 1890, Utah achieved statehood in 1896, with women's suffrage guaranteed by the state constitution. Women in Idaho also achieved the vote in 1896, by a state constitutional amendment. In other states, owing to women's involvement in the temperance movement, the equal suffrage campaign became associated with prohibition, and, as a result, lost some support. Testimonials from the four original suffrage states finally offered proof of satisfaction with the results, but it took well-organized drives by women in Washington, California, and Oregon from 1910 to 1912 to win the vote in those states. In California, San Francisco voters strongly opposed the measure, but the rest of the state prevailed, despite some local opposition in San Diego (Document 3). Other state victories soon followed, and finally, in 1920, the Nineteenth Amendment gave women the vote nationwide.

Oppressive conditions for migratory agricultural and other workers had long troubled the West. In response, William Haywood and a coalition of radicals from the Western Federation of Miners, socialists Eugene V. Debs and Daniel DeLeon, and disgruntled workers from the American Federation of Labor founded the Industrial Workers of the World (IWW) in Chicago in 1905. The IWW embraced unhappy laborers and hoped to bring about a working-class revolution. The organization's direct-action tactics of strikes and free-speech movements were often peaceful, but some of its actions triggered violence. IWW members appealed to dock and lumber workers in Washington and Oregon and in 1912 carried their movement as far south as San Diego. In 1913 a bloody confrontation broke out at the Durst Ranch in Wheatland, California (Document 4), resulting in four deaths and many injuries. The governor sent the National Guard to Wheatland, and several IWW members were jailed. Although the riot solved little and farmworkers failed to organize, the state legislature began to improve conditions for migratory laborers.

The Pacific Northwest also had its share of labor problems just prior to World War I but defense demand soon changed the picture. Seattle became a hub of shipbuilding activities, and former lumberman William E. Boeing started producing airplanes. A number of superpatriotic organizations sprang up after the war in the West, particularly in Oregon, as Document 5 reveals. The Russian Revolution of 1917 created a "red scare," but some Americans simply disliked those whom they considered foreigners.

On the lighter side, millionaire newspaper publisher William Randolph Hearst planned the building of a home at San Simeon that would become a veritable castle. Hearst had inherited considerable wealth from his parents, former senator and silver magnate George Hearst and education pioneer Phoebe Apperson Hearst, and he had made a substantial fortune himself. Architect Julia Morgan designed what later was known as Hearst's Castle, a showplace then (Document 6) and today a popular California state park. Hearst ran a private motion-picture theater and tried his luck in Hollywood making movies starring his good friend Marian Davies.

Aimee Semple McPherson, a Canadian evangelist with a wide appeal to newcomers in southern California, enjoyed tremendous popularity during the early 1920s with her Four Square Gospel: conversion, physical healing, the second coming, and redemption. Although McPherson never claimed that she could miraculously heal people, followers traveled miles to experience the touch of her hand. An attractive and accomplished performer, she was one of the first to reach a large audience by means of radio. Claiming to be the victim of a mysterious kidnapping in 1926, she was nevertheless charged with falsifying the entire event (Document 7). A Los Angeles jury acquitted Sister Aimee, who maintained significant popularity until her death in 1946.

Women had gained the right to vote in this era, and some, like McPherson, did achieve wealth and fame, but they had made only partial strides in business compared with men. The final selection (Document 8) captures what women in Idaho in 1929 considered appropriate business demeanor. Their outlook previewed the depression era of the 1930s, a time when women considered themselves fortunate to have a job and declined to make demands.

Questions for Analysis

1. Do you think that it is a good idea for people to challenge the work of the legislature and recall office-holders? Does this activity slow the legislative process?
2. Did women influence national trends after gaining the right to vote? Were prohibition and women's suffrage related?
3. Can you sympathize with the IWW at the Durst Ranch? What could Durst have done to improve conditions?
4. How did World War I affect the West?
5. Hearst Castle is a major tourist attraction. Do you think that William Randolph Hearst spent his money wisely?
6. Why are people attracted to evangelists and, more recently, televangelists? Why do you think they give them so much money?
7. Would many women today agree with Aurvilla Green's speech?

1. Edward Francis Adams Argues Against the Initiative, Referendum, and Recall, 1911

If the referendum be bad the initiative is worse. It is the uncorking of all the bottles of crankiness, and it is one of the strongest arguments of the proponents of the initiative that the people will probably vote down most of the laws that are proposed. But why subject ourselves to the torment and expense? Any law that ought to be passed, and any law that the people really demand, whether it ought to be passed or not, will be passed by a Legislature; but in the process of legislation it will be licked into some kind of reasonable shape, and can be amended if not right, or repealed when we are tired of it. The more direct legislation you have, the greater and the more costly will be our litigation, and the greater the body of our judge-made law.

The recall is an abomination. It is evidence of almost inconceivable hysteria in the American people that they cannot wait to get rid of an official, whom in the fulness of their wisdom they have just elected, until the expiration of his brief term of office. What we seem to need is a dose of soothing syrup. The recall of judges would be an atrocity. The talk about the people being as competent to recall as to elect is nonsensical. Personally I do not believe the people more competent to elect judges than to elect railroad commissioners, and I heartily favor that change in the glorious constitution of 1879, which takes from us that power which we have shown our incompetence to use wisely, and place it in the hands of our good Governor and his successors forever. But when we do elect judges we elect them on their general reputation at the bar or on the bench, and if we ever recall them we shall do it not because of their general conduct on the bench, but because we are mad about some particular decision—which the recall will not change—just as some of the people in one of the judicial districts of Oregon are now trying to recall a judge whose charge to the jury on the Oregon law of self defense is assumed to have set free a murderer whom the recallers think should be hanged. What is wanted of the recall is that judges may be terrorized into deciding law points to produce the result which popular clamor demands, regardless of what the judge thinks the law really is. It would never be invoked in a single instance except as the result of popular clamor against some special decision, in which the judge is far more likely to be right than the people. It is as wicked to terrorize a judge as to bribe him, and far more dangerous to society. . . .

2. Women Demand Pay Equality, 1910

The Women's Union Label League No. 197 participates in the 1910 Labor Day Parade in San Diego.

3. Leroy Cummings Believes Women Have No Need to Vote, 1911

What could women gain by depositing a piece of paper in a ballot box? As voters: they still would have to depend upon men for protection, support and employment. They would be independent in no substantial sense for the reason that they could not construct business blocks or heavy machinery, or do a thousand other tasks that men perform.

Before women can enjoy equality of wages with men, they must be able and willing to do their share of the work now done exclusively by men. How would the suffragettes like to shoulder shovels, axes and sledges, to do their part of toil in the mines, forests and foundries? Are they willing to become pumpkin rollers on the farm and endure sunburned noses and a mussy appearance for the sake of producing their share of the food supply?

Does any one imagine that the "eternal feminine" would be changed by any hocus-pocus at the ballot box? Would an enfranchised woman be less likely to look under the bed for a burglar, or be less skittish in the dark without a male escort than she was before being initiated into politics?

With female suffrage in vogue, the vote of the most profound scholar could be annulled by the ballot of a giggling damsel whose head might be composed mostly of false hair. In reply, it can be said with truth that male dunces are doing the same thing now at every election. But as two wrongs never right each other, the use of female ignorance as an antidote for male ignorance would be like eating more green apples to cure the colic.

Luckily, only a small and strenuous minority of women have political bees buzzing in their bonnets, and the intrepid men of California will risk being stung to save these ladies from themselves. After the first wild burst of grief is over, the suffragettes can find consolation in the thought that they have escaped the necessity of revealing in the election registers how long they have been on earth.

Cheer up, girls (spinsters and great-grandmothers included), in the next incarnation you may be men and get all that is coming to you. Meantime, you can do business at the old stand and rule the rulers with your smiles and tears.

Leroy Cummings

870 Logan avenue.

4. IWW Editor Mortimer Downing Reports on the Wheatland Riot, 1913

Bloody Wheatland is glorious in this, that it united the American Federation of Labor, the Socialist Party and the I.W.W. in one solid army of workers to fight for the right to strike.

Against the workers are lined up the attorney general of the state of California, the Burns Agency, the Hop Growers' Association, the ranch-owners of California, big and little business and the district attorney of Yuba County, Edward B. Stanwood. For the army of Burns men, engaged in this effort to hang some of the workers, somebody must have paid as much as $100,000. The workers have not yet gathered $2,000 to defend their right to strike.

Follow this little story and reason for yourself, workers, if your very right to strike is not here involved.

By widespread lying advertisements Durst Brothers assembled twenty-three hundred men, women and children to pick their hops last summer. A picnic was promised the workers.

They got:

Hovels worse than pig sties to sleep in for which they were charged seventy-five cents per week, or between $2,700 and $3,000 for the season.

Eight toilets were all that was provided in the way of sanitary arrangements.

Water was prohibited in the hop fields, where the thermometer was taken by the State Health Inspector and found to be more than 120 degrees. Water was not allowed because Durst Brothers had farmed out the lemonade privilege to their cousin, Jim Durst, who offered the thirsting pickers acetic acid and water at five cents a glass.

Durst Brothers had a store on the camp, and would not permit other dealers to bring anything into the camp.

Wages averaged scarcely over $1 per day.

Rebellion occurred against these conditions. Men have been tortured, women harassed, imprisoned and threats of death have been the portion of those who protested.

When the protest was brewing, mark this: Ralph Durst asked the workers to assemble and form their demands. He appointed a meeting place with the workers. They took him at his word. Peaceably and orderly they decided upon their demands. Durst filled their camp with spies. Durst went through the town of Wheatland and the surrounding country gathering every rifle, shot gun and pistol. Was he conspiring against the workers? The attorney general and the other law officers say he was only taking natural precautions.

When the committee which Ralph Durst had personally invited to come to him with the demands of the workers arrived, Durst struck the chairman, Dick Ford, in the face. He then ordered Dick Ford off his ground. Dick Ford had already paid $2.75 as rental for his shack. Durst claims this discharge of Ford broke the strike.

This was on Bloody Sunday, August 3, 1913, about two o'clock in the afternoon.

Ford begged his fellow committeemen to say nothing about Durst's striking him.

At 5:30 that Sunday afternoon the workers were assembled in meeting on ground rented from Durst. Dick Ford, speaking as the chairman of the meeting reached down and took from a mother an infant, saying, "It is not so much for ourselves we are fighting as that this little baby may never see the conditions which now exist on this ranch." He put the baby back into its mother's arms as he saw eleven armed men, in two automobiles, tearing down toward the meeting place. The workers then began a song. Into this meeting, where the grandsire, the husband, the youth and the babies were gathered in an effort to gain something like living conditions these armed men charged. Sheriff George Voss has sworn, "When I arrived that meeting was orderly and peaceful." The crowd opened to let him and his followers enter. Then one of his deputies, Lee Anderson, struck Dick Ford with a club, knocking him from his stand. Anderson also fired a shot. Another deputy, Henry Dakin, fired a shot gun. Remember, this crowd was a dense mass of men, women and children, some of them babies at the breast. Panic struck the mass. Dakin began to volley with his automatic shot gun. There was a surge around the speaker's stand. Voss went down. From his tent charged an unidentified Puerto Rican. He thrust himself into the mass, clubbed some of the officers, got a gun, cleared a space for himself and fell dead before a load of buckshot from Henry Dakin's gun.

Thirty seconds or so the firing lasted. When the smoke cleared, Dakin and Durst and others of these bullies had fled like jack rabbits. Four men lay dead upon the ground. Among them, District Attorney Edward T. Manwell, a deputy named Eugene Reardon, the Puerto Rican and an unidentified English lad. About a score were wounded, among them women.

Charges of murder, indiscriminative, have been placed for the killing of Manwell and Reardon. This Puerto Rican and the English boy sleep in their bloody graves and the law takes no account—they were only workers.

Such are the facts of Wheatland's bloody Sunday. Now comes the district attorney of Yuba County, the attorney general of the state of California and all the legal machinery and cry that these workers, assembled in meeting with their women and children, had entered into a conspiracy to murder Manwell and Reardon. They say had no strike occurred there would have been no killing. They say had Dick Ford, when assaulted and discharged by Durst, "quietly left the ranch, the strike would have been broken." What matters to these the horrors of thirst, the indecent and immodest conditions? The workers are guilty. They struck and it became necessary to disperse them. Therefore, although they, the workers were unarmed and hampered with their women and children, because a set of drunken deputies, who even had whiskey in their pockets on the field, fired upon them, the workers must pay a dole to the gallows. . . .

5. The Ku Klux Klan Marches in Oregon, c. 1921

The Ku Klux Klan, prominent in 1921, all but disappeared by 1926.

6. Julia Morgan Furnishes Hearst's Castle at San Simeon, 1921

. . . So far we have received from him [William Randolph Hearst], to incorporate in the new buildings, some twelve or thirteen carloads of antiques, brought from the ends of the earth and from prehistoric down to late Empire in period, the majority, however, being of Spanish origin.

They comprise vast quantities of tables, beds, armoires, secretaries, all kinds of cabinets, polychrome church statuary, columns, door frames, carved doors in all stages of repair and disrepair, over-altars, reliquaries, lanterns, iron-grille doors, window grilles, votive candlesticks, all kinds of chairs in quantity, and six or seven well heads.

I don't see myself where we are ever going to use half suitably, but I find the idea is to try things out and if they are not satisfactory, discard them for the next thing that promises better. There is interest and charm coming gradually into play. . . .

7. *Aimee Semple McPherson Describes Her Background to a Los Angeles Jury, 1926*

I want to say that if character counts a little, that I want you to look back: my mother gave me to God before I was born; my earliest training had been in Bible and religious work; I lined up the chairs and preached to them as early as five years of age, and gave my testimony; I was converted at seventeen, married an evangelist, preached the gospel in my humble way at home and then sailed for China, never expecting to come back to this land, but willing to give my life for Jesus. They buried my precious husband there. I came back with my little baby in my arms, born a month after her father died. I took up the Lord's work as soon as I was able to go on.

I had no great denominations back of me, but I began very humbly. Until this crushing thing that none of us can explain why even God would permit [her kidnapping], although we cannot question that—it would be wrong to do that—I was on the pinnacle of success so far as my work for God was concerned, but I have not always been there. I began preaching to farmers, ranchers, under the trees to farmers in their blue overalls sitting on the grass and using the piazza as a mourner's bench. But from there, with the sixty dollars that came in the collection, I bought a little tent, a poor little tent very full of holes, and from that I saved my money and bought a bigger one, and that has been the history. I drove my own stakes, patched the tent and tied the guy ropes almost like a man; and then came the times when we began to get bigger buildings and theaters and buildings costing sometimes as much as a hundred dollars a day, in buildings where I have preached to as many as sixteen thousand in a day.

Then came the building of Angelus Temple. I came here to a neighborhood that had no special buildings in it, got a piece of land and hired horses and scrapers and bossed the men myself and went out to build the foundation with my little capital. I told people my dream to preach the gospel as God had given it to me, and they came to help me, not here, but from other cities, through the *Bridal Call*, my little magazine. I have never put my money in oil wells or ranches or even clothes or luxuries. My great thought has always been—and this can be absolutely proved—for the service of the Lord and my dear people. . . .

Naturally, I have preached a gospel which made some enmity: I have gone unmercifully after the dope ring, gambling, liquor, tobacco, dancing, and made the statement that I would rather see my children dead than in a public dance hall. I have perhaps laid myself open in these lines about evils in the schools, et cetera; but in everything, I have tried to live as a lady and a Christian.

Perhaps you are skeptical. I don't blame anyone who should doubt my story, because it does sound absurd. But it did happen, ladies and gentlemen. I would not work with one hand seventeen years, and, just as I saw my dearest dream coming true, sweep it over! . . .

8. *Aurvilla Green Supports Women in Business, 1929*

. . . [W]ithin the last twenty years woman has made herself absolutely indispensable to business; and not only in minor positions, because some of the biggest positions in the country are today being held by women.

I believe we can attribute the success of Women in Business to the development of a high average level of education, of culture and well-being. Poise is the business woman's greatest asset. Calm, rest, quiet, repose, balance—*poise.* Cultivate and make use of this valuable asset. It gives you power, relieves tension, spares your nerves, strengthens your personality. . . .

The privilege of being able to follow one's own inclinations is a very recent one for women. The opportunities have been so limited, and much of the training so poor, that it was too often a case of doing anything one could get to do—

and liking it if one could. Fortunately that is passing. Women have proved that they can do almost any work well.

. . . [I]n brief, the requirements of a successful business woman are: complete training for vocation chosen; able to meet, interview, and handle tactfully and diplomatically visitors, patients, or customers as the case may be; . . . must be willing to study the particular need and temperament of her supervising executive; and be able to adapt herself loyally to his requirements, both business and personal; must have a pleasing appearance and personality, be cheerful, unobtrusive, willing and close-mouthed, must have good health and keep reliable attendance.

Success is doing all we can do, not just doing better than someone else.

References

1. Edward Francis Adams Argues Against the Initiative, Referendum, and Recall, 1911
   "Direct Legislation," *Transactions of the Commonwealth Club of California,* Vol. 6 (September 1911): 286–296, quoted in Leonard Pitt, *California Controversies: Major Issues in the History of the State* (Arlington Heights, Ill.: Harlan Davidson, 1987), p. 97.
2. Women Demand Pay Equality, 1910
   Photograph courtesy of the San Diego Historical Society Research Archives, Ticor Collection.
3. Leroy Cummings Believes Women Have No Need to Vote, 1911
   "Why These Suffragettes?" *San Diego Union,* September 8, 1911.
4. IWW Editor Mortimer Downing Reports on the Wheatland Riot, 1913
   Solidarity, January 3, 1914, quoted in Joyce L. Kornbluh, ed., *Rebel Voices: An I.W.W. Anthology* (Ann Arbor: University of Michigan Press, 1964).
5. The Ku Klux Klan Marches in Oregon, c. 1921
   Photograph courtesy of the Oregon Historical Society, Portland.
6. Julia Morgan Furnishes Hearst's Castle at San Simeon, 1921
   Quoted in William Randolph Hearst, Jr., with Jack Casserly, *The Hearsts: Father and Son* (New York: Roberts Rinehart Publishers, 1991), p. 75.
7. Aimee Semple McPherson Describes Her Background to a Los Angeles Jury, 1926
   Lately Thomas, *The Vanishing Evangelist: The Aimee Semple McPherson Kidnapping Affair* (New York: Viking Press, 1959), pp. 130–131.
8. Aurvilla Green Supports Women in Business, 1929
   Susan M. Stacy, *Legacy of Light: A History of Idaho Power Company* (Boise: Idaho Power Company, 1991), p. 90.

Document Set 11

Depression and the New Deal, 1930–1940

It took some time before California and the West felt the full effects of the October 1929 stock market crash. As the crisis took its toll, migratory farm workers remained unorganized, city workers competed for a limited number of jobs, and newcomers pouring in from the Midwest found little work and abundant prejudice. The administration of President Herbert Hoover floundered. Democratic presidential candidate Franklin Roosevelt campaigned throughout the West in 1932 promising a "New Deal" that would halt the downward economic spiral and put the nation back on its feet.

By the mid-1930s federal relief projects such as the Civilian Conservation Corps (CCC) and National Youth Administration (NYA) employed young men to work in forests and parks. The Works Progress Administration (WPA) directed a broad range of activities, and the Public Work Administration (PWA) provided jobs for men in construction. Water and power projects from the state of Washington to the Mexican border took thousands off bread lines and yielded a tremendous amount of water and hydroelectric power for future development in the West. The states themselves also launched projects to combat the depression's effects. By the end of the decade, the outbreak of World War II in Europe created a demand for war-related materials. Economic problems in the West gave way to a new set of tensions as westerners concerned themselves with providing housing and an adequate labor supply and managing the shipment of raw materials to coastal ports.

During the early 1930s Diego Rivera, one of Mexico's foremost muralists, worked in San Francisco, where he introduced the themes of twentieth-century industry with a focus on the laborer. His mural shown in Document 1 represents California with its three bases of wealth—gold, petroleum, and fruits—and stresses rail and marine transportation with its motifs of energy and speed. A radical and controversial figure in Mexico, the warm and jovial Rivera, accompanied by his talented wife Frida Kahlo, also an artist, won over the local populace.

Although federal projects such as the Grand Coulee and Bonneville dams in Washington and Oregon employed numerous workers during the depression, conditions for migrants in the Yakima Valley (Document 2) remained difficult because large numbers of apple and hop pickers were needed only for short periods of time. Disease raced through the crowded camps, and other problems, such as a lack of sanitary facilities, poor food, and scarcity of clean drinking water, plagued the workers during the height of the season. Employers kept a strict watch to guard against labor uprisings.

In California two plans to boost the depressed economy gained prominence in the mid-1930s. Dr. Francis E. Townsend, a Long Beach physician, proposed a pension plan for senior citizens (Document 3) and started a weekly newspaper to unite that group for the first time. The second plan was suggested by controversial muckraker Upton Sinclair, author of *The Jungle* (1906), an exposé of the Chicago meat-packing industry. Sinclair, who ran for governor of California in 1926, 1930, and 1934 as the Socialist candidate, failed to gain the Democratic nomination. He also outlined ideas for his EPIC (End Poverty in California) crusade in a pamphlet (Document 4) published before the election. After Sinclair lost to Republican governor Frank Merriam by just 259,063 votes, many people continued to support his philosophy.

San Diegans brightened the gloomy days of the Great Depression by holding a world's fair in Balboa Park in 1935. Well-known politicians and other celebrities visited the area (Document 5). The Old Globe Theater, brought in from the Chicago Century of Progress Exposition of the previous year, especially caught the crowd's attention. Critics warned that five or six abridged Shakespearean plays given daily would bore visitors, but the performances almost always sold out. San Diego preserved the Old Globe and kept it open until World War II. It reopened after the war.

Congressman Phil Swing from San Diego and Senator (and former governor) Hiram Johnson had introduced the Swing-Johnson bill in 1928 to permit construction of the federal Boulder Canyon Project on the Colorado River. Work on the Hoover and Parker dams, completed on March 1, 1936, provided jobs for hundreds of workers in southern California, Arizona, and Nevada. The Hoover Dam, the highest in the world at that time (Document 6), held a record capacity of more than 30 million acre-feet of water and harnessed enough power to meet the estimated needs of the still-growing state of California far into the future.

Despite recovery programs and job opportunities, some immigrant groups still fared badly in depression-era California. Filipinos, struggling to adjust to hard times and to save money, often worked for very low wages around Salinas and in the San Joaquin Delta area. Subjected to prejudice and disappointment (Document 7), many looked forward to making enough money to return to their homeland. Others adapted well and joined the mainstream of American culture.

Although foreigners faced prejudice because of their skin color and unfamiliarity with English, many families who migrated westward from the Midwest received equally poor treatment. Called Okies or Arkies (though they may have hailed from Kansas, Texas, or Tennessee), these newcomers were despised for their poverty and unemployment. John Steinbeck (Document 8), in his Pulitzer Prize–winning fictional best-seller *The Grapes of Wrath* (1939), interpreted why Californians lacked sympathy for the midwesterners' plight. Jobs finally became available with the advent of World War II.

Questions for Analysis

1. What do you think of Diego Rivera's interpretation of California history?
2. How could the migratory farm labor problem be solved? Does the problem still exist?
3. What was wrong with Dr. Townsend's and Upton Sinclair's plans to end poverty?
4. Why are fairs so appealing to the public? What results can be attributed to fairs?
5. How did dams in the United States compare with those in foreign countries prior to the 1940s?
6. Why were Americans prejudiced against the Filipinos?
7. Why were people in the West prejudiced against the Okies and Arkies?

1. Diego Rivera Portrays California, 1931

The heroic figure of California, the mother, gives gold, fruit, and grain. Man's will and spirit transform the raw materials into goods for a better future.

2. Workers in the Yakima Valley Struggle, 1934

. . . In Yakima for a few weeks in September, 33,000 workers are needed in the hop fields; and in October about 12,000 are required in the apple orchards. Since both major crops are highly commercialized and keenly sensitive to market conditions, growers want to crowd the maximum amount of work out of employees in the briefest period of time. There is, therefore, really no norm for the number of workers who, during a period of a few weeks, can find some employment. Both crops, moreover, attract a different type of labour: large migrant families for hops; smaller resident families for apples. Agricultural labour has its own hierarchy and hop picking is universally regarded as about the lowest form of field labour. Nearly three-fourths of the hop pickers are non-agricultural workers by vocation; the apple knockers, on the contrary, are usually professional migratory workers. Fruit pickers, also, generally come from a greater distance than hop pickers.

Workers are recruited in Yakima by various means: by advertisements; by placards put up in gas stations, tourist camps, and posted on the highways; and, in former years, by "labour bosses" paid 50 cents a head to bring workers into the valley. Nowadays, since the influx of migrants, most of the labour is of the "drive-in" variety; it appears at the gate and seeks employment. The apple knockers and hop pickers travel to Yakima by all sorts of conveyances: 75.1 per cent by automobile (five or more to a car); 15.4 per cent by riding the freights; 7.9 per cent by hitch-hiking; and 5.2 per cent—the élite—by rail or bus as paid passengers. Single men ride the freights; families travel by car. "The car," writes Dr. Landis, "is petted and the family denies itself necessities of life that it may be kept in running condition." Most of the cars are old-model sedans—ten and twelve years old in need of constant repairs; but of late trucks and trailers have come into more general use. According to Dr. Carl F. Reuss, the average distance travelled in a year by these migrants is 1,226 miles. Allowing 2 1/4 cents per mile as a minimum cash cost for car operation, he concluded that families were spending 11 per cent of their annual cash income for travelling expenses.

Migrants are not encouraged to remain in Yakima once the season is over. Law-enforcement officials raid the camps, round up the migrants, and "encourage" the stragglers to be on their way. During the summer, one clerk in the welfare office is kept busy preparing notices to be served on the families who during the season have applied for assistance. Once the apples and hops are picked, the notices are served. Reciting the provisions of the Pauper Act, the notice "warns" the migrant "to get out" and advises him that no relief will be granted if he stays. Despite these precautions, many workers, failing to make their expenses in the summer, are compelled to wait around until spring before they can leave. Of the transient families studied by Dr. Reuss, 54 per cent reported that they had received relief during the year. "It is extremely significant," comments Dr. Reuss, "that such a high proportion of persons deriving private employment solely from farm labour were aided by relief funds. The relief programme in Yakima County in effect becomes a subsidy to agriculture, raising the less than living wages paid farm labourers to a minimum subsistence level." . . .

The living conditions of migratory workers in the Yakima Valley have long been regarded as about the worst to be found in the entire West. One of the four richest agricultural counties in the United States, Yakima has had one of the highest typhoid-fever rates of any county in America. It is not uncommon to see mountain streams in the valley, crystal clear above a hop pickers' camp, muddy with filth and debris for miles downstream. Other areas in the North-west have long provided private labour camps; but Yakima has had the reputation of not providing camps. Camps near the orchards, according to the growers, would provide workers with too good an opportunity to steal fruit. It would require too much space to describe the existing camps; full descriptions, with photographs, can be found in a study made by Dr. Marion Hathway in 1934 and in a later study by Dr. Landis.

3. Dr. Francis E. Townsend Gives Hope to Senior Citizens, 1933

If the human race is not to retrogress, two facts of essential importance must be recognized; the stimulus to individual effort must be maintained by the certainty of adequate monetary reward.

If business is good at all times, we need not worry about the reward of individual effort; and if money is plentiful we need have no fears that business will become bad.

Of late years it has become an accepted fact that because of man's inventiveness less and less productive effort is going to be required to supply the needs of the race. This being the case, it is just as necessary to make some disposal of our surplus workers, as it is to dispose of our surplus wheat or corn or cotton. But we cannot kill off the surplus workers as we are doing with our hogs; nor sell them to the Chinese on time as we do our cotton. We must retire them from business activities and eliminate them from the field of competitive effort.

What class should we eliminate, and how should it be done: Wars have served in the past to hold down surplus population, but the last big war, in spite of the unprecedented slaughter, served only to increase production, while reducing the number of consumers.

It is estimated that the population of the age of 60 and above in the United States is somewhere between nine and twelve millions. I suggest that the national government retire all who reach that age on a monthly pension of $200 a month or more, on condition that they spend the money as they get it. This will insure an even distribution throughout the nation of two or three billions of fresh money each month. Thereby assuring a healthy and brisk state of business, comparable to that we enjoyed during war times.

"Where is the money to come from? More taxes?" Certainly. We have nothing in this world we do not pay taxes to enjoy. But do not overlook the fact that we are already paying a large proportion of the amount required for these pensions in the form of life insurance policies, poor farms, aid societies, insane asylums and prisons. The inmates of the last two mentioned institutions would undoubtedly be greatly lessened when it once became assured that old age meant security from want and care. A sales tax sufficiently high to insure the pensions at a figure adequate to maintain the business of the country in a healthy condition would be the easiest tax in the world to collect, for all would realize that the tax was a provision for their own future, as well as the assurance of good business now.

Would not a sales tax of sufficient size to maintain a pension system of such magnitude exhaust our taxability from our sources?, I am asked. By no means—income and inheritance taxes would still remain to us, and would prove far more fertile sources of Government income than they are today. Property taxes could be greatly reduced and would not constitute a penalty upon industry and enterprise.

Our attitude toward Government is wrong. We look upon Government as something entirely foreign to ourselves; as something over which we have no control, and which we cannot expect to do us a great deal of good. We do not realize that it can do us infinite harm, except when we pay our taxes. But the fact is, we must learn to expect and demand that the central Government assume the duty of regulating business activity. When business begins to slow down and capital shows signs of timidity, stimulus must be provided by the National Government in the form of additional capital. When times are good and begin to show signs of a speculative debauch such as we saw in 1929, the brakes must be applied through a reduction of the circulation medium. This function of the Government could be easily established and maintained through the pension system for the aged. . . .

4. Upton Sinclair Plans to End Poverty in California, 1934

. . . The Legislature will create a public body to establish and conduct land colonies. The act will be known as the California Land Colonies Act, and the body will be the California Authority for Land (the CAL). It will be empowered to exercise the right of eminent domain and condemn land required for colony purposes. It will be authorized to take over all land which has been sold or may in future be sold for taxes, whether by cities or by counties, and to retain this land and put it to use. It will be authorized to bid for land sold under foreclosure proceedings. It will establish colonies, erect buildings, conduct all business operations, and make regulations for the governing of the colonies. It will be authorized to open stores for its members, and conduct a merchandising business.

The same principles apply to the acquiring of factories and production plants. This act will be the California Production Act, and the public body the California Authority for Production (the CAP). This body will be authorized to acquire factories by condemnation proceedings, to purchase those sold at foreclosure sales, and put these plants to productive use; to purchase raw materials and sell the finished products; to erect buildings, and make regulations for the governing of the factories; to open stores for its members and conduct a merchandising business.

The act for the financing of these undertakings will be known as the California Money Act, and the public body will be the California Authority for Money (the CAM): the three agencies for the realizing of EPIC [End Poverty in California] thus being the CAL, the CAP, and the CAM.

The CAM will be authorized to issue scrip for the purposes of both CAL and CAP. These bodies will pay scrip for services rendered, and for goods purchased from one another, and for the handling and distributing of goods. The CAM will also be authorized to issue bonds to the amount of three hundred million dollars to finance the operations of CAL and CAP. These bonds will be sold directly to the people without commissions to any bankers, and CAM will establish an educational department for the purpose of explaining the value and importance of the bonds to the public. The issues will be of denominations of from ten dollars to one thousand, and of two kinds, long term bonds and those redeemable upon thirty days' notice. The latter will constitute in effect a state savings bank.

The remainder of the legislative program of EPIC is as follows:

An act of the Legislature repealing the present sales tax, and substituting a tax on stock transfers at 4 cents per share.

An act of the Legislature providing for a State income tax, beginning with incomes of $5000 and steeply graduated until incomes of $50,000 pay 30% tax.

An increase in the State inheritance tax, steeply graduated and applying to all properties in the State regardless of where the owner may reside. This law will take for the State 50% of all money above $50,000 bequeathed *to* an individual and 50% of all money above $250,000 bequeathed *by* an individual.

A law increasing taxes on privately owned public utility corporations and banks.

A constitutional amendment revising the tax code of the State and providing that cities and counties shall exempt from taxation all homes occupied by the owners, and ranches cultivated by the owners, when the assessed value of such homes and ranches is less than $3000. Assessments between $3000 and $5000 will pay a normal tax, as at present, and above $5000 there will be an increase of one-half of one per cent for each $5000 of additional assessed valuation. Similar provisions will be made for graduated taxes upon all other real property.

A constitutional amendment providing for a graduated land tax upon all unimproved building land and all agricultural land which is not under cultivation. The enabling act providing for this tax will contain exact and careful provisions to avoid evasion. The law will specify what constitutes cultivation, and will provide that crops must not merely be planted but must be harvested and used or sold. Improvements must bear a certain relation to the assessed valuation of the building sites. A valuable city lot will not be considered to be improved because a shack is hurriedly erected upon it, nor will thousands of acres of land be kept out of productive use because a million-dollar palace occupies a small part. Individual holdings assessed at less than $1000 will be exempted.

A law providing for the payment of a pension of $50 per month to every person over sixty years of age who is in need, and who has lived in the State of California three years prior to the date of the coming into effect of the law.

A law providing for the payment of $50 per month to all needy persons who are blind, or who by medical examination are proved to be physically unable to earn a living; these persons also having been residents of the State for three years.

A pension of $50 per month to all widowed women who have dependent children; if the children are more than two in number, the pension to be increased by $25 per month for each additional child. These to have been residents for three years. . . .

5. President Franklin D. Roosevelt Tops the List of Visitors to the San Diego World's Fair, 1935

The name of the President of the United States today stood at the top of a list of visitors to the California Pacific International Exposition that reads like a "who's who" of the world.

With less than 35 days of the Exposition season left, leaders of scores of foreign nations, foremost representatives of every profession and trade in the United States, statesmen, and craftsmen already have visited 1935's biggest show.

After the nation's chief executive and that of the First Lady, there stood the names of the only living ex-president, Herbert Hoover; a former ruler of Mexico, Plutarco Elias Calles; and the commander-in-chief of the United States navy, Adm. Joseph Mason Reeves.

Newsmakers, too, there were in numbers. Gen. Hugh S. Johnson, No. 1 new dealer and administration "stormy petrel," was among them. Dr. F. E. Townsend, who has been in the nation's news more in the last two years than almost any other one person. Aimee Semple McPherson, evangelist, who held the nation's headlines for almost four years.

Jack Dempsey represented the "tops" in fisticuffs. From the movies came Mae West, Edward G. Robinson, Gloria Swanson, Jean Harlow, Joe Penner, complete with duck; Joe E. Brown and many another favorites of the galloping celluloids.

Death of Will Rogers and his famous flying companion, Wiley Post, sent the Exposition into mourning, for the revered Rogers had shortly before completed arrangements to appear at the world's fair on crippled children's day, to entertain the shut-ins.

Congressmen, army, and navy leaders. Edsel Ford and other giants of industry and transportation, Dr. C. H. Mayo and many other expert physicians and surgeons, lawyers, Amelia Earhart, and fliers whose names are household words throughout the world. Mme. Ernestine Schumann-Heink and singers of national note—from every walk of life came the hundreds of famous visitors to the giant Exposition.

Approximately one-third of the 3,730,198 persons who have visited the California Pacific International Exposition here to date are from states east of the Rocky mountains, according to an exhaustive study made of attendance completed today by Tom Thienes, manager of the central coast counties' exhibit in the California State building.

6. Hoover (Boulder) Dam, Completed on March 1, 1936, Holds the Most Water

Hoover (Boulder) Dam Compared with Other Great Dams[a]

Dam	*Location*	*Cost*	*Year Completed*	*Maximum Height (feet)*	*Crest Length (feet)*	*Volume (cubic yards)*	*Reservoir capacity (acre-feet)*[b]
Hoover (Boulder)	Arizona-Nevada	$ 70,600,000	1936	727	1,282	3,250,335	30,500,000
Shasta	California	. . . .	. . . .	560	3,400	5,610,000	4,500,000
Grand Coulee	Washington	118,600,000	. . . .	550	4,200	10,500,000	9,640,000
Hetch Hetchy	California	10,000,000	1938	427	. . . .	. . . . . .	359,000
Owyhee	Oregon	5,672,000	1932	417	833	556,471	1,120,000
Sautet Drac	French Alps	. . . .	1936	414	. . . .	. . . .	106,000
San Gabriel	California	15,746,251	. . . .	381	. . . .	. . . .	. . . .
Arrowrock	Idaho	4,928,000	1915	354	1,100	602,200	286,500
Shoshone	Wyoming	1,439,000	1910	328	200	78,576	445,700
Esla	Zamora, Spain	12,000,000	. . . .	328	. . . .	. . . .	810,800
Parker	Arizona-California	8,805,000	. . . .	322	800	268,000	720,000
Elephant Butte	New Mexico	4,538,000	1916	306	1,162	605,200	2 ,637,700
Horse Mesa	Arizona	2,873,000	1927	305	784	147,357	244,900
Jandula	Andujar, Spain	5,000,000	1930	295	. . . .	. . . .	364,900
Friant	California	15,000,000	. . . .	290	3,330	1,600,000	400,000
Roosevelt	Arizona	3,806,000	1911	284	1,125	242,970	1,420,000
Bartlett	Arizona	4,472,000	. . . .	270	950	162,825	200,000
Norris	Tennessee	13,800,000	1936	265	. . . .	. . . .	3,401,500
Marshall Ford	Texas	17,700,000	. . . .	265	2,325	. . . .	3,068,900
Seminoe	Wyoming	4,360,000	. . . .	265	560	161,000	1,000,000
Barberine	Switzerland	20,000,000	1921	259	. . . .	. . . .	254,100
Coolidge	Arizona	4,500,000	1928	249	. . . .	. . . .	1,200,000
Fort Peck	Montana	86,000,000	. . . .	242	20,000	100,000,000[b]	20,000,000
Tygart River	West Virginia	15,700,000	. . . .	232	. . . .	. . . .	327,100
Dnieprostroy	Russia	110,000,000	1932	200	. . . .	. . . .	895,500
Hartebeestpoort	South Africa	8,000,000	1923	193	. . . .	. . . .	1,258,200
Lloyd Barrage	British India	73,730,000	1928–32	190	. . . .	. . . .	. . . .
Marathon	Greece	2,200,000	1929	177	. . . .	. . . .	33,100
Bonneville	Oregon-Washington	51,000,000	1938	170	1,090	1,000,000	480,000
Assuan	Egypt	29,000,000	1912	144	. . . .	. . . .	4,060,000
Sennar	Sudan	43,000,000	1928	128	. . . .	. . . .	429,700
Krishnaraja	British India	13,000,000	. . . .	124	. . . .	. . . .	138,100
Imperial	Arizona-California	7,551,800	. . . .	45	3,430	2,191,800	85,000
Laguna	Arizona-California	1,921,492	1909	40	4,844	451,000	. . . .

[a]Bureau of Reclamation, *Dams and Control Works* (1938), pp. 1, 7, 20, 28, 31, 44–46, 49, 57, 85–86, 137, 258–60.
[b]One acre-foot is the amount of water needed to cover one acre of land one foot deep; about 325,900 gallons.

7. *A Filipino Immigrant Decries Prejudice, 1937*

. . . Western people are brought up to regard Orientals or colored people as inferior, but the mockery of it all is that Filipinos are taught to regard Americans as our equals. Adhering to American ideals, living American life, these are contributory to our feeling of equality. The terrible truth in America shatters the Filipino's dream of fraternity.

I was completely disillusioned when I came to know this American attitude. If I had not been born in a lyrical world, grown up with honest people and studied about American institutions and racial equality in the Philippines I should never have minded so much the horrible impact of white chauvinism. I shall never forget what I have suffered in this country because of racial prejudice. . . .

8. *John Steinbeck Writes About the Okies in* The Grapes of Wrath, *1939*

. . . And then the dispossessed were drawn west—from Kansas, Oklahoma, Texas, New Mexico; from Nevada and Arkansas families, tribes, dusted out, tractored out. Carloads, caravans, homeless and hungry; twenty thousand and fifty thousand and a hundred thousand and two hundred thousand. They streamed over the mountains, hungry and restless—restless as ants, scurrying to find work to do—to lift, to push, to pull, to pick, to cut—anything, any burden to bear, for food. The kids are hungry. We got no place to live. Like ants scurrying for work, for food, and most of all for land.

We ain't foreign. Seven generations back Americans, and beyond that Irish, Scotch, English, German. One of our folks in the Revolution, an' they was lots of our folks in the Civil War—both sides. Americans.

They were hungry, and they were fierce. And they had hoped to find a home, and they found only hatred. Okies—the owners hated them because the owners knew they were soft and the Okies strong, that they were fed and the Okies hungry; and perhaps the owners had heard from their grandfathers how easy it is to steal land from a soft man if you are fierce and hungry and armed. The owners hated them. And in the towns, the storekeepers hated them because they had no money to spend. There is no shorter path to a storekeeper's contempt, and all his admirations are exactly opposite. The town men, little bankers, hated Okies because there was nothing to gain from them. They had nothing. And the laboring people hated Okies because a hungry man must work, and if he must work, if he has to work, the wage payer automatically gives him less for his work; and then no one can get more.

And the dispossessed, the migrants, flowed into California, two hundred and fifty thousand, and three hundred thousand. Behind them new tractors were going on the land and the tenants were being forced off. And new waves were on the way, new waves of the dispossessed and the homeless, hardened, intent, and dangerous.

And while the Californians wanted many things, accumulation, social success, amusement, luxury, and a curious banking security, the new barbarians wanted only two things—land and food; and to them the two were one. And whereas the wants of the Californians were nebulous and undefined, the wants of the Okies were beside the roads, lying there to be seen and coveted: the good fields with water to be dug for, the good green fields, earth to crumble experimentally in the hand, grass to smell, oaten stalks to chew until the sharp sweetness was in the throat. A man might look at a fallow field and know, and see in his mind that his own bending back and his own straining arms would bring the cabbages into the light, and the golden eating corn, the turnips and carrots.

And a homeless hungry man, driving the roads with his wife beside him and his thin children in the back seat, could look at the fallow fields which might produce food but not profit, and that man could know how a fallow field is a sin and the unused land a crime against the thin children. And such a man drove along the roads and knew temptation at every field, and knew the lust to take these fields and make them grow strength for his children and a little comfort for his wife. The temptation was before him always. The fields goaded him, and the company ditches with good water flowing were a goad to him.

And in the south he saw the golden oranges hanging on the trees, the little golden oranges on the dark green trees; and guards with shotguns patrolling the lines so a man might not pick an orange for a thin child, oranges to be dumped if the price was low.

He drove his old car into a town. He scoured the farms for work. Where can we sleep the night?

Well, there's Hooverville on the edge of the river. There's a whole raft of Okies there.

He drove his old car to Hooverville. He never asked again, for there was a Hooverville on the edge of every town.

The rag town lay close to water; and the houses were tents, and weed-thatched enclosures, paper houses, a great junk pile. The man drove his family in and became a citizen of Hooverville—always they were called Hooverville. The man put up his own tent as near to water as he could get; or if he had no tent, he went to the city dump and brought back cartons and built a house of corrugated paper. And when the rains came the house melted and washed away. He settled in Hooverville and he scoured the countryside for work, and the little money he had went for gasoline to look for work. In the evening the men gathered and talked together. Squatting on their hams they talked of the land they had seen.

There's thirty thousan' acres, out west of here. Layin' there. Jesus, what I could do with that, with five acres of that! Why, hell, I'd have ever'thing to eat.

Notice one thing? They ain't no vegetables nor chickens nor pigs at the farms. They raise one thing—cotton, say, or peaches, or lettuce? 'Nother place'll be all chickens. They buy the stuff they could raise in the dooryard.

Jesus, what I could do with a couple pigs!

Well, it ain't yourn, and it ain't gonna be yourn.

What we gonna do? The kids can't grow up this way.

In the camps the word would come whispering, There's work at Shafter. And the cars would be loaded in the night, the highways crowded—a gold rush for work. At Shafter the people would pile up, five times too many to do the work. A gold rush for work. They stole away in the night, frantic for work. And along the roads lay the temptations, the fields that could bear food.

That's owned. That ain't our'n. . . .

References

1. Diego Rivera Portrays California, 1931
   Laurance P. Hurlburt, *The Mexican Muralists in the United States* (Albuquerque: University of New Mexico Press, 1989), pp. 107–108.
2. Workers in the Yakima Valley Struggle, 1934
   Carey McWilliams, *Ill Fares the Land: Migrants and Migratory Labour in the United States* (London: Faber and Faber Limited, 1945), pp. 57–59.
3. Dr. Francis E. Townsend Gives Hope to Senior Citizens, 1933
   Dr. Francis E. Townsend, *New Horizons (An Autobiography)*, Jesse George Murray, ed. (Chicago: J. L. Stewart Publishing Company, 1943), pp. 137–140.

4. Upton Sinclair Plans to End Poverty in California, 1934
   Upton Sinclair, *The EPIC Plan for California* (Los Angeles, 1934), pp. 21–23.
5. President Franklin D. Roosevelt Tops the List of Visitors to the San Diego World's Fair, 1935
   San Diego Herald, October 10, 1935, 3:1–2.
6. Hoover (Boulder) Dam, Completed on March 1, 1936, Holds the Most Water
   Compiled from Bureau of Reclamation, *Dams and Control Works* (1938), by Paul L. Kleinsorge, *The Boulder Canyon Project: Historical and Economic Aspects* (Stanford: Stanford University Press, 1941), table 12, p. 228.
7. A Filipino Immigrant Decries Prejudice, 1937
   H. Brett Melendy quoting Carlos Bulosan in "Filipinos in the United States," *Pacific Historical Review* (November 1974): 537–538.
8. John Steinbeck Writes About the Okies in *The Grapes of Wrath*, 1939
   John Steinbeck, *The Grapes of Wrath* (Cleveland, Ohio: World Publishing Company, 1947), pp. 246–247.

Document Set 12

World War II and Postwar America, 1941–1960

The U.S. entry into World War II came as a shock to most residents of the Far West. Although the conflict had begun in Europe, and the United States had stepped up production for defense and for aid to the Allies, the fighting seemed far removed from the Pacific coast. Japan's unexpected attack on Pearl Harbor on December 7, 1941, suddenly shifted the theater of operations and brought the war literally to America's doorstep.

The war years brought an economic boom, a population spurt, transportation and housing difficulties, shortages of vital materials, and the expansion of all military facilities in the West. Even before Pearl Harbor, the Pacific Northwest had increased production of ships, aircraft, lumber, machinery, food, clothing, munitions, and armaments. Seattle experienced unprecedented growth as its metropolitan population soared from 368,000 in 1940 to 650,000 by 1944. Kaiser shipyards and Boeing aircraft plants virtually turned the city into a company town. Nearby Portland also recorded spectacular growth but handled its early expansion with admirable cooperation among government officials (Document 1).

After the attack on Pearl Harbor, Californians feared for their safety, and the Japanese became targets of a kind of mass hysteria. General John L. DeWitt, in Document 2, explains the military motives for the evacuation of Japanese-Americans into internment camps. *Korematsu* v. *United States,* concerning the right of the military to issue the order, reached the U.S. Supreme Court in 1944. In a split decision, Justice Robert Jackson wrote a dissenting opinion (Document 3) that made clear the potentially dangerous consequences of the evacuation. In Document 4, a Japanese woman summarizes her experiences in an internment camp during the war years.

Postwar peacetime adjustments lasted until the outbreak of fighting in Korea in 1950, when many World War II veterans returned to military service. With the onset of the Cold War in Europe, companies based in California and the Pacific Northwest continued to manufacture military aircraft and joined the race for weapons superiority. The 1950s also ushered in the jet age, and a few advanced thinkers made plans for the United States to conquer space. In the meantime, people relaxed in front of their small, black-and-white television screens and marveled at the possibility of programs in color.

Ansel Adams, a native San Franciscan and one of the best-known and most admired contemporary photographers, gives his opinion about photography as a profession in Document 5. Photographs, paintings, and sketches enhance the historical record. Indeed, as the saying goes, "A picture is worth a thousand words." We can open our minds to fresh interpretations of the past if we can visualize the action, the setting, or the people involved. Adams tried to establish himself as a musician during the 1920s and took photographs to earn extra money. By the 1930s he had achieved national recognition as a photographer, and he followed that profession for the rest of his life.

Another extremely talented and creative individual had begun his career in California in the 1920s. Dreaming of making cartoons, Walt Disney, with his brother Roy, had taken his ideas to Hollywood and almost immediately scored a success with *Steamboat Willie* (1928), starring Mickey Mouse—the first animated film to use sound. Disney's achievements continued through the 1930s and 1940s with cartoons and feature-length films. In 1953 Disney Studios, in tune with public trends, added a weekly television show to reach a wide audience and to stimulate interest in full-length Disney movies (Document 6). Disney also persuaded the television network to invest in his new venture, an amusement park called Disneyland, which opened in 1955. Walt Disney wanted to make people smile and to banish ugliness from their lives, even if only briefly.

Disney epitomized all that was fun in postwar life, but the exhaust from the million-plus automobiles on the freeways that led to the Magic Kingdom, and the smoke from nearby industries, gave rise in this era to a dirty new word: *smog*. New smog-control devices required on automobiles, along with other pollution controls, were developed during the late 1950s, about the time that John Beecher wrote a poem about bad air (Document 7).

The exposure of past injustices perpetrated on western Indians—prominently including reservation Indians in California, the Klamaths of Oregon, and the Flatheads of Montana—also tarnished the tranquility of the postwar years. After World War II the federal government had turned its attention to problems encountered by tribes seeking compensation for lands unfairly lost through cession treaties or by other means. With the advent of the Indian Claims Commission in 1946, Indians proceeded with their lawsuits, establishing claims and collecting judgments against the United States. In 1953 Congress provided what it considered the next step in Indian independence by terminating certain Indian reservations, abolishing federal supervision over these tribes, and subjecting members to the same laws, privileges, and responsibilities as other citizens of the United States. Because of strong Native American opposition to this reform, and in view of new concerns for minority rights, congressional members spoke out against reservation termination. On September 18, 1958, the secretary of the interior urged the nation to reconsider termination (Document 8). Presidential candidates Richard Nixon and John Kennedy in 1960 agreed, and both political parties supported changes in federal Indian policy. As president, Kennedy encouraged a shift from termination to the development of the human and natural resources on Indian reservations.

Questions for Analysis

1. Why do some people believe that war is good for the country?
2. How would you feel about the internment of a particular group of people? What are some alternatives to internment?
3. Do you think that relocation of immigrants could occur today?
4. How might a photograph be historically inaccurate?
5. What is the role of cartoons in society? Do you think that it is harmful for children to view violence in the world of make-believe?
6. Has air pollution increased or decreased in your area during the past decade? Why?
7. Should American Indians be compensated for lands lost more than a hundred years ago? Do you think that Indians should be protected on reservations, or should they join the mainstream of American life?

1. *Edgar Kaiser Praises Portland's Wartime Expansion, 1943*

No community can expand as this one has done, without it being a strain on the entire population. . . . You may properly ask why, in our opinion, the condition of the Portland-Vancouver area is best of any congested area on the Pacific Coast. The reason for this is that . . . State and city officials, community organizations, Government agencies involved, and industry have met together and discussed each particular problem. . . . In other areas of the Pacific Coast there has been a considerable divergence of opinion. Industry has not been able to get together; city and State officials have had one program, portions of industry another with the result . . . that what was finally done was inadequate or too late. . . .

2. *General John L. DeWitt Explains Why the Japanese Were Evacuated, 1942*

1. I transmit herewith my final report on the evacuation of Japanese from the Pacific Coast.

2. The evacuation was impelled by military necessity. The security of the Pacific Coast continues to require the exclusion of Japanese from the area now prohibited to them and will so continue as long as the military necessity exists. The surprise attack at Pearl Harbor by the enemy crippled a major portion of the Pacific Fleet and exposed the West Coast to an attack which could not have been substantially impeded by defensive fleet operations. More than 115,000 persons of Japanese ancestry resided along the coast and were significantly concentrated near many highly sensitive installations essential to the war effort. Intelligence services records reflected the existence of hundreds of Japanese organizations in California, Washington, Oregon and Arizona which, prior to December 7, 1941, were actively engaged in advancing Japanese war aims. These records also disclosed that thousands of American-born Japanese had gone to Japan to receive their education and indoctrination there and had become rabidly pro-Japanese and then had returned to the United States. Emperor-worshipping ceremonies were commonly held and millions of dollars had flowed into the Japanese imperial war chest from the contributions freely made by Japanese here. The continued presence of a large, unassimilated, tightly knit racial group, bound to an enemy nation by strong ties of race, culture, custom and religion along a frontier vulnerable to attack constituted a menace which had to be dealt with. Their loyalties were unknown and time was of the essence. The evident aspirations of the enemy emboldened by his recent successes made it worse than folly to have left any stone unturned in the building up of our defenses. It is better to have had this protection and not to have needed it than to have needed it and not to have had it—as we have learned to our sorrow.

3. On February 14, 1942, I recommended to the War Department that the military security of the Pacific Coast required the establishment of broad civil control, anti-sabotage and counter-espionage measures, including the evacuation therefrom of all persons of Japanese ancestry. In recognition of this situation, the President issued Executive Order No. 9066 on February 19, 1942, authorizing the accomplishment of these and any other necessary security measures. By letter dated February 20, 1942, the Secretary of War authorized me to effectuate my recommendations and to exercise all of the powers which the Executive Order conferred upon him and upon any military commander designated by him.

3. Justice Robert Jackson Warns Against a Dangerous Precedent, 1944

. . . The limitation under which courts always will labor in examining the necessity for a military order are illustrated by this case. How does the Court know that these orders have a reasonable basis in necessity? No evidence whatever on that subject has been taken by this or any other court. There is sharp controversy as to the credibility of the DeWitt report. So the Court, having no real evidence before it, has no choice but to accept General DeWitt's own unsworn, self-serving statement, untested by any cross-examination, that what he did was reasonable. And thus it will always be when courts try to look into the reasonableness of a military order.

In the very nature of things military decisions are not susceptible of intelligent judicial appraisal. They do not pretend to rest on evidence, but are made on information that often would not be admissible and on assumptions that could not be proved. Information in support of an order could not be disclosed to courts without danger that it would reach the enemy. Neither can courts act on communications made in confidence. Hence courts can never have any real alternative to accepting the mere declaration of the authority that issued the order that it was reasonably necessary from a military viewpoint.

Much is said of the danger to liberty from the Army program for deporting and detaining these citizens of Japanese extraction. But a judicial construction of the due process clause that will sustain this order is a far more subtle blow to liberty than the promulgation of the order itself. A military order, however unconstitutional, is not apt to last longer than the military emergency. Even during that period a succeeding commander may revoke it all. But once a judicial opinion rationalizes such an order to show that it conforms to the Constitution, or rather rationalizes the Constitution to show that the Constitution sanctions such an order, the Court for all time has validated the principle of racial discrimination in criminal procedure and of transplanting American citizens. The principle then lies about like a loaded weapon ready for the hand of any authority that can bring forward a plausible claim of an urgent need. Every repetition imbeds that principle more deeply in our law and thinking and expands it to new purposes. All who observe the work of courts are familiar with what Judge Cardozo described as "the tendency of principle to expand itself to the limit of its logic." A military commander may overstep the bounds of constitutionality, and it is an incident. But if we review and approve, that passing incident becomes the doctrine of the Constitution. There it has a generative power of its own, and all that it creates will be in its own image. Nothing better illustrates this danger than does the Court's opinion in this case. . . .

4. A Japanese Woman Describes Her Life in an Internment Camp During World War II, 1942–1944

We stayed in Stockton Assembly Center for two or three months until the camps in Arkansas were ready. We traveled there by train with the shades drawn down. It was better that way because quite a few Japanese people were killed by Americans before we were interned.

People closely affiliated with Japan were rounded up and imprisoned earlier. There was a young Japanese man in our town who told the FBI everything. He received money for being a rat. People said after the war they would kill him. The FBI also approached me and offered to pay me money but I said, "What are you talking about! You're crazy!" But that young man told. I would never do anything like that—tell on others to pull them down. Even if your mouth is rotten, you should never be a spy. No matter how poor I was, even if I couldn't eat tomorrow, I could not be that rotten. My lips were sealed tightly but there were people who told. A person must be human. You can't say things about others that would bring them down . . . even for money.

My biggest worry had been money for food and shelter. In camp that burden was wiped out. The government fed us and gave us a monthly allowance for $10.50. Food came out from early morning. The camp was divided into blocks and each block had a big kitchen. Everyone lined up to eat in the mess hall. Do you know what they fed us at the beginning? Corned beef and cabbage every day. Then it slowly changed.

People tried to think of things to occupy their spare time. There were English classes, flower-arrangement classes, and dance classes. They asked me to teach Japanese, but I didn't because I was pregnant again. It looks bad when you're already old [age 40] and pregnant. The pregnancy was hard on me physically but I had nothing but good thoughts.

One day our block would have a talent show, the next day a different block. Papa got pulled from block to block. They called for him constantly. He was never home to fight with. What an actor he was! When they did plays, he would always perform in them. No one could sing *Yasuki Bushi* [a Japanese folk song] better than he: Everybody said that. He would sing among thousands . . . even a professional would have run away barefooted from stage fright. When I was young . . . I always remember thinking how good he was.

The winters were cold, but we had a big stove. A fire was always burning. People went to the mountains and collected wood. They carved and polished the wood, making *obutsudans* [Buddhist altars], drawers, chairs, all sorts of things. No matter which way you faced, there were mountains. You couldn't tell which direction was east or west. Many got lost and search parties went out to look for them. There were quite a few who died there.

I grew vegetables. Everyone grew them in front of their barracks. Watermelons, eggplants, sweet potatoes . . . everything grew well. The soil was rich because no one had grown things there before. That's why Papa wanted to stay and farm.

There were two factions in camp: one who said they would stay in America, and another who said they wanted to return to Japan. About half returned to Japan. I didn't want to return to Japan. America was my home. I know I made the right decision.

In camp the Yamaguchis asked for Nesan. There were many seekers after her hand in marriage. But we knew the Yamaguchis back in Liberty. Everyone knew the Yamaguchis. There were *bigu shatsu* [big shots]. Although they were one of the wealthiest families in Liberty, we didn't gain anything from marriage: we just lost a daughter.

We couldn't have a real wedding because it was camp time. Just the immediate relatives attended. I think Hana got married to the Maedas in camp too, but I can't remember any more.

Before the War ended, we left the camp with the Yamaguchis. We promised that we would grow food toward the war effort and they let us go. Several families left at the same time. We were already there for two years. . . .

5. Ansel Adams Describes the Profession of Photography, 1952

A profession is a vehicle for the social realization of the creative spirit. Whether the profession be an art, science, or craft, this definition holds. Photography is all of these—science, craft, and art. Photography, now accepted as an art, *could* be a noble profession. . . .

In the first place, a profession is not defined merely by the money-making aspects of an art. We all have to live somehow, and we must all receive something for our efforts. But the doing of the job is the prime consideration; the returns are secondary in this discussion. We will simply assume they are essential and that any intelligent professional can properly adjust them.

We will open our discussion by presenting two very important and basic statements on the subject:

> It is true that photography, next to the printed word, reaches, instructs, interprets, clarifies, and modulates opinion more than any other medium of communication and expression. Therefore, it is deserving of attention and respect equal to that accorded painting, literature, music and architecture.
>
> Unless photographers establish for themselves some severe standards of professional training and professional certification the art will never achieve its potentially high position among the creative professions of modern society. . . .

In the mid-twentieth century, a little more than a hundred years after the discovery of the medium, the profession of photography is more a trade than an art; more a business than a profession. The general standards do not encourage devotion to ideals. Definition, clarification and enforcement of high standards are, to me, self-evident necessities. . . .

6. Walt Disney Plays to the Public and Goes on Television, 1954

. . . I've always had this confidence since way back when we had our first upsets and lost Oswald[1] and went to Mickey Mouse. Then and there I decided that in every way we could, we would build ourselves with the public and keep faith with the public. We felt that the public were really the people we had to play to, you know? We didn't care about anybody in between. Once when I was trying to sell Mickey Mouse, a fellow told me something. He said, "Mickey Mouse? What is it? Nobody knows it. Why, I can get cartoons that I know for the same amount of money you're asking." Then he held up a package of Lifesavers. He said, "Now if you're inclined to sell me Lifesavers, that would be different. Because the public knows Lifesavers. They don't know you and they don't know your mouse."

That hit me. I said, "From now on, they're *going* to know. If they like a picture, they're going to know who made it. They're going to know what his name is." And I stuck Mickey Mouse so darn big on that title that they couldn't think it was a rabbit or anything else. The public has been my friend. The public discovered Mickey Mouse before the critics and before the theatrical people. It was only after the public discovered it that the theatrical people became interested in it. Up to that time the critics wouldn't be bothered to give it any space, you see?

So it all boils down that the newspapers and the people who write the newspapers are only interested in things after the public is interested—or if they think they can create some interest on the part of the public. So in all of our exploitation, everything from then on we kept directly at the public. I never went to motion-picture fan magazines. I said, "No, that is not the public. That's a segment of the motion-picture audience, but not the whole motion-picture audience." I always wanted to go for the big periodicals. I told my publicity boys, "Look, when you get the big magazines, then you're reaching a broader segment of the audience."

Now, when television came, I said, "There's a way we can get to the public. Television is going to be my way of going direct to the public, bypassing the others who can sit there and be the judge on the bench. Maybe they never see any more of the public than those in their offices or those they see at the cocktail hour. In other words, the world is that small to them."

---

[1]Oswald the rabbit was a character in Disney's first series, done in 1927.

I decided when we got into television, we would have to control it. Now everybody wanted to buy all our old product. We wouldn't sell it. We wouldn't hear of it. We wanted to handle it ourselves, make good use of it. Some of the old product that should not be shown we would not show. Some of it we would frame so it would have a proper presentation for today. . . . We won't throw any piece of junk at the public and try to sell 'em. We fight for quality. All we're trying to do through television is to let 'em know what we've done. And if they're interested in what we do, they'll come to the theaters to see it. There's a loyalty there. . . .

7. *John Beecher's Poem About Smog, 1956*

An Air That Kills

Times were worse then
Jobs were hard to get
People were suffering more
but do you know
a man could breathe

It's as if the oxygen
were all exhausted
from the atmosphere
That's how I feel
and why I quit

Same land same sky same sea
same trees and mountains
I painted then
I guess the light went out
I saw them by

Don't make politics
out of what I say
It's just that something isn't here
that used to be
and kept us going

8. *Interior Secretary Fred Seaton Signals the End of Coercive Termination of Indian Reservations, 1958*

On August 1, 1953, House Concurrent Resolution No. 108 was adopted expressing the sense of the Congress of the United States to be that of ending the wardship status of Indian tribes as rapidly as possible. Certain additional provisions applied to Indian tribes located in the States of California, Florida, New York, and Texas, and to some other tribes in other States, with relation to the earliest possible elimination of Federal control over their persons and properties.

This stands as the most recent congressional declaration upon the subject.

Since that time—that is since 1953—the pros and cons of public opinion relative to congressional policy on Indian affairs have been given wide expression in the press and in other media throughout the country. Some people have interpreted these statements to mean that it is the intention of Congress and the Department of the Interior to abandon Indian groups regardless of their ability to fend for themselves.

In my opinion, the stated intentions of the Congress to free Indian tribes from Federal supervision, and to eliminate the need for the special services rendered by the Bureau of Indian Affairs to Indian citizens, is more than adequately counterbalanced in the congressional resolution itself. I now refer you to such qualifying phrases as, and I quote, "at the earliest possible time," and "at the earliest practicable date." The intent is clear, I believe. What the Congress intended was to state an objective, not an immediate goal.

To be specific, my own position is this: no Indian tribe or group should end its relationship with the Federal Government unless such tribe or group has clearly demonstrated—first, that it understands the plan under which such a program would go forward, and second, that the tribe or group affected concurs in and supports the plan proposed.

Now, ladies and gentlemen, it is absolutely unthinkable to me as your Secretary of the Interior that consideration would be given to forcing upon an Indian tribe a so-called termination plan which did not have the understanding and acceptance of a clear majority of the members affected. Those tribes which have thus far sought to end their Federal wardship status have, in each instance, demonstrated their acceptance of the plan prior to action by the Congress. I shall continue to insist this be the case and I hope and believe that Congress and its leaders will pursue the same course. To make my position perfectly clear, as long as I am Secretary of the Interior, I shall be dedicated to preserving the principle which I have just enunciated.

I further believe the Commissioner of Indian Affairs tried to make the position of the Congress and the Department of the Interior clear when in the fall of 1953, he stated, and I quote, "We want to give the Indians the same opportunities for advancement—the same freedom and responsibility for the management of their properties—as have other American citizens." Then Mr. Emmons continued, "I know that there are some tribes which are ready and anxious to take over full responsibility for their own affairs at the earliest possible time, and that others will have to move along toward that objective much more slowly and gradually." He then added he recognized that in many areas there is a real need for a continuation of the trusteeship and will be for a span of years. And so it seems to me the intent has never been one of precipitating Indian groups into a position for which they were unprepared.

True enough, Indian groups can continue to exist as cultural islands in the midst of our national populations, isolated from the main group by language and custom, and living at standards far below those of the average American citizen. They can do this. In fact, many of them have done so for many years. But let me put this question to you: "Does the majority of the population of such tribes prefer to live in that manner, or does it do so because there seems to be no other choice? Or, does it do so because there is no general awareness of the alternatives?" I believe the majority of our Indian citizens are as desirous and capable of exercising all of the duties and responsibilities of citizenship as are the rest of us, provided they have equal opportunities with their fellow citizens. And having said that, I want to add this: under no circumstances could I bring myself to recommend the termination of the Federal relationship with any Indian tribe in this country until the members of that tribe have been given the opportunity of a sound and effective education. To me it would be incredible, even criminal, to send any Indian tribe out into the stream of American life until and unless the educational level of that tribe was one which was equal to the responsibilities which it was shouldering. . . .

References

1. Edgar Kaiser Praises Portland's Wartime Expansion, 1943
   Edgar F. Kaiser, *Congested Area Hearings: Columbia River Area,* p. 1662, quoted by Gerald D. Nash, *The American West Transformed: The Impact of the Second World War* (Bloomington: Indiana University Press, 1985), pp. 78–79.
2. General John L. DeWitt Explains Why the Japanese Were Evacuated, 1942
   Lt. Gen. J. L. DeWitt to Chief of Staff, U.S. Army, June 5, 1943, in U.S. Army Western Defense Command and Fourth Army, *Final Report, Japanese Evacuation from the West Coast, 1942* (Washington, D.C.: U.S. Government Printing Office, 1943), p. vii.

3. Justice Robert Jackson Warns Against a Dangerous Precedent, 1944
   Korematsu v. *United States*, 323 U.S. 244–247 (1944).
4. A Japanese Woman Describes Her Life in an Internment Camp During World War II, 1942–1944
   Akemi Kikumura, *Through Harsh Winters: The Life of a Japanese Immigrant Woman* (Novato, Calif.: Chandler & Sharp Publishers, 1981), pp. 51–53.
5. Ansel Adams Describes the Profession of Photography, 1952
   Ansel Adams, *The Profession of Photography* (1952), quoted in *Nine Classic California Photographers,* ed. William Hively (Berkeley: Friends of the Bancroft Library, 1980), pp. 81–83.
6. Walt Disney Plays to the Public and Goes on Television, 1954
   Bob Thomas, *Walt Disney: An American Original* (New York: Simon and Schuster, 1976), pp. 253–255.
7. John Beecher's Poem About Smog, 1956
   "An Air That Kills," in *Land of the Free* (Oakland, Calif.: Morningstar Press, 1956), p. 21.
8. Interior Secretary Fred Seaton Signals the End of Coercive Termination of Indian Reservations, 1958
   Broadcast address over Radio Station KCLS, Flagstaff, Arizona, September 18, 1958, quoted in 105 *Congressional Record* 3105 (1959).

Document Set 13

The Modern Era, 1960–1975

The year 1960 ushered in a decade of unrest characterized by protests against the Vietnam War, student uprisings (sometimes violent) on university campuses, and youthful dissatisfaction with "the Establishment." An underground culture based on nonconformity spawned a new breed of rebels—"flower children," who favored long hair, communal living, health foods, and not-so-healthful drugs. The Haight-Ashbury district of San Francisco became the hippie headquarters as young men and women dropped out of mainstream society.

The antimaterialistic youths of the sixties, whether hippies or members of the mainstream culture, widely promoted love, a return to the simple life, environmental protection, minority rights (including gay rights), a revitalized university curriculum, and a ban on nuclear weapons. Unfortunately, the intemperate methods and radical leanings of some activists frightened adults and at first prevented productive dialogue with those in positions of responsibility. Nevertheless, the young voices eventually were heard. As the energy crisis of the 1970s struck, the assumption that bigger is better came into question in American society at large.

In Document 1, Mario Savio, spokesman for the Berkeley Student Free Speech Movement, examines the relationship of students and faculty to the university administration. Sit-ins, demonstrations, and strikes took place across the nation during the next few years as students expressed disillusionment with higher education. By the end of the decade, school administrators and students reached compromises on free expression, speech, assembly, and distribution and sale of literature on many university campuses.

The 1960s were also turbulent years for African-Americans. The McCone Commission Report (Document 2) lists the problems that blacks faced in the 1960s that led to the Watts riots in August 1965. It also points out conditions in Los Angeles that would breed future riots. Although city and county officials solved some urban problems, others haunted Los Angeles for the next three decades. Eugene Burdick, a popular writer of the 1960s, earned acclaim for his best-selling book *The Ugly American* (1958), which criticized Americans for their ignorance of other countries' cultures. In Document 3, Burdick takes a lighthearted look at California and finds three geographic divisions.

After the violence of the 1960s, including the assassinations of President John F. Kennedy, Attorney General Robert Kennedy, and Dr. Martin Luther King, Jr., labor and farmworkers, another oppressed group, resisted the temptation to use protest methods that caused injury or rioting. One union organizer in California stands above the rest as an advocate of nonviolence. César Chávez (Document 4), a migrant farmworker of Hispanic heritage, led a peaceful boycott of the grape fields of Delano during the mid-1960s. His success convinced others that his methods worked.

As the 1970s opened, those in charge turned their efforts to solving underlying social problems. Although some of their solutions succeeded, others provided little more than a temporary bandage. As in the past, no one had clear-cut answers. By 1973, however, the energy crisis demanded resolution. Americans enacted previously considered conservation measures when oil prices soared and shipments of the vital commodity to the United States dropped. Secretary of State Henry Kissinger summarized the need for action in a national policy statement on energy in 1975 (Document 5). The days of unlimited, cheap gasoline were over, and the country looked to the deregulation of fuel and the development of potential resources in Alaska and offshore sites. "Save" instead of "use" became the byword as prices skyrocketed. Energy suppliers throughout the West began exploring alternative sources of power.

Like other minority groups, Native Americans organized demonstrations during this era to publicize their plight. In the Pacific Northwest, resident Indians claimed that despite later state laws, federal treaties dating to 1854 and 1855 gave them the right to continue fishing in their traditional areas. They staged several protests during the early 1970s and triumphed in the case of *United States* v. *Washington* in 1974. As a result of the dispute, federal district judge George Boldt ruled that treaty Indians of Puget Sound were entitled to catch half of all fish that passed by, or that normally would pass by, their usual locations, as long as they took care not to endanger the runs. Non-Indian fishers protested that they now could compete for only half as many fish as before. An appeal was denied (Document 6), and the U.S. Supreme Court upheld Boldt's decision in 1979.

In western Canada the Métis, a group born of a mixture of European (mainly French) fur traders and native-born (Indian) women, finally achieved recognition as a distinct culture with special needs and problems. As one writer put it, the Métis were the true natives of Canada, for Indians and Europeans were both immigrants—their arrival separated only by time. The meeting of Native Americans and Europeans produced a mixture (*mestizo* in Spanish) rooted solely in the New World—a truly bilingual, bicultural nation. The Métis still exist in Canada, as do many other racial mixtures in the United States. Document 7 captures the dilemma of those facing a clash of cultures.

Questions for Analysis

1. The 1960s have stimulated a variety of interpretations. Gather several opinions from people who remember those times and see whether they agree or disagree on the meaning of the decade.
2. What conditions lead people to riot?
3. Do stereotypes such as those that Eugene Burdick has created for California have value in an analysis of the state's development?
4. Why do you think César Chávez's methods succeeded?
5. Why do residents of the American West take the supply of energy for granted?
6. Do Indians deserve to be favored in fishing rights? Do you think it is fair to penalize non-Indians today to make up for past wrongs? Are there other recent cases in which Indians have secured favorable decisions?
7. Should native peoples be encouraged to maintain their own identity, or should they attempt to work within the mainstream of society?

1. Mario Savio Challenges University Leaders, 1964

. . . Those who should give orders—the faculty and students—take orders, and those who should tend to keeping the sidewalks clean, to seeing that we have enough classrooms—the administration—give orders. . . . As [social critic] Paul Goodman says, students are the exploited class in America, subjected to all the techniques of factory methods: tight scheduling, speedups, rules of conduct they're expected to obey with little or no say-so. At Cal you're little more than an IBM card. For efficiency's sake, education is organized along quantifiable lines. One hundred and twenty units make a bachelor's degree. . . .

The university is a vast public utility which turns out future workers in today's vineyard, the military-industrial complex. They've got to be processed in the most efficient way to see to it that they have the fewest dissenting opinions, that they have just those characteristics which are wholly incompatible with being an intellectual. . . . People have to suppress the very questions which reading books raises. . . .

. . . The business of the university is teaching and learning. Only people engaged in it—the students and teachers—are competent to decide how it should be done. . . .

America may be the most poverty-stricken country in the world. Not materially. But intellectually it is bankrupt. And morally it's poverty-stricken. But in such a way that it's not clear to you that you're poor. It's very hard to know you're poor if you're eating well.

In the Berkeley ghetto—which is, let's say, the campus and the surrounding five or six blocks—you bear certain stigmas. They're not the color of your skin, for the most part, but the fact that you're an intellectual, and perhaps a moral nonconformist. You question the mores and morals and institutions of society seriously. This creates a feeling of mutuality, of real community. Students are excited about political ideas. They're not yet inured to the apolitical society they're going to enter. But being interested in ideas means you have no use in American society . . . unless they are ideas which are useful to the military-industrial complex. That means there's no connection between what you're doing and the world you're about to enter.

At first we didn't understand what the issues were. But as discussions went on, they became clear. The university wanted to regulate the content of our speech. . . . The Free Speech Movement has always had an ideology of its own. Call it essentially anti-liberal. By that I mean it is anti a certain style of politics prevalent in the United States: politics by compromise—which succeeds if you don't state any issues. You don't state issues, so you can't be attacked from any side. . . . By contrast our ideology is issue-oriented. We thought the administration was doing bad things and we said so. Some people on the faculty repeatedly told us we couldn't say or do things too provocative or we'd turn people off—alienate the faculty. Yet, with every provocative thing we did, more faculty members came to our aid. And when the apocalypse came, over 800 of them were with us.

. . . We have a society which has many social evils, not the least of which is the fantastic presumption in a lot of people's minds that naturally decisions which are in accord with the rules must be right—an assumption which is not founded on any legitimate philosophical principle. In our society, precisely because of the great distortions and injustices which exist, I would hope that civil disobedience becomes more prevalent than it is. . . .

2. The McCone Commission Reports on Causes of the Watts Riots, 1965

In examining the sickness in the center of our city, what has depressed and stunned us most is the dull, devastating spiral of failure that awaits the average disadvantaged child in the urban core. His home life all too often fails to give him the incentive and the elementary experience with words and ideas which prepares most children for school. Unprepared and unready, he may not learn to read or write at all; and because he shares his problem with 30 or more in the same classroom, even the efforts of the most dedicated teachers are unavailing. Age, not achievement, passes him on to higher grades, but in most cases he is unable to cope with courses in the upper grades because they demand basic skills which he does not possess. . . .

Frustrated and disillusioned, the child becomes a discipline problem. Often he leaves school, sometimes before the end of junior high school. (About two-thirds of those who enter the three high schools in the center of the curfew area do not graduate.) He slips into the ranks of the permanent jobless, illiterate and untrained, unemployed and unemployable. . . .

Reflecting this spiral of failure, unemployment in the disadvantaged areas runs two to three times the county average, and the employment available is too often intermittent. A family whose breadwinner is chronically out of work is almost invariably a disintegrating family. Crime rates soar and welfare rolls increase, even faster than the population.

This spiral of failure has a most damaging side effect. Because of the low standard of achievement in the schools in the urban core and adjacent areas, parents of the better students from advantaged backgrounds remove them from these schools, either by changing the location of the family home or by sending the children to private school. In turn, the average achievement level of the schools in the disadvantaged area sinks lower and lower. The evidence is that this chain reaction is one of the principal factors in maintaining de facto school segregation in the urban core and producing it in the adjacent areas where the Negro population is expanding. From our study, we are persuaded that there is a reasonable possibility that raising the achievement levels of the disadvantaged Negro child will materially lessen the tendency towards de facto segregation in education and that this might possibly also make a substantial contribution to ending all de facto segregation. . . .

The Commission recognizes that much of what it has to say about causes and remedies is not new, although it is backed up by fresh additional evidence coming out of the investigation of the Los Angeles riots. At the same time, the Commission believes that there is an urgency in solving the problems, old or new, and that all Americans, whatever their color, must become aware of this urgency. Among the many steps which should be taken to improve the present situation, the Commission affirms again that the three fundamental issues in the urban problems of disadvantaged minorities are: employment, education and police-community relations. Accordingly, the Commission looks upon its recommendations in these three areas as the heart of its plea and the City's best hope.

As we have said earlier in this report, there is no immediate remedy for the problems of the Negro and other disadvantaged in our community. The problems are deep and the remedies are costly and will take time. However, through the implementation of the programs we propose, with the dedication we discuss, and with the leadership we call for from all, our Commission states without dissent, that the tragic violence that occurred during the six days of August will not be repeated. . . .

3. Eugene Burdick Describes Three Californias, 1965

The feeling of rootlessness, of obscure origin, of not knowing where one came from or where one is going, is typical of California. . . . Like people are attracted to like places, and after centuries there develops a kind of homogeneity about fellow citizens. . . . History, intermarriage, selective migration, the old Darwinian processes usually create a people who look enough alike to be a nation of sisters and brothers. California has not had the time. Everything happened so fast. California has had to make a merit of the novel, the unique, the *sui generis,* the new, the rejected, the unarticulated, the emerging, the unformed, the rebellious. . . .

On most outsiders, the state makes a surrealistic and conflicting impression that hazes wildly different things together: Disneyland, sport shirts, sun, oranges, religious cults, Hollywood, white beaches, women in bathing suits wearing high heels and mink stoles; college kids with beards, college kids with surf boards, old people—many old people—sin, everyone tanned, everyone in cars roaring down insane freeways. . . . When pressed, the outsider will confess that he thinks the place is not quite real, but if it is real it is childish, and below the childishness there is a smell of evil. . . . It lacks authority, civility, tradition. It is a sensual paradise where practical things cannot be done. Serious people cannot abide it. The place is lush and wanton. It is—well it is like Disneyland. Not real. . . .

The vision of the outsider is true—in part. The vision is based on the South of California, which is the most publicized, visible and colorful part of the state. But it is not the character of the whole state. . . .

The North is north of San Francisco. . . . There is a staidness to the North. People walk slower, the accents are a mixture of Nebraska, Iowa and an undertone of New England. . . . The houses have a sturdy look to them. The people in the North use the word "uppity" more often. . . . The term is used to describe a man who drinks Martinis, or gets his suits in San Francisco, or gets a new car every year, or buys his wife a full-length mink. . . .

The North is not seductive. The people who went to the North were not looking for a bonanza, the soft life or excitement. They came with a thirst for land, a low, steady metabolic rate and a very high sense of what is practical. . . . The North is inhabited by country people frightened by the intimacy of city life, high on self-confidence, low on "showing off," with a reverence for courage and respect for the slow-speaking person who bulls ahead and wins out. *Work* is the word that describes good character in the North. . . .

In the South—south of the Tehachapi Mountains, that is—the immigrants are different. First of all, more of them are fresh first-generation immigrants. They come from Texas and New Orleans and Alabama and New York City. More of them are Negroes. The sounds of jazz are louder in the night, and wailing out of the cheap apartments of North Hollywood and San Diego, day and night. . . . Cool, hip and classical music are big in the South. . . . Rumor is a principal means of communication. Rumor about movie stars, the path of the newest freeway, the "inside" of the latest property development or divorce case; about stocks, . . . the horsepower of the new Mustang, . . . why Bing Crosby moved away, IBM's future. . . . On and on it goes.

One of the least publicized statistics of California is that for every two migrants who come in to stay, someone *leaves*. Who stays? And why? When asked, most of them say "health" or "sunshine" or "a healthy place for the kids to grow up," and right behind this, "better chance to get ahead—better luck out here." *Luck*. There is no word you hear more often in the South. In the South people came with a hard drive and a sense that their luck would turn. They are the optimists of the United States, the advocates of causes, the believers in faiths, the youngest sons who rebelled, the visionaries, the discontented. All of them with the hope of "lucking out" under the sun and beside the sea. . . .

If the mystique word that drew them to the South is "luck," the object that enthralls the Southerner is that seductive possession, "the car." The South depends on the car, and not just in some dim Freudian sense. The South is the only place in the world so geared to the automobile that if it were eliminated the whole region would collapse. Outsiders stare with a barely disguised horror at the white, wormlike freeways of the South. . . . The freeways are expensive, hideous, congested and self-defeating. They are obsolete the day they are finished. But the Southerner cares little. He plans his life so that he can roar to work on the freeway in off-hours. . . . It is not uncommon for the Southerner to drive sixty miles to work; 120 miles on a date; and fifty miles to shop for loss leaders at the colossal supermarkets. . . .

The City is the central part of California. It takes in everything from the Tehachapis in the South, to a line somewhere in Marin County, just across the Golden Gate Bridge. Above that is the North. The City, San Francisco, is a living fiction. It is an invention, a manufactured thing, contrived and not wholly true. Everyone within the pull of the City "lives" there. People from Palo Alto, San Jose, Santa Cruz, Berkeley, Orinda, Piedmont, Atherton and Oakland always say to an outsider that they are "from the City—I mean San Francisco."

. . . The City is unlike anything else in America. . . . There are two causes for the City's feeling of uniqueness: the Bay and the Great Fire. . . . People of the City never grow tired of the Bay. Apartments that have a view of the Bay command approximately twice the rent of viewless apartments. Even those that have no view but are in earshot of a foghorn fetch relatively higher prices. People who have lived in the City all their lives still fall silent when the fog comes rolling in through the great arches of the Golden Gate Bridge.

The Great Earthquake and Fire gave the City a shared catastrophe, something that not only bound immigrants to citizens but also marked a point of time when chaos was destroyed and a culture emerged. Each detail of the Fire is perfectly remembered, sharply etched but softened in some golden way. . . . The City emerged from the Fire like a place cleansed. It now had a history; a grinding, searing history, but a history. . . . The City had another great advantage: it is a snug little community. There is no way for the City to expand except upward. . . . The suburbs that grew down the Peninsula and into Marin County adopted the City's manners.

Just as the City influences the thinking of millions of Californians who live outside its physical boundaries, it also works a strong magnetism on the rest of the country. Untold millions have tried to push into the gleaming, fog-washed, tight little city by the Bay. Most return whence they came, but some wriggle in—and often they are miserable. . . .

But the City has begun to lose its grip on its chunk of California. It has, most significantly, become narcissistic—which is the first step toward decay. . . . The South grows strong and powerful. It is designed for the mass man and there is no hiding the fact. But along with the mass man it also has gathered most of the writers, sculptors, painters, designers, dancers, actors and artists in California. If culture follows the dollar, the South is going to get the culture. The North finds the South lascivious and wanton. The City has few attractions for the Northerner. He is self-contained, remote, certain and insular, and wants to remain that way. . . .

. . . There are three Californias—the North, the South and the City. Each is made up of immigrants from other states. But the immigrants do not just come to California; they come to one of the three Californias.

4. *César Chávez Advocates Nonviolence Among Farmworkers, 1965*

DiGiorgio didn't spend much time fighting us on the picket lines. As they were more mature than other growers, they spent their time gathering information, getting police to do their dirty work, and filing suits against us. Finally, on May 20, they obtained a court order restricting the number of pickets.

We believe that each worker must have the right to protest, and if he can't be on the picket line to do his own protesting, his right for effective striking is taken away.

We saw this injunction as especially unfair because there had been no violence on the picket line. It also threw all of our strategy into a turmoil, because we couldn't use our source of strength, which was the people. We began to struggle desperately for other ways of putting the pressure on the scabs and on the company.

But after several days of particularly futile picketing, people were getting impatient and discouraged. As I just couldn't come up with any solution, I called a meeting at the American Legion Hall in Delano.

The meeting soon got around to the idea that we were losing because we weren't using violence, that the only solution was to use violence. We spent most of the day discussing that. Then, although we had taken a vote at the beginning of the strike to be nonviolent, we took another vote. Except for one older fellow, all voted to continue nonviolently.

Before ending the meeting, I told them that I had run out of ideas of things to do, but I knew that in them, the people, there were answers, and I needed their help to find those answers.

They said yes, but still they left without suggesting anything.

A couple of hours later, three ladies said they wanted to see me. In those days the question of money was extremely severe. We just didn't have it. So the first thing that came to my mind was that the ladies wanted money for some very special personal need. I asked them to come into my little office.

First they wanted to make sure that I wouldn't be offended by what they wanted to tell me. Then they wanted to assure me that they were not trying to tell me how to run the strike.

After we got over those hurdles, they said, "We don't understand this business of the court order. Does this mean that if we go picket and break the injunctions, we'll go to jail?"

"Well, it means that you go to jail, and that we will be fined," I said.

"What would happen if we met across the street from the DiGiorgio gates, not to picket, not to demonstrate, but to have a prayer, maybe a mass?" they asked. "Do you think the judge would have us arrested?"

By the time they got the last word out, my mind just flashed to all the possibilities.

"You just gave me an idea!" I said, then I was away and running. They didn't know what hit me.

I got Richard and had him take my old station wagon and build a little chapel on it. It was like a shrine with a picture of Our Lady of Guadalupe, some candles, and some flowers. We worked on it until about 2:00 in the morning. Then we parked it across from the DiGiorgio gate where we started a vigil that lasted at least two months. People were there day and night.

The next morning we distributed a leaflet all the way from Bakersfield to Visalia inviting people to a prayer meeting at the DiGiorgio Ranch and made the same announcement on the Spanish radio. People came by the hundreds. You could see cars two miles in either direction.

We brought the loud-speakers and tried to get the people in the camp to come to the mass, but I don't think more than ten came out. Most of them were out at the fence looking and seeing a tremendous number of people. They were very impressed.

There also was so much confusion, our guys found themselves talking to our members inside the camp for the first time in about three weeks.

The next day at noon something very dramatic happened. When the trucks brought the people from the fields to eat at the company mess hall, about eight women decided to come to where we had the vigil instead of going into the mess hall. The supervisors got the trucks in the way to keep them from coming, but the women went way out through the vines and wouldn't be stopped. They knelt down and prayed and then went back.

That was the beginning.

The same evening about fifty women came. The next evening half of the camp was out, and from then on, every single day, they were out there. Every day we had a mass, held a meeting, sang spirituals, and got them to sign authorization cards. Those meetings were responsible in large part for keeping the spirit up of our people inside the camp and helping our organizing for the coming battle.

It was a beautiful demonstration of the power of nonviolence.

5. Henry Kissinger Asks Cooperation in the Energy Crisis, 1975

The events set in motion by the October 1973 war exposed the dangerous vulnerability we had incurred as a result of our growing dependence on imported oil. The oil embargo and the series of massive oil price increases which followed underscored the degree to which we had lost control over the price of a central element of our economic system. We also found that our own economic well-being and security were threatened by the energy vulnerability of our allies and that the escalating price of energy had wreaked havoc on the programs of developing countries.

Over the past two years our objective has been to develop a comprehensive strategy to end our domestic and international energy vulnerability. Our goal has been to build a series of policies which would:

—Protect us against short-term dangers such as embargoes and the destabilizing movements of assets held by oil countries;

—Provide support for developing countries hard hit by high oil prices;

—Make possible a return to noninflationary growth, and

—Create the political and institutional conditions for a productive dialogue between consumer and producer countries.

We have made substantial progress in meeting the immediate crisis.

Despite this progress much remains to be done if we are to overcome the impact of the energy crisis.

Here at home we must move rapidly in reducing our dependence on imported oil. Our present vulnerability will continue, and indeed increase, unless we intensify our conservation efforts and promptly initiate those programs and policy measures which will insure the availability of major amounts of new energy by the end of this decade and into the 1980's.

For the short term we look to conservation as the primary means of reducing our import dependence. In this regard, the decontrol of domestic oil prices is the single most important conservation measure we can take.

But there should also be other elements in our domestic energy policy, including the deregulation of natural gas, as well as the accelerated exploration of potential resources in Alaska and on the outer continental shelf.

We cannot succeed alone in this effort. We must work closely with other major consuming countries if we expect to end the monopoly power of the producer countries in unilaterally setting oil prices.

Regardless of the decisions of the oil producers, the United States must regain control of its own economic future. Our leadership role in the world demands that we demonstrate our national resolve to overcome the problems we face and our determination not to entrust our political and economic destiny to others.

6. Judge George Boldt's Decision Finds in Favor of Native American Fishermen in Western Washington, 1974

[The] United States, on its own behalf and as trustee for several Western Washington Indian tribes, brought action against the State of Washington seeking declaratory and injunctive relief concerning off-reservation treaty right fishing. The District Court for the Western District of Washington, George H. Boldt, J., granted relief in part and all parties appealed. The Court of Appeals, Choy, Circuit Judge, held that state could regulate fishing rights guaranteed to the Indians only to the extent necessary to preserve a particular species in a particular run; that trial court did not abuse its discretion in apportioning the opportunity to catch fish between whites and Indians on a 50–50 basis; that trial court properly excluded Indians' catch on their reservations from apportionment; and that certain tribes were properly recognized as descendants of treaty signatories and thus entitled to rights under the treaties.

Historical Background

In the early 1850's, an increasing flow of American settlers poured into the lowlands of Puget Sound and the river valleys north of the Columbia. Washington Territory was organized in 1853. Isaac Stevens, its first governor, was commissioned to smooth the way for settlement by inducing the Indians of the area to move voluntarily onto reservations.

George Gibbs' official chronicle of the treaty proceedings reveals the governor as a tactful and effective negotiator. He united the scattered Indian communities into a number of tribes and selected "chiefs" from each tribe with whom to bargain. The Indians west of the Cascade Mountains were known as "fish-eaters"; their diets, social customs, and religious practices centered on the capture of fish. Their fish-oriented culture required them to be nomadic, moving from one fishing spot to another as the runs varied with the seasons. Stevens nevertheless persuaded them to settle down on designated reservations, thus freeing the great bulk of the land for American settlement without a bloody war of conquest. In exchange, he promised the tribes money and the benefits of the white man's civilization—material goods and education. Governor Stevens assured them, moreover, that they were restricted to the reservations only for the purpose of residence; he explained that they would remain free to fish off the reservations at their traditional fishing places in common with the white settlers.

In negotiating the treaties, Stevens read a predrafted document and asked for the Indians' comments and approval. Although the treaties read as typical legal documents, few if any of the Indian negotiators read or spoke English. The treaties and the Americans' explanation of their terms were translated into Chinook jargon, a trade medium of some 300 words common to most Northwest Indians. The district court found that the jargon was inadequate to express more than the general nature of the treaty provisions.

During 1854 and 1855, Stevens executed treaties with all of the treaty tribes. Each treaty contained a provision guaranteeing off-reservation fishing rights similar to that found in the Treaty of Medicine Creek:

> The right of taking fish, at all usual and accustomed grounds and stations, is further secured to said Indians, in common with all citizens of the Territory.

To this day, fishing remains an important aspect of Indian tribal life, providing food, employment, and an ingredient of cultural identity. Indians have adopted modern techniques of sport and commercial fishing. They share the concern of other citizens with preservation of runs of anadromous fish. Some tribes regulate the times and manner of fishing by their members.

Decree of the District Court

The district court held that the state and its agencies can regulate off-reservation fishing by treaty Indians at their usual and accustomed grounds only if the state first satisfies the court that the regulation is reasonable and necessary for conservation. The court defined "conservation" as the perpetuation of a run or of a species of fish. The state must also show that the conservation objective cannot be attained by restricting only citizens other than treaty Indians. In addition, the regulation must not discriminate against treaty Indians and must meet appropriate due process standards.

Each year, a certain escapement of fish is necessary to preserve the run. After this escapement has been allowed by either state or tribal regulation, the remainder of the run is available for harvest. The court decreed an allocation of this harvestable run between the treaty tribes and other citizens. The state may not regulate treaty Indians' taking of this harvestable run at their "usual and accustomed grounds and stations" unless necessary to limit them to 50 percent of the harvest at those grounds. Treaty Indians thus are to have the opportunity to take up to 50 percent of the available harvest at their traditional grounds.

The harvest to be allocated comprises not merely those fish which actually pass the traditional fishing grounds, but also those captured en route and those bound for those grounds but caught in marine waters by non-treaty fishermen. The court decreed an "equitable adjustment" to the harvestable catch to compensate for attrition from these sources. On the other hand, those fish caught by treaty Indians on reservations or taken for traditional tribal ceremonies or personal consumption by tribal members and their immediate families are to be totally disregarded in calculating the harvestable catch.

The state and its agencies challenge virtually all of these features of the district court's decision.

The treaties were "not a grant of rights to the Indians, but a grant of rights from them—a reservation of those not granted." The extent of that grant will be construed as understood by the Indians at that time, taking into consideration their lack of literacy and legal sophistication, and the limited nature of the jargon in which negotiations were conducted. Although ceding their right to occupy the vast territories in which they had been accustomed to roam unimpeded, the Indians reserved their traditional right to fish at their accustomed places. They granted the white settlers the right to fish beside them. In a sense, the treaty cloaks the Indians with an extraterritoriality while fishing at these locations. Although present Indian status is not understood in terms of tribal sovereignty, recalling past acceptance of that concept aids in perceiving the Indians' understanding of the effect of the treaties which they signed. They retained the right to continue to fish as they were accustomed. Certainly, they did not understand that in permitting other citizens access to their traditional fishing areas they were submitting to future regulations calculated to benefit those other citizens.

Nevertheless, this is precisely how the state of Washington has regulated fishing for years. In treating treaty Indian fishermen no differently from other citizens of the state, the state has rendered the treaty guarantees nugatory [invalid]. As the non-Indian population has expanded, treaty Indians have constituted a decreasingly significant proportion of the total population, catching a decreasing proportion of a fixed or decreasing number of fish. "This is certainly an impotent outcome to negotiations and a convention, which seemed to promise more and give the word of the Nation for more."

In summary, the Indians negotiated the treaties as at least quasi-sovereign nations. They relinquished millions of acres of their lands, retiring to reservations carved out of those lands. But they expressly reserved their indispensable rights to fish at their traditional places. The United States obtained for the settlers and for the subsequently-admitted state only the right of equal access to these fishing grounds. The treaty provision at issue grants the state's other citizens only a limited right to fish at treaty places; it thus is "express federal law" preempting all state regulation of Indian fishing at the treaty fishing grounds, except as hereafter stated.

Today, the treaty Indians' "usual and accustomed" fishing grounds in general are located upstream from sites of intensive non-treaty Indian fishing. Because the parties to the treaties did not anticipate shortages of harvestable fish, they did not foresee that downstream fishing by non-Indians would someday injure the Indians' right to fish at their usual places. Therefore, the Indians are entitled to catch 50 percent not simply of the fish passing the traditional grounds, but also of those destined for those grounds but captured downstream or in marine waters. . . .

7. *Stan Dodman Laments the Loss of the Indian Way of Life, 1975*

Urban Halfbreed

I dream of buffalo that I've never seen,
I dream of places where I've never been;
I dream of customs that I've never known,
And dream of going where the spirit is flown.

I long for trails that I'll never run,
I long for a hunt in the autumn sun;
I long for a way that is no more,
Lost here amidst concrete and smoke.

I curse this place where I was born,
And curse these walls where I do mourn;
I curse these ties that hold me here,
And think of names that I hold dear.

I remember Isadore their first victim,
And then Gabriel, the warrior grim;
I remember Louis, on the scaffold high,
For his people was unafraid to die!

Though a century has passed this way,
I'll not forget their glorious day;
So Métis warriors, Do not despair,
You are not lost, for your children care.

In your efforts there is a start,
For your dreams have won my heart;
I'll take the torch, that you held high,
And in your paths I'll walk with pride!

References

1. Mario Savio Challenges University Leaders, 1964
"The University Becomes a Factory," interview edited by J. Fincher, *Life,* February 26, 1965, quoted in James Haskins and Kathleen Benson, *The 60s Reader* (New York: Viking Kestrel, 1988), pp. 55–57.

2. The McCone Commission Reports on Causes of the Watts Riots, 1965
State of California, Governor's Commission on the Los Angeles Riots, "Violence in the City—An Ending or a Beginning" (Los Angeles, 1965), quoted in Leonard Pitt, *California Controversies: Major Issues in the History of the State,* 2d ed. (Arlington Heights, Ill.: Harlan Davidson, 1987), pp. 229, 235.

3. Eugene Burdick Describes Three Californias, 1965
Holiday (October 1965), in W. Storrs Lee, *California: A Literary Chronicle* (New York: Funk & Wagnalls, 1968), pp. 523–528.

4. César Chávez Advocates Nonviolence Among Farmworkers, 1965
Jacques E. Levy, *César Chávez: Autobiography of La Causa* (New York: W. W. Norton & Company, 1975), pp. 225–227.

5. Henry Kissinger Asks Cooperation in the Energy Crisis, 1975
Congressional Research Service, *United States—OPEC Relations: Selected Materials* (Washington, D.C.: U.S. Government Printing Office, 1976), pp. 195–196.

6. Judge George Boldt's Decision Finds in Favor of Native American Fishermen in Western Washington, 1974
United States v. *State of Washington,* 520 F. 2d 677, 682–685, 688–689 (1975).

7. Stan Dodman Laments the Loss of the Indian Way of Life, 1975
John W. Friesen, *When Cultures Clash: Case Studies in Multiculturalism* (Calgary: Detselig Enterprises, 1985), pp. 119–120.

Document Set 14

The Environmental Age, 1976–1990s

The dream of sunshine and plenty turned into a nightmare of drought, overdevelopment, and recession for many Californians during the late 1980s and early 1990s. Popular optimism resulting from decades of continuous growth gave way to uncertainty and fear as personal bankruptcy and business and banking failures received increasing attention in the news. Real estate sales plummeted, and more and more houses in sparkling new developments stood empty.

Internationally, the Berlin Wall fell, the Soviet Union dissolved, and Eastern Europeans gained the freedom to travel to the West. Removal of the communist threat allowed cuts in U.S. defense spending but also forced laid-off military and war industry workers from San Diego to Seattle to look elsewhere for work. High taxes, environmental concerns, and a state budget crisis in turn discouraged out-of-state businesses from locating in California. In the other western states, controversies over logging, mining, fishing, oil reserves, nuclear power, and even recreation and tourism added to the pressure.

Nevertheless, as 1992 ended, California and the American West had dramatically assumed an international role. The commemoration of the Columbus quincentennial prompted residents of the American West to reexamine their history, their values, interracial contact, past mistakes, and future directions. New relationships with Latin America included a free trade agreement with Mexico, and the western states began to look toward the nations rimming the Pacific Ocean for economic exchange. Japanese investment in the West reached an all-time high. Political leaders at every level searched for the answer to a balance of trade.

The protests of the 1960s, though volatile, had yielded gains in civil rights and a new awareness of social issues. With the end of the Vietnam War in 1973, however, the economy took a downward turn, and a recession hit in 1974. Unemployment provoked legal challenges to such programs as affirmative action. The hiring of minorities, some the victims of age-old prejudices and others the victims of oppression or war, had sparked controversy in the West from the earliest days, when the railroads laid off thousands of Chinese workers.

Minority quotas in school admission policies also contributed to the tension. Allan Bakke, a white student, sued the Regents of the University of California because he had been denied admission to the medical school at Davis solely on the basis of race. He won his case in 1978, when the U.S. Supreme Court ruled that a school could not specify an exact number of minority seats (quotas) but could use race or ethnicity, along with other factors, in making admissions decisions. Although Bakke triumphed, the case also upheld the general principle of affirmative action. Justice Thurgood Marshall, in a dissenting opinion (Document 1), nevertheless called the decision a blow to blacks.

Despite persistent concerns about the economy, the environment, social problems, and world peace, Americans still enjoyed watching movies and reliving nostalgically the days of the West, when life was simple and the greatest danger came from outlaws robbing the stage or rustling cattle. (No one cared whether the steers were fed steroids or antibiotics.) As the 1970s closed, John Wayne, one of Hollywood's heroes—a symbol of life in the rugged West—passed away. Document 2 honors the memory of a motion picture actor who received a congressional Gold Medal for his contributions to American life.

Document 3 takes a refreshingly positive look at the California freeway system, a phenomenon not often praised in contemporary literature. Because freeways have affected nearly everyone's life in the West, it is a rewarding exercise to extract some meaning or even cultural enjoyment from these massive structures. David Brodsly discusses the Los Angeles freeways, but his analysis applies to any freeway upon which commuters may be trapped.

Continuing deterioration of the environment and the ongoing depletion of life-sustaining natural resources remain serious concerns in the West. Among all environmental issues in the region, one of the most difficult to assess accurately and rationally is water. This precious commodity is unpredictable and unevenly distributed. Many people wonder why hydrologists cannot desalinate seawater to relieve Pacific coastal regions of drought. Document 4 explains why this solution to water shortages usually is not practical.

Nearly a century after acquiring Hawaii and Guam, the United States has reached its ultimate "manifest destiny" in the Pacific Rim. In contrast to the imperialism of the late nineteenth and the early twentieth centuries, however, the watchword is not *annexation* but *economic cooperation.* Alaska is a close neighbor, and the ports of Seattle, Tacoma, Portland, San Francisco, Los Angeles, and San Diego are important gateways to the Pacific. Observers predict that the American West, with Hawaii as a focal point of Pacific Ocean travel, will continue to forge strong links with the countries of Asia, Latin America, the South Pacific, and Australia. Document 5 notes the tension, a half-century after World War II in the Pacific, between the Atlantic Alliance and the Pacific Basin.

The problem of integrating diverse peoples into the mainstream of life while respecting cultural differences long has challenged California and the rest of the West. Document 6 is taken from a collection of autobiographical statements that accompanied photographs of recent immigrants. Their collective experiences show how widely scattered groups of people, for different reasons, have come together in the West. Twentieth-century views possibly expand Frederick Jackson Turner's concept of the West as a safety valve for discontented easterners. The West, in fact, has served as a kind of *world* safety valve, where people of many different nationalities and backgrounds have gained a fresh start. In a way, the history of the American West is not so different from the beginnings of the United States, when English, German, Irish, and other European immigrants arrived to take advantage of a new land and new economic opportunities.

In many areas of the West, different racial groups live or work together amicably, but true integration has often failed to take place. The Los Angeles riots of 1992, although triggered by sensational media reporting of an unpopular jury verdict, had long-standing, deep-rooted causes. The riots stemmed in part from the same conditions that precipitated the Watts riots of 1965. The later outbreaks, however, had underlying tensions between African-Americans and Korean-Americans as well. Document 7 illustrates the significant role played by the latter in Los Angeles and the unclear relationship that immigrants have with their countries of origin. By contrast, Document 8, written by Antonia Hernandez, president and general counsel of the Mexican American Legal Defense and Educational Fund, paints a positive picture. She predicts Mexican-Americans as having greater political power and holding more highly skilled jobs and management positions by the year 2000.

In her highly acclaimed book *The Legacy of Conquest* (1987), historian Patricia Nelson Limerick discusses the unbroken continuity of western history. She explores the diversity of the characters who have inherited the West's complex past and believes that "it is a disturbing element of continuity in Western history that we have not ceased to be strangers." Document 9, the final selection, shows how history is a sum of its parts—and how no part can be overlooked. This lesson applies to all of history, and each generation must rewrite the past in view of new insights.

Questions for Analysis

1. Do you agree with Justice Marshall that the Supreme Court should have established quotas for minority admission?
2. What values can a movie star like John Wayne instill in a younger generation?
3. How have freeways affected the life-style of residents in the West?
4. In what areas has desalination been successful?
5. Do you think that the United States should allow friendly refugees from countries such as Vietnam or Cuba to come into the United States? What has been the economic impact of these newcomers?
6. What do you think could have been done to prevent the rioting in Los Angeles in 1992?
7. What have been the major contributions of Mexican-Americans to the American West?
8. What do you think have been the most important factors influencing the history of California and the West? Are there any major differences between the states first settled by Spain and those settled by other countries?

1. Justice Thurgood Marshall Challenges the Bakke *Decision, 1978*

. . . [I]t is more than a little ironic that, after several hundred years of class-based discrimination against Negroes, the Court is unwilling to hold that a class-based remedy for that discrimination is permissible. In declining to so hold, today's judgment ignores the fact that for several hundred years Negroes have been discriminated against, not as individuals, but rather solely because of the color of their skins. It is unnecessary in 20th century America to have individual Negroes demonstrate that they have been victims of racial discrimination; the racism of our society has been so pervasive that none, regardless of wealth or position, has managed to escape its impact. The experience of Negroes in America has been different in kind, not just in degree, from that of other ethnic groups. It is not merely the history of slavery alone but also that a whole people were marked inferior by the law. And that mark has endured. . . .

2. John Wayne, Folk Hero of Hollywood, Dies, 1979

John Wayne was an American folk hero by reason of countless films in which he lived bigger, shot straighter and loomed larger than any man in real life ever could.

His death in Los Angeles on Monday at the age of 72 deprived the world of the last active survivor and exponent of the classic American action film. In the more than 200 features in which he appeared in a career that spanned half a century, "Duke" Wayne projected an image of rugged, sometimes muleheaded and always formidable masculinity.

His name was synonymous with the Western and, beyond that, with Hollywood and with what many Americans would like to believe about themselves and their country. He became a figure whose magnitude and emotional conviction took on an enduring symbolic importance.

Mr. Wayne's films earned about $700 million. For 25 consecutive years, he was listed among the top 10 box office attractions of American films. His only Academy Award came late in his career for his role as the cantankerous Marshal Rooster Cogburn in "True Grit" in 1969. The critics as well as the public thought it was well deserved.

Perhaps no Hollywood actor had a more distinctive appearance—a slightly tilted stance and a loping stride, an emphatic, syncopated way of speaking which delighted many a mimic, professional and amateur, and an awesome physical presence. His physicality was expressed most engagingly, perhaps, in a peerless ability to kick in locked doors.

In an interview in 1976, Mr. Wayne described the typical hero he portrayed:

"The man I played," he said slowly, "could be rough, he could be immoral, he could be cruel, tough or tender, but" his hand hit the table smartly—"he was never petty or small. Everyone in the audience wants to identify with that kind of character. He may be bad, but if he's bad, he's BAD. He's not just a petty little whiner."

Mr. Wayne died of cancer at 8:35 P.M. (Eastern time) at the UCLA Medical Center in Los Angeles. His death was announced three hours later by Dr. Bernard R. Strohm, the hospital administrator. The actor's seven children were at his bedside at the end.

The character Mr. Wayne played on the screen and the gallantry and stubbornness with which he fought repeated illnesses in recent years were evoked in the messages of sympathy that came from around the world.

In a statement issued by the White House, President Carter said that "in an age of few heroes" Mr. Wayne was "the genuine article."

"But he was more than just a hero," the president said. "He was a symbol of many of the most basic qualities that made America great. The ruggedness, the tough independence, the sense of personal conviction and courage—on and off the screen—reflected the best of our national character. It was because of what John Wayne said about what we are and what we can be that his great and deep love of America was returned in full measure." . . .

Mr. Wayne starred in Hollywood action films beginning with a grandiose Western epic, "The Big Trail," and ending with "The Shootist" in 1976. Although he enjoyed success in many non-Western roles—at one time his identity as a movie soldier probably took precedence over his identity as a movie cowboy—Mr. Wayne's fame and appeal are likely to rest on such Westerns as John Ford's "Stagecoach," "She Wore a Yellow Ribbon," "Rio Grande," "The Searchers," and "The Man Who Shot Liberty Valance," Howard Hawks' "Red River" and "Rio Bravo," and Henry Hathaway's "North to Alaska" and "True Grit."

At once the most venerable and durable of Western stars, Mr. Wayne sustained this genre by the force and clarity of his personality years after other stars of his generation had abandoned it. Although some critics have felt that Mr. Wayne did little more than play himself in his movies, the image he projected was one he devised with considerable art. His walk and his manner of speaking, for example, were copied from his friend Yakima Canutt, the stunt man.

Film historian David Thomson wrote that "Wayne's sincere wrong-headedness may yet obliterate the fact he is a great screen actor. . . . It is a matter of some . . . importance that the student of film appreciate that Wayne is an actor of noble bearing. Good enough to survive innumerable bad films, he is a presence that makes meaning and appearance exactly congruent—one can ask for no more."

3. David Brodsly Praises Los Angeles Freeways, 1981

The freeway is literally a concrete testament to who we are, and it continues to structure the way we live. Both the dominant role the freeways play in transportation and their sheer permanence have made them the backbone of southern California. They rank with the mountains and the rivers in influencing the organization of a changing city, and uncontestably they are the single most important feature of the man-made landscape. Driving the freeway is absolutely central to the experience of living in Los Angeles, and any anthropologist studying our city would head for the nearest onramp, for nowhere else would he or she observe such large-scale public activity. Time spent on the freeway is for many of us a significant chunk of our lives. The way we think about place, both the city at large and our home turf, is intimately tied to cars and freeways. Perhaps the most basic feature of freeways, and the one most overlooked by the preoccupied commuter, is that they are impressive structures, the most awesome works of design in the daily lives of most of us. They can even be beautiful.

Although tourists and schoolchildren look to Olvera Street for a visible sign of Los Angeles' illusive history, the freeway stands as a living monument to our past. It is a final product of succeeding generations of transportation systems which have been superimposed on the southern California landscape. . . .

The relationship of the freeways to their highway predecessors is the most obvious and the easiest to understand. The freeways were built to relieve the most popular surface highways of through traffic. The names associated with the freeways in the early master plans of the 1930s and 1940s make this intended superimposition particularly clear: Sepulveda Parkway, Colorado Parkway, Ramona Parkway, Atlantic Parkway, Olympic Parkway, Crenshaw Parkway, and so on. The parallel was even more pronounced in the plan for a freeway and expressway system adopted by the state legislature in 1959, which was to replace practically every major state highway with a freeway. What was actually built, however, more closely resembles the earlier rail patterns than a comprehensive highway grid. The radial routes usually received higher priority and were constructed first, and several major bypass routes were subsequently deleted owing to funding shortages and routing controversies.

The Los Angeles freeway is a silent monument not only to the history of the region's spatial organization, but to the history of its values as well. Rather than representing a radical departure from tradition, the freeway was the logical next step in making the Los Angeles dream a reality. Los Angeles' appeal lay in its being the first major city that was not quite a city, that is, not a crowded industrial metropolis. It was a garden city of backyards and quiet streets, a sprawling small town magnified a thousandfold and set among palms and orange trees and under a sunny sky. When the city began drowning in the sheer popularity of this vision, the freeway was offered as a lifeline. The L.A. freeway makes manifest in concrete the city's determination to keep its dream alive. . . .

Joan Didion . . . calls the freeway experience "the only secular communion Los Angeles has." The more I think about the parallel, the more I realize how correct she is. Every time we merge with traffic we join our community in a wordless creed: belief in individual freedom, in a technological liberation from place and circumstance, in a democracy of personal mobility. When we are stuck in rush-hour traffic the freeway's greatest frustration is that it belies its promise.

The L.A. freeway is the cathedral of its time and place. It is a monumental structure designed to serve the needs of our daily lives, at the same time representing what we stand for in this world. It is surely the structure the archaeologists of some future age will study in seeking to understand who we were.

4. *Ross Hallwachs Evaluates Desalination, 1991*

You can wade in it, swim and fish in it, and sail on it. You can revel in the vivid colors as the sun sets into it, bask in the breezes that blow from it in the summer and luxuriate in the warmth of the Santa Ana winds it draws in the winter.

But you can't drink it.

For all the good the Pacific Ocean does Southern California's water needs, it might as well be a desert mirage. Technology to desalinate oceanwater has existed for some time, but the cost has put it out of reach.

Now, however, with Southern California's reliable supplies of freshwater decreasing as its population rises; with the quality of Sacramento–San Joaquin Delta water tainted by agricultural drainwater and saltwater, with the delta's very existence threatened by earthquake; and with a statewide drought now in its fifth year, a thorough look at desalination is warranted.

In fact, a growing number of California water suppliers—including Metropolitan Water District and the San Diego County Water Authority—are giving desalination serious consideration; a few agencies already have small desalination plants in operation.

Marin Municipal Water District began a pilot desalination project in September, and may ask voters to approve a major desalting plant that would provide about one-seventh of that district's needs. Cornered by dry times, the city of Morro Bay has rented desalination units to produce 40 percent of the city's drinking water; Santa Barbara has contracted the use of temporary desalination units to meet about a third of the city's water needs. Santa Catalina Island has a new desalination plant producing 25 percent of the island's tapwater.

Metropolitan is participating in a $600,000 study to evaluate the feasibility of constructing and operating a facility capable of producing up to 100 million gallons of water per day and 500 megawatts of electricity along the Pacific Coast near Tijuana, Mexico, and intends to have a 5-million-gallon-per-day (mgd) distillation plant of its own in operation by 1995, and is determining at which of 13 Southern California power plants it can be built. That desalination facility will be the pilot project for Met's eventual construction of a 100 mgd distillation plant.

But these projects are miniscule compared to what would be required to provide the additional freshwater Southern California will need in the coming decades, or even replace the water Metropolitan currently draws from the delta. . . .

Is desalting oceanwater the answer?

Approximately 8,000 desalination plants are in operation around the world, producing about 10,000 acre-feet of water a day, close to 4 million acre-feet a year, according to Patricia Burke, executive director of the International Desalination Association. Many plants use reverse osmosis, which forces seawater through membranes, screening out salts and contaminants. But distillation—heating saltwater into steam and condensing the vapor—produces most of the world's desalinated water. The largest plant, at Al-Jubail, Saudi Arabia, distills 300 million gallons per day, 336,000 acre-feet a year. One expert estimated that one out of every 30 barrels of oil pumped out of the ground in Saudi Arabia is used to distill that country's water.

What exactly would be required to build and operate desalination plants that could replace the 1.5-million-acre-feet of water Metropolitan uses from the delta and provide the additional 1.2 million acre-feet the district is expected to need in 20 years? What would be the cost? What environmental and economic effects could be expected?

The 100 mgd distillation plant Metropolitan is planning would be the nation's largest desalination facility. But it would take 24 such plants to replace the water Met is receiving from the delta and to provide the freshwater Southern California is expected to need in just 20 years.

Gary Snyder, chief engineer at Metropolitan, says the number of plants needed in such a hypothesis could be reduced by doubling their capacity. "Conceivably, you could string any number of desalination plants together at the same site," Snyder says. But reducing the number of plants wouldn't eliminate the practical considerations accompanying a giant desalination project: location and cost. In fact, it might magnify them.

Desalination plants have to be built right on the coast or very close to it, Snyder says. Why not build them inland and pump seawater to them? "Distillation uses five times as much saltwater as the freshwater produced, so pipeline sizes and pumping costs would be enormous," Snyder explains.

Locating a chain of mammoth desalination plants along the Southern California coast would not be easy. Wayne Lusvardi, who handles real estate for Metropolitan, estimates that a 200 mgd desalination plant with an adjoining power station might need up to a hundred acres for facilities and to buffer the plant from neighbors. And, the so-called NIMBY ("Not in my backyard") factor shouldn't be underestimated.

Could a dozen 100-acre sites be found along the Southern California coast between San Diego and Ventura, some of the most scenic and expensive real estate in the United States?

"Improbable," Lusvardi says. "Even with our right of eminent domain, it's doubtful we could assemble sites that large. Even if the sites could be found, the price would be enormous. You're talking between $500,000 and $1 million an acre," or a possible $100 million per site.

Less expensive but still difficult to acquire would be the "ocean lots" needed for the saltwater intake and return, Lusvardi says. This offshore property, acquired through the State Lands Commission, is typically granted to public entities at the price of the commission's administrative costs.

Once the land is acquired, construction costs are not small. The Catalina Island plant cost $2.5 million and will produce only 132,000 gallons per day. Construction cost of the 5 mgd plant Marin Municipal Water District hopes to build is estimated at $60 million. And that doesn't include power plants. A consultant's study for Metropolitan in 1987 estimated the cost of a 100-mgd desalination plant and adjoining power plant at about $2 billion.

Finally, a mammoth pipeline and pumping system would have to be built to connect the coastal desalting plants with Metropolitan's existing water delivery system. Because the existing system flows mostly downhill, it needs few pumps to push the water to its destinations. With coastal plants, however, all the water would have to be pumped uphill, which increases construction costs and adds ongoing operating costs.

But perhaps the most important considerations are the possible effects of a major desalination program on Southern California's coastal scenery and air quality. Desalting plants could be buffered with land and screened by landscaping, but locating a string of large structures along some of the nation's most scenic coastline would doubtless raise public ire and face a difficult if not impossible administrative review process.

The impact of a major desalination program on Southern California air quality also would be a probable bone of public contention. Desalination requires enormous amounts of power. It takes the energy equivalent of five barrels of oil per acre-foot to pump freshwater through the California Aqueduct, but 30 barrels to desalt the same amount of oceanwater.

"For a 200-mgd desalination plant, you'd need to either refurbish an existing power plant and tie the desalting plant to it, or build a whole new generating plant," Snyder says.

Traditional power plants use fossil fuels—coal, oil and gas—that produce air pollution. If oil were used, generating electricity to desalinate 2.7 million acre-feet would consume about 81 million barrels of oil. That's about 73.5 million barrels more than are needed for moving Southern California's share of the State Water Project. A representative of the South Coast Air Quality Management District estimated that burning 81 million barrels of oil would release about 3,300 tons of pollutants into the atmosphere.

Even assuming that permits could be obtained to burn that much oil—and the AQMD says they couldn't—fuel cost would be extremely high. When oil prices jumped to $40 a barrel due to the Persian Gulf crisis, the cost of 81 million barrels was $3.2 billion. Metropolitan's entire 1990–1991 annual operating budget is $628 million.

Natural gas is cleaner burning, but desalinating 2.7 million acre-feet of water would require about a 50 percent increase over the amount now used for all purposes in the southland. A Southern California Gas Co. engineer estimates that would add about 1,600 tons of pollutants a year to the air; other experts estimate that such a hike in use would require a pipeline be built from Texas or Canada at a cost of about $1 billion.

The obvious alternative to fossil-fuel-burning power plants is nuclear energy, which doesn't pollute the air with smoke and other emissions. Though a new breed of reactors incorporating advanced safety features is being developed, public opinion remains vehemently opposed to nuclear power. Until a safe, economic form of fusion is perfected, it appears that public opinion will remain opposed to nuclear power plants.

What at first glance would seem an economic, ecologic and publicly popular solution to Southern California's water quality and supply problems could be exactly the opposite: enormously expensive, environmentally damaging and widely *un*popular.

Until the economic and environmental considerations can be resolved, Metropolitan will continue to view large-scale desalination cautiously and to see the impact of that technique on the state's water resources as limited.

"When those problems *are* solved," says Metropolitan's General Manager Carl Boronkay, "desalination, unquestionably, will play a major role in the state's future water resources."

5. *James Kurth Hopes That the Pacific Basin Remains Pacific, 1989*

The 1990s, a half century after the Pacific War, will be a period of tension between two international relations paradigms: (1) the declining one of international liberalism and extended deterrence, created by the United States in the Atlantic/European world and extended by it into the Pacific/Asian world, the paradigm of the American half century; and (2) the rising one of international mercantilism and finite deterrence, created by the Pacific/Asian powers themselves, the paradigm of the future. The two paradigms are in an uneasy but symbiotic relationship. The relationship between the Atlantic Alliance and the Pacific Basin paradigms is rather like the relationship between yin and yang, that famous Asian symbol that appears in many places in Asian life, including the center of the South Korean flag. The Atlantic Alliance paradigm is waning and the Pacific Basin paradigm is waxing, but each is intimately—and dialectically—connected to the other.

In its contemporary version, international mercantilism can mean economic cooperation between the states of the Pacific Basin in a reasonable but changing division of labor based upon dynamic, not static, comparative advantage in the international market. Similarly, comprehensive security can mean comprehensive cooperation between the states of the Pacific Basin, with military deterrence directed only at the most finite security objective, the protection of the national territory.

A half century ago Japan adhered to a harsher version of international mercantilism and comprehensive security: imperial mercantilism and East Asian hegemony. In pursuit of these policies, Japan warred upon the other great Asian power, China. In doing so, it came into conflict with the American paradigms of international liberalism—the open door in China—and extended deterrence—the U.S. forces in the Philippines and the fleet at Pearl Harbor. This is turn opened the way for the Pacific War, the American victory, and the American half century.

If Japan and China should again come into conflict, as they did a half century ago, the outcome of the tension between the Atlantic Alliance and the Pacific Basin paradigms is likely to be a descent into chaos and a journey into the unknown, although, of course, not necessarily in a way like the Pacific War. Conversely, if Japan and China should come into cooperation, even more than they have in the past decade, the outcome of the tension between the Atlantic Alliance and the Pacific Basin paradigms is likely to be the gradual waning of the first and waxing of the second, the dialectic of yin and yang.

The Atlantic Alliance paradigm and the American Century entered into their historic moment through the Pacific War. The Pacific Basin paradigm and the Pacific Century will enter into their historical moment only if the Pacific Basin remains pacific.

6. New Americans Find a Home in the West, 1988

Mai Khan *(Vietnam)*

It was almost empty in our hands when we arrived here. We had to leave because the Vietcong government took our house and property. We could not take job because we are Chinese born in Vietnam. They didn't like Chinese, though the Chinese government helped Vietnam a lot. They closed our fabric export business and said we must do the farmers' job—grow vegetables. There was no food or water. You could grow something or just die.

Before escaping we had to pay ten ounces of gold per person to the boat owner. We were caught and they took all our cash and gold. The second time we took no risk. My mother and brother slipped out and then my sister and I so the guard wouldn't notice. The boat was very crowded with over 300 people. On the way we hit a big storm. The boat was small and we were very scared. We were finally picked up by a Panamanian freighter.

People here are generous and kind, not selfish. They found us an apartment and jobs. My brother, sister, and I all work the same shift at the same company, so we can drive together. Mother stays home and cooks our meals. We feel satisfied with what we have now. Our salary is not too high because of our language problem, but we were able to each buy our favorite thing. My brother owns a stereo, sister bought a TV, and I got a sewing machine. Together we share the living room furniture and chose the Mickey Mouse telephone. These are our only possessions. We celebrate in our mind every day. A lot of people died on their way to freedom.

Wichharak Nai *(Cambodia)*

Long Beach

According to my age and to my tradition, I could be someone's husband, but my father changed my age when we crossed the Cambodian border into Thailand six years ago. I have had to fake it ever since, act like I was a kid, like I was four years younger. I almost got conditioned that way. My father wanted us to have a good education, go to school here like other children. Had they known that I was already over 16 years old they would have never allowed me to enter junior high school. Now I am a junior, only my guidance counselor knows my real age.

I have two things against me: my language and my size. The language problem can be gotten under control. I just study and study and don't do too much else, because it hurts a lot to be put down as being stupid just because you have not mastered the new language yet. I have been here already for three years, long enough to speak English fluently, but still, from time to time I find myself translating in my mind.

It is my size that really bothers me. I don't get to be on any team. They don't pick you if you are not an athletic figure. I have been wrestling, doing push-ups, I lift weights, and I eat a lot, but I guess I won't grow any more. Cambodians are smaller than Americans to start with, but I also had to work hard and carry heavy loads when I was a young boy.

Santiago Aguilar (Mexico)

Farmworker

Nine years ago my mother sent me up here. I was 14 and in love with a 24-year-old girl. That's no good, said my mother, and off I went to live with my uncles in National City. For most of these years I have been working on farms, but once a year I go to see my mother in Guadalajara.

A friend of mine has been teaching me English. She knows nothing at all Spanish and I know nothing at all English. Now I am going to school to learn to write. I should have gone long ago. I didn't know it was important.

When we go to Escondido we sometimes get picked up by the Border Patrol. If it is before 9 A.M. they take us to the border at 10 A.M. In that case we can be back at work by two or three in the afternoon. A waste of time. I hope to get my papers soon. I want to stay here.

Vu Uy Thang (Vietnam)

Auto Body Shop Owner, Santa Ana

I am 54 years old. In Vietnam a man my age and his wife don't work; they stay home and let the children take care of them. In America you work hard and you keep on working hard. Everything is hard. Our children don't live with us as they do at home. They have to live close to where their job is. They have to look after themselves. The good life is gone. Everybody looks after themselves.

Anonymous (Russia)

Cab Driver

I have been here for almost 10 years. I come from Russia, I am a Jew. Right from the beginning I've been driving a cab. It would be all right, but this place is not safe. Six times I was robbed, lost all the money I made that day. Don't get me wrong, I like it here, but the government is too much nice. You have too many freedoms. People here don't know how to handle their freedoms.

Sal Salem (Iraq)

Part Owner of a Liquor Store

If you enter this country as a legal immigrant, all you have to worry about is the cultural adjustment and the language. That is not easy. Especially for the older people, that is a struggle. But for us, the young ones, we've got as good a chance as anybody else and better because we work harder. If we keep our principles and values, we can make a good living.

There must be at least 2,000 people from Iraq in San Diego. Most of us are Catholics. People here think we are all Muslims just because we come from the Middle East. There is a lot of ignorance here and people pass judgment before they know you. After you talk with them and tell them how you think and who you are, they are usually happy to accept you.

7. *The Los Angeles Riots Dramatize Racial Tensions, 1992*

In an emotional encounter at the heavily guarded South Korean Consulate in Los Angeles on 4 May between leaders of the Korean American community and California Governor Pete Wilson, David Kim, the head of the community grocers' association put the crucial question: "Where were those [the police and the National Guard] who are supposed to protect and serve their people when we needed them most?"

Kim called on government help to rebuild Korean American businesses, devastated in the three-day riot that raged from 29 April to 1 May, and added the ominous warning: "If we do not have a reply . . . there will be uncontrollable demonstration of our frustration, anger and disappointment—in huge numbers."

As Los Angeles citizens pick up the pieces and start to rebuild, and as the US ponders the riot's broader meaning, the Korean American community stands polarized, still shell-shocked and enraged by the destruction wrought on it. Korean American entrepreneurs were by no means the only victims of the rioting, nor were the perpetrators of arson, looting and vandalism all blacks.

But there is no question that the long standoff between Korean Americans and blacks in this city has turned into overt confrontation and that unless the situation is handled delicately, more trouble could follow. Observers worry that Korean American demands for separate compensation and the Seoul government's reported call for "reparations" for Korean American businesses could prove counterproductive.

The Los Angeles riot, triggered by the acquittal on 29 April of four city policemen who had severely beaten a black motorist after a chase in March last year, is now described as the worst in this century, with the death toll surpassing 50. Some 3,600 fires were reported in three days in the city and adjacent areas. About 1,600 businesses were burned down or otherwise damaged seriously, and double this number were looted, according to preliminary reports.

At least 100 Korean American–owned groceries, liquor stores and other shops were hit on the first night, mainly in the city's predominantly black South-Central district, where few Korean Americans actually live. Violence spread in the following two days to Koreatown and beyond, and a tally by the *Korea Times* newspaper showed, as of 5 May 1,867 community businesses reporting total damage of US$346 million.

Two Korean Americans were killed by gunfire: one in an accident, by fellow Korean Americans protecting their property from their attackers, and the other when he was coming out of a bank having withdrawn some money. Many others were wounded.

Korean Americans arming themselves heavily in self-defence made some of the most disturbing and memorable images of this riot, shown repeatedly on television and in newspapers. Korean Americans complain bitterly that they had no other choice, given that the police and the National Guard had abandoned them.

Prof. Eui-young Yu of California State University protests further that the media took these images out of context to frame the black–Korean American conflict as the central feature of the riots. Yu and others feel Korean Americans are being blamed for the failure of mainstream America to integrate the blacks. But many conservative Americans seem to applaud the Korean Americans' action; a segment of the anti-gun control lobby has already made them its hero.

Minimizing black–Korean American racial tensions, some observers point out that Korean Americans happen to own the majority of groceries in South-Central Los Angeles. Koreatown lies directly north of South Central and was thus a natural target. Some reports stress that Hispanic and white Americans as well as blacks were involved in the violence in Koreatown.

But the racial tensions are out in the open. As Congresswoman Maxine Waters from South-Central said: "Let us not deny that there are tensions [and] suspicions. Let us not deny that there are people down here who believe that people coming from some place else are doing better."

Tense relations between blacks and Korean American shopowners are seen throughout the US. Blacks complain of rude treatment and high prices in these stores, and Korean Americans complain of losses from shoplifting. Feelings reached a new height last year when a white judge gave not a prison sentence but probation to a Korean American woman who had shot dead a black teenager she suspected of shoplifting a bottle of orange juice.

On 4 May, the day the dusk-to-dawn curfew was lifted in Los Angeles, the police opened a "storefront" at the massive Oriental Mission Church at the edge of Koreatown to allow Korean Americans to report the damages they had suffered. Asked about Korean Americans' anger at the failure of the system, and in particular of law enforcement, to protect them, Sgt Gary Farmer said: "When something happens to you personally, it means everything to you." He hastened to add that such a reaction was understandable from the many Korean American businessmen whose insurance does not cover damages suffered from civil unrest and who may not be able to restart their businesses.

But the community's strong demand for special compensation—including debt and tax relief, emergency credit and contributions to relief funds—is making some city and state officials uncomfortable. The officials, citing budgetary constraints, have been less than forthcoming with specifics.

One Asian American notable laments that recent immigrants are not required or prepared to give up part of their old selves to become American and work with other Americans. . . .

Observers suspected that the coming presidential election in South Korea was one reason behind Seoul's interest in the Los Angeles riot. . . .

The sudden rush to Los Angeles prompted concern that some South Koreans might have forgotten that the 400,000 Koreans living in Los Angeles are immigrants who have adopted a new country. Expressions of support sometimes appeared excessive, with students holding demonstrations in front of the US Embassy in Seoul and the local press reporting that the Korean Embassy in Washington might ask for US Government "compensation."

The riot is likely to have a profound long-term effect on the Asian American community as on the rest of the US. "Suddenly, I am scared to be Asian. More specifically, I am afraid of being mistaken for a Korean [American]. Having acknowledged those fears, I feel shame, guilt and a . . . puzzlement over where to go from here," wrote *Los Angeles Times* columnist Elaine Woo, who is Chinese American.

Although the Bush administration is obviously reluctant to spend great amounts of money to improve the lot of Korean Americans, it will nonetheless divert more of its dwindling resources to domestic programmes, making the US more inward-looking, analysts say. If, on top of that, Asian companies decide that Los Angeles is no longer a safe and pleasant place in which to do business, the city's position as US' strongest link with Asia could be diminished, a city official says.

8. A Mexican-American Speaks Out About the Future, 1992

The rest of this country is discovering what many of us have known for quite some time: Our Hispanic roots are showing. And with this awakening come the realization and understanding that the Hispanic population in the United States is growing, not only in number but also in influence.

For the Mexican American community, the deserved recognition has been long in coming, and it hasn't been because we're the invisible minority. There are over 11.8 million Mexican Americans living in this country, by far the largest Hispanic subgroup in the country. We make up about 8 percent of the population, although we are little known on the East Coast, where many people have heard about Mexican Americans but have never known any. People think of us as the ethnic minority population with strong ties—often family ties—to our neighbor to the south, Mexico.

For those who haven't noticed, however, the Mexican American is no longer a Southwest phenomenon. We have gone beyond the borders of California, Arizona, New Mexico, Colorado, and Texas. We now have substantial communities in the Midwest—in Chicago, Minneapolis, and St. Paul. Our numbers are also growing in Florida, New York, New Jersey, and Washington State.

Increased numbers can mean that more individuals will participate in, contribute to, and enrich our society, and indeed Mexican Americans have begun to do so. But we must take additional steps to ensure that we are able to fully participate in the economic, political, and social spheres.

Mexican Americans will face two fundamental issues between now and the next century. Clearly, the most important of these is education. Without a strong educational background, many doors will be closed to our community. Educational achievement is directly tied to occupational mobility—you must have an education if you are going to succeed—and with our changing society, that is truer today than ever before.

The United States is moving farther away from a manufacturing-based to a service-based economy, and the occupations of the future will require more education and specialized training. The future of the Mexican American depends on how well our existing labor force is trained and prepared to work in a changing economic setting.

Shifts in population have made it increasingly clear that Mexican Americans are going to play a significant role in the employment picture during the next 30 years. By the year 2020, the elderly population will nearly double as the baby-boom generation begins to retire. The expectation is that a largely white aging population will rely upon the support of a shrinking work force that is composed largely of ethnic minorities. The economic implications are tremendous. Are we preparing our labor force to effectively adjust to these changing demographics?

By 1995, Los Angeles, which has the nation's largest Hispanic population, will be on the verge of becoming the first region in the country where minorities will make up more than 50 percent of the population. Also, between now and the year 2000, the number of high-skill jobs will increase as the number of low-skill employment opportunities shrinks. Unfortunately, research shows that Mexican Americans are underrepresented in the fastest-growing occupations—like health care, management, and administration—and overrepresented in the shrinking job categories. These changes in the employment market demand greater levels of training for Mexican Americans. If we don't better train this work force for an increasingly technological economy, we are going to face serious problems.

Political Power

A second major challenge facing Mexican Americans is the development of our newly discovered political power. There will be more than 13 million Hispanics, or 7 percent of the nation's 183 million citizens of voting age, for the November election. Our numbers indicate a dramatic potential for Hispanics to become an electoral power, especially when congressional districts are redrawn following the 1990 census. I faintly recollect that someone said the eighties were going to be the decade of the Hispanic, but that simply didn't materialize. I believe the time for Hispanics has not yet arrived, but it is coming. . . .

Mexican Americans, like other Hispanics, possess and maintain a strong, diverse, and rich cultural history. We love our language, music, food, art, and, of course, traditions. We are happy to see that others too are recognizing the unique qualities of being Hispanic.

Mexican Americans have contributed and continue to contribute greatly to the development of this country. We have played a critical role in creating a diverse, strong, and proud country. Through our toil in the fields and factories, we've helped to create a life-style that today is enjoyed by relatively few Hispanics. We also recognize that in the past these contributions often have been ignored by non-Hispanics. Out of necessity, all of this will change in the future. . . .

We want the same kinds of things that most Americans want: a good life for our families, a good education for our children, full participation in the political processes of this country, and the pursuit of happiness.

Yes, our numbers are growing and so is our influence. We recognize that culture precedes politics in America. We accept that as we prepare for the future. As this country becomes better acquainted with its Hispanic roots, a new era for Mexican Americans is beginning in the United States. We've only begun to demonstrate what we can do.

9. *The American West: A Complicated Place, 1987*

Western historians, like Western people throughout the centuries of contact between formerly separate worlds, have been desperate for categories in which they could place these perplexing and unsettling "others" whose existence made life unmercifully complicated. For more than a century, Americans thought they had found the key in "race." Race would provide a filing system, a set of conceptual containers in which one could place troubling individuals, understand them as much as they needed to be understood, and get on with one's business. But the West, from the beginning, overloaded the concepts; Indian diversity alone would eventually have demonstrated the inadequacy of racial categories. Unsure of an alternative, Americans still held on to the filing system, as well to the faith that Congress could fine-tune the system and make it work.

When the weight of Southern civilization fell too heavily on Huckleberry Finn, Mark Twain offered the preferred American alternative: "I reckon I got to light out for the Territory ahead of the rest, because Aunt Sally she's going to adopt me and sivilize me, and I can't stand it. I been there before." The West, the theory had gone, was the place where one escaped the trials and burdens of American civilization, especially in its Southern version. Those "trials and burdens" often came in human form. Repeatedly, Americans had used the West as a mechanism for evading these "problems." Much of what went under the rubric "Western optimism" was in fact this faith in postponement, in the deferring of problems to the distant future. Whether in Indian removal or Mormon migration, the theory was the same: the West is remote and vast; its isolation and distance will release us from conflict; this is where we can get away from each other. But the workings of history carried an opposite lesson. The West was not where we escaped each other, but where we all met.

That has made for a very complicated history. The histories of minorities, written in the last few decades, have made those complications unavoidable. But how, with the addition of these various points of view, is Western history to regain coherence?

When the advance of white male pioneers across the continent was the principal concern of the Western historian, the field had coherence to spare. But two or three decades of "affirmative action history" have made hash of that coherence. Ethnocentricity is out, but what alternative center is in?

When it comes to centers, Western history now has an embarrassment of riches—Indian-centered history, Hispanic-centered history, Asian-centered history, black-centered history, Mormon-centered history, and (discredited though it may be) white-American-mainstream-centered history. If historians were forced to choose one of those centers, hold to it, and reject all others, we would be in deep professional trouble. But that is by no means the only choice available.

Take, for instance, a thoroughly un-Western metaphor for a complicated phenomenon—a subway system. Every station in the system is a center of sorts—trains and passengers converge on it; in both departure and arrival, the station is the pivot. But get on a train, and you are soon (with any luck) at another station, equally a center and a pivot. Every station is at the center of a particular world, yet that does not leave the observer of the system conceptually muddled, unable to decide which station represents the true point of view from which the entire system should be viewed. On the contrary, the idea of the system as a whole makes it possible to think of all the stations at once—to pay attention to their differences while still recognizing their relatedness, and to imagine how the system looks from its different points of view.

What "system" united Western history? Minorities and majority in the American West occupied common ground—literally. A contest for control of land, for the labor applied to the land, and for the resulting profit set the terms of their meeting. Sharing turf, contesting turf, surrendering turf, Western groups, for all their differences, took part in the same story. Each group may well have had its own, self-defined story, but in the contest for property and profit, those stories met. Each group might have preferred to keep its story private and separate, but life on the common ground of the American West made such purity impossible.

Everyone became an actor in everyone else's play; understanding any part of the play now requires us to take account of the whole. It is perfectly possible to watch a play and keep track of, even identify with, several characters at once, even when those characters are in direct conflict with each other and within themselves. The ethnic diversity of Western history asks only that: pay attention to the parts, and pay attention to the whole. It is a difficult task, but to bemoan and lament the necessity to include minorities is to engage, finally, in intellectual laziness. The American West was a complicated place for its historical participants; and it is no exercise in "white guilt" to say that it is—and should be—just as complicated for us today. . . .

References

1. Justice Thurgood Marshall Challenges the *Bakke* Decision, 1978
   Regents of the University of California v. *Bakke* 438 U.S. 265 (1978).
2. John Wayne, Folk Hero of Hollywood, Dies, 1979
   Gary Arnold and Kenneth Turan, "The Duke: More Than Just a Hero," *Washington Post*, June 13, 1979.
3. David Brodsly Praises Los Angeles Freeways, 1981
   David Brodsly, "L.A. Freeway: An Appreciative Essay," 2–5, University of California Press, 1981.
4. Ross Hallwachs Evaluates Desalination, 1991
   Ross Hallwachs, "How Close Are We to Harnessing the Ocean to Our Taps?" *Focus* (publication of the Metropolitan Water District of Southern California), no. 3 (1991): 7–9.
5. James Kurth Hopes That the Pacific Basin Remains Pacific, 1989
   James R. Kurth, "The Pacific Basin Versus the Atlantic Alliance: Two Paradigms of International Relations," *Annals of the American Association of Political Science* (September 1989): 44–45.
6. New Americans Find a Home in the West, 1988
   Ulli Steltzer, *The New Americans: Immigrant Life in Southern California* (Pasadena, Calif.: Newsage Press, 1988), pp. 25, 101, 115, 139, 145.
7. The Los Angeles Riots Dramatize Racial Tensions, 1992
   Susumu Awanohara and Shim Jae Hoon, "Melting Pot Boils Over," *Far Eastern Economic Review*, May 14, 1992, pp. 10–11.
8. A Mexican-American Speaks Out About the Future, 1992
   Antonia Hernandez, "The Political Awakening of Mexican Americans," *Latino Stuff Review* (Spring 1992): 3–4.
9. The American West: A Complicated Place, 1987
   Patricia Nelson Limerick, *The Legacy of Conquest: The Unbroken Past of the American West* (New York: W. W. Norton, 1987), pp. 290–292.

Credits

p. 4 "The Miwok Tell the Story 'Mouse Steals Fire'" in Edward W. Gifford and Gwendoline Harris Block, eds. *Californian Indian Nights Entertainments*, Arthur H. Clark Company, 1930, pp. 135–136. Reprinted by permission of Arthur H. Clark Co.

p. 8 From Doyce B. Nunis, ed. *The Drawings of Ignacio Tirsch: A Jesuit Missionary in Baja California*, 1972, pp. 89–95. Reprinted by permission of Dawson's Book Shop, Los Angeles.

pp. 8–10 From *Font's Complete Diary: A Chronicle of the Founding of San Francisco*, translated and edited by Herbert Eugene Bolton, pp. 109–112. Copyright © 1931 The Regents of the University of California. Reprinted with permission.

pp. 10–11 From *Noticias de Nutka: An Account of Nootka Sound in 1792,* translated and edited by Iris H. W. Engstrand, 1970, revised 1991, pp. 24–28. Reprinted by permission of University of Washington Press.

pp. 11–12 From *California in 1792: A Spanish Naval Visit*, by Donald C. Cutter, pp. 144–149. Copyright © 1990 by the University of Oklahoma Press.

pp. 12–13 Reprinted from *The Journals of the Lewis and Clark Expedition, July 28–November 1, 1805*, Volume 5, edited by Gary E. Moulton, pp. 119–121. Reprinted by permission of the University of Nebraska Press. Copyright © 1988 by the University of Nebraska Press.

p. 18 From Herbert E. Bolton, trans. and ed., *Fray Juan Crespí: Missionary Explorer on the Pacific Coast, 1769–1774*, pp. 229–231. Copyright © 1927 The Regents of the University of California.

pp. 19–20 From Herbert E. Bolton, trans. and ed., *Anza's California Expeditions,* Vol. III, 1966, pp. 33–37, Russell and Russell Publishers.

pp. 23–24 From Charles N. Rudkin, trans. and ed., *The First French Expedition to California: Laperouse in 1786*, 1959, pp 61–67. Reprinted by permission of Dawson's Book Shop, Los Angeles.

pp. 24–25 From Marguerite Eyer Wilbur, ed., *Vancouver in California 1792–1794: The Original Account of George Vancouver,* 1954, pp. 230–233. Reprinted by permission of Dawson's Book Shop, Los Angeles.

pp. 26–27 From *A Voyage to the Northwest Coast of America,* Milo Milton Quaife, ed., Chicago: The Lakeside Press, 1954, pp. 35–40.

p. 33 William Smyth of the H.M.S. Blossom Sketches Native Bidarkas in Alaska (1826), in John Frazier Henry, *Early Maritime Artists of the Pacific Northwest Coast, 1741–1841*, 1984, p. 126, University of Washington Press.

pp. 36–37 From *Voyage of the Venus: Sojourn in California*, translated by Charles N. Rudkin, 1956, pp. 10-12, 36-37. Reprinted by permission of Dawson's Book Shop, Los Angeles.

pp. 37–38 Reprinted by permission of The Putnam Publishing Group from *Sutter's Own Story* by Erwin G. Gudde, pp. 74–80. Copyright © 1936 by Erwin G. Gudde.

pp. 42–43 From *Jim Beckwourth: Black Mountain Man and War Chief of the Crows*, by Elinor Wilson, pp. 34–35. Copyright © 1972 by the University of Oklahoma Press.

pp. 44–45 From David J. Webber, *The Californios Versus Jedediah Smith, 1826–1827: A New Cache of Documents*, 1990, pp. 44–46, 51–55. Reprinted by permission of Arthur H. Clark Co.

pp. 53–54 From William Henry Thomes, *Recollections of Old Times in California* (original 1887 manuscript in the Bancroft Library) edited by George R. Stewart, 1974, pp. 22–25. Reprinted with permission of the Friends of The Bancroft Library.

pp. 55–56 From "The Diary of Patrick Breen" in George R. Stewart, *Ordeal by Hunger: The Story of the Donner Party*, 1960, pp. 323–328.

pp. 59–61 From *The Original Journals of Henry Smith Turner: With Stephen Watts Keamy to New Mexico and California, 1846–1847*, by Henry Smith Turner, pp. 144–148. Copyright © 1966 by the University of Oklahoma Press.

pp. 69–70 From Charles W. Churchill in *Fortunes Are Few: Letters of a Forty-Niner*, edited by Duane A. Smith and David J. Weber, San Diego Historical Society, 1977, pp. 55–59. Reprinted by permission of the San Diego Historical Society.

p. 81 Newspaper clips compiled by Remi Nadeau in *Westways*, September 1962, p. 17.

p. 93 Reprinted from *The Pacific Northwest: An Interpretive History*, by Carlos A. Schwantes, p. 185. Reprinted by permission of the University of Nebraska Press. Copyright © 1989 by the University of Nebraska Press.

p. 99 Photograph of the Haas-Lilienthal House used by permission of the Library of Congress.

p. 100 (top) Photograph of the Long-Waterman House used by permission of the San Diego Historical Society; (bottom) photograph of the Dickinson-Boals House used by permission of the Title Insurance and Trust Company, San Diego, California, Historical Collection.

p. 103 Photograph of miners used by permission of the Anchorage Museum of History and Art.

p. 112 Photograph of the Women's Union Label League No. 197 used by permission of the San Diego History Society, Title Insurance and Trust Collection.

p. 115 Photograph of the Ku Klux Klan used by permission of the Oregon Historical Society.

p. 121 Photograph of "Allegory of California," by Diego Rivera, used by permission of Stock Exchange Tower Associates.

pp. 116–117 From Susan M. Stacy, *Legacy of Light: A History of Idaho Power Company,* 1991, p. 90. Reprinted by permission of Idaho Power Company.

p. 122 From Carey McWilliams, *Ill Fares the Land: Migrants and Migratory Labour in the United States*, Faber and Faber, Ltd., 1945.

pp. 57–59 From *In California Before the Gold Rush*, by John Bidwell, 1948. Reprinted by permission of Laurence Pollinger Limited, Author's Agents.

pp. 127–128 From *The Grapes of Wrath* by John Steinbeck. Copyright © 1939, renewed © 1967 by John Steinbeck. Used by permission of Viking Penguin, a division of Penguin Books USA Inc.

pp. 134–135 Reprinted by permission of the publisher from *Through Harsh Winters: The Life of a Japanese Immigrant Woman*, Akemi Kikumura, pp. 51–53. Copyright © 1981 by Chandler & Sharp Publishers. All rights reserved.

p. 137 Poem by John Breecher, "An Air That Kills" from *Land of the Free*, Morningstar Press, 1956, p. 21.

pp. 142–143 From "The University Becomes a Factory" an interview edited by J. Fincher, *Life* Magazine, February 26, 1965.

pp. 143–146 Eugene Burdick Describes Three Californias in 1965, in *Holiday* Magazine, October 1965, as condensed by W. Storrs Lee in *California: A Literary Chronicle*, New York: Funk & Wagnalls, 1968, pp. 523–528.

pp. 146–147 From *César Chávez: Autobiography of La Causa*, by Jacques E. Levy, pp. 225–227. Copyright © 1975 by W. W. Norton. Reprinted by permission.

p. 150 "Urban Halfbreed" from John W. Friesen, *When Cultures Clash: Case Studies in Multiculturalism*, 1985, pp. 119–120. Reprinted with permission of Detselig Enterprises, Ltd.

pp. 155–156 Article by Gary Arnold and Kenneth Turan, "The Duke: More Than Just a Hero," *The Washington Post*, June 13, 1979. Copyright © 1979, The Washington Post. Reprinted by permission.

p. 157 David Brodsly, *L. A. Freeway: An Appreciative Essay*, pp. 2–5. Copyright © 1981 The Regents of the University of California.

pp. 160–161 From James R. Kurth, "The Pacific Basin Versus the Atlantic Alliance: Two Paradigms of International Relations," *Annals of the American Association of Political Science* (Sept. 1989), pp. 44–45. Reprinted by permission of Sage Publications Inc.

pp. 161–162 From Ulli Steltzer, *The New Americans: American Life in Southern California*, 1988, pp. 25, 101, 115, 139, 145, Newsage Press.

pp. 162–164 From Susumu Awanohara and Shim Jae Hoon, "Melting Pot Boils Over," *Far Eastern Economic Review* (4 May, 1992), pp. 10–11. Reprinted by permission of Far Eastern Economic Review, Hong Kong.

pp. 164–165 From Antonia Hernandez, "The Political Awakening of Mexican Americans," *Latino Stuff Review* (Spring/Primavera 1992), pp. 3–4. Reprinted by permission of the author.

pp. 166–167 From Patricia Nelson Limerick, *The Legacy of Conquest: The Unbroken Past of the American West,* p. 290–292, Copyright © 1987 by W. W. Norton. Reprinted by permission.